COMMUNICATING
ORGANIZATIONAL CHANGE

SUNY Series in International Management
Andrzej K. Kozminski, Patricia Sanders, and Sarah Sanderson
King, Editors

COMMUNICATING ORGANIZATIONAL CHANGE:

A MANAGEMENT PERSPECTIVE

Edited by

DONALD PETER CUSHMAN

and

SARAH SANDERSON KING

State University
of New York
Press

Published by
State University of New York Press, Albany

© 1995 State University of New York

Production by Susan Geraghty
Marketing by Fran Keneston

Printed in the United States of America

For information, address State University of New York
Press, State University Plaza, Albany, N.Y., 12246

10 9 8 7 6 5 4 3 2 1

Library of Congress Cataloging-in-Publication Data

Communicating organizational change : a management perspective /
    Donald Peter Cushman and Sarah Sanderson King, editors.
        p.   cm. —(SUNY series in international management)
    Includes bibliographical references and index.
    ISBN 0-7914-2495-2 (acid-free paper). —ISBN 0-7914-2496-0 (pbk.:
acid-free paper)
        1. Communication in mangement.   2. Organizational change.
    3. Communication in organizations.   I. Cushman, Donald P.
    II. King, Sarah Sanderson.   III. Series.
    HD320.3.C637   1995
    658.4′5—dc20   94-27492
                                                                CIP

To
Tony and Robyn Loquet
Ron and Mary Cullen
T. J. and Sandar Larkin
who taught us both a great deal about communication
and change, friendship, colleagueship, and a rich, high-
quality life.

CONTENTS

Chapter 1   Communicating Organizational Change
by Donald P. Cushman and Sarah S. King   1

Part 1   Private Sector Organizations   7

Chapter 2   Communicating Change: A High-Speed
Management Perspective
by Sarah S. King and Donald P. Cushman   9

Chapter 3   Leading Organizational Change: A High-
Speed Management Perspective
by Donald P. Cushman and Sarah S. King   35

Chapter 4   Improving Community Service: Strategic
Cooperation Through Communication
by Rod Miller   65

Chapter 5   Stereotypes and Organizational Learning:
Lessons from Mergers and Acquisitions of Multinational
Corporations in Post-Communist Countries
by Krzysztof Obloj   83

Chapter 6   Organizational Inertia or Corporate Culture
Momentum
by Michael Goodman   95

Chapter 7   Communicating the Need for Change in a
Multinational Pharmaceutical Corporation: A Case Study
by Giuseppe Raimondi   113

Chapter 8   Communicating the Need for Shared
Responsibility in Nongovernment Joint Venture Projects:
Lessons from Years of Experience
by Gordon Knowles   127

Part 2   Public Sector Organizations   145

Chapter 9   Public Sector Performance and Private Sector
Management
by Ron Cullen   147

Chapter 10   Communicating Health Care Reform: A
Change for the Better?
by John Johnson   161

Chapter 11   Communication and Role Stress in a
Government Organization
by John Penhallurick   191

Part 3   Organizations in Regional Cultures   225

Chapter 12   Communicating Change in China
by Yanan Ju   227

Chapter 13   Communicating Change in Australia
Robyn Johnston   251

Chapter 14   Communication in Asian Job Interviews
by Ernst Martin   275

Chapter 15   Lessons from the Restructuring of Post-
Communist Enterprises
by Andrzej K. Kozminski   311

Contributors   329

Index   333

CHAPTER 1

Communicating Organizational Change

Donald P. Cushman and Sarah S. King

Rapidly changing technologies, the globalization of economic forces, unexpected competition, and quick market saturation are creating an increasingly complex and volatile business climate. As environmental turbulence increases, the rate of organizational change necessary for survival also increases. . . . In the final analysis, it is the innovative, adaptable, flexible, efficient use of information and communication which allows an organization to reorient rapidly and successfully in a volatile business environment.

Cushman and King (1995, 1)

The Center for Information Systems Research at the MIT Sloan School of Management in 1985 argued that an organization's ability to continuously improve its effectiveness in managing organizational interdependencies will be the critical element in successfully responding to the competitive forces of the 1990s (Rockart and Short 1989). Effectiveness in managing organizational interdependencies refers to a firm's ability to achieve coalignment among its internal and external resources in a manner equal to or greater than existing world class benchmarks. *assumes all org. operate in the same environment —*

Coalignment is a unique form of communication linkage in which each of a firm's stakeholders and subunits clearly articulates its needs, concerns, and potential contributions to the organization's functioning in such a manner that management can forge an appropriate value added configuration and linkages between units.

An appropriate value added configuration and linkage between units and stakeholders integrates, coordinates, and controls each participant's needs, concerns, and contributions so that the outcome is mutually satisfying to the participants involved and optimizing in value added activities to the organizational functioning as a whole, thus creating a sustainable competitive advantage (Cushman and King 1995, 2–6).

Several studies regarding how such communications must proceed to achieve this goal generate eight benchmarks for effective communication:

1. The CEO must function as an open communication champion.
2. There must be a match between management's words and actions.
3. There must be a commitment to two-way communication.
4. There must be an emphasis on face-to-face interaction.
5. There must be shared responsibility for employee input.
6. Good and bad news traveling up to management should be encouraged.
7. Stakeholders' interests, contributions, and concerns must be known.
8. Employees should be encouraged to use an open communication strategy (Young and Post 1994, 34).

When such communication benchmarks are met, then a firm's organizational alignments and realignments with its environment in times of rapid change produces supernormal profits (Powell 1992, 119).

Organizational change can be of two types—incremental and discontinuous. Incremental change requires the use of self-managed and cross-functional teamwork between stakeholders to achieve world class benchmarking targets. Discontinuous change involves stopping all that one is doing and adopting a totally new approach. Here benchmarking teams which take ideas from world class performance and adjust them to one's own use and outside linking teams which form joint ventures, outsource, and so forth allow the world class benchmark to provide the product to one's own firm so as to achieve a competitive advantage.

Organizations, like people, must adapt their response to rapid environmental change so they can perform at least at the speed of change (Conners 1993, 5). Optimally a firm would like to anticipate important changes and position the firm to achieve supernormal profits from such changes (Hodgetts, Luthans, and Lee 1994, 10). In either case, effective communication as just discussed must be utilized to rapidly orient and reorient a firm's internal and external resource and stakeholders to rapid environmental change.

In January 1994, some twenty researchers of organizational communication processes from throughout the world met in Sydney, Australia, to discuss communication and organizational change. This book contains the most suggestive papers from that conference. The papers contained in this volume are divided into three sections, addressing the issues involved in communication and change in (1) private sector firms, (2) public sector firms, and (3) regional markets.

The Introduction and the seven chapters in Part I explore coalignment problems in private sector firms. In Chapter One, we provide definitions of communication and change and a framework for understanding the relationship of communication to organizational change.

In Chapter 2, "Communicating Change: A High-Speed Management Perspective," King and Cushman draw upon their thirty years of teaching, research, and consulting experience to discuss high-speed management as a general theory of the relationship between communication and organizational change. This discussion explores in detail high-speed management's three subtheories, indicating how a firm obtains information and opens up communication with customers and competitors, the coalignment of a firm's decisions, and the ways in which the use of teamwork can be employed to continuously improve performance.

Then, in Chapter 3, "Leading Organizational Change: A High-Speed Management Perspective," Cushman and King outline a new theory of organizational leadership focusing on how to handle discontinuous change. This theory draws upon transformational leadership, network leadership, and leading discontinuous change.

In Chapter 4, "Community Service: Strategic Cooperation Through Communication," Rod Miller, head of the community relations unit at Queensland University of Technology, discusses the unique interface between a high-speed management firm and the community in adapting communication to change. High-speed management theory is applied to an analysis of focusing, meeting, and executing an organization's expectations and developing cost expedient programs.

In Chapter 5, "Stereotypes and Organizational Learning: Lessons from Mergers and Acquisitions of Multinational Corporations in Post-Communist Countries," Krzysztof Obloj, a teacher, researcher, and consultant in Europe, discusses the role organizational stereotypes play in a firm's communicative adaptation to change. He explores how organizational structures, layoffs, training, and performance are influenced positively and negatively by stereotypes.

In Chapter 6, "Organizational Inertia or Corporate Cultural Momentum," Michael Goodman explores several examples of the attempt to move organizations in new directions and the role corporate culture plays in assisting or retarding that movement. In so doing he explores the NASA Challenger accident, McDonnell Douglas DC10 door blowouts, and C17 TQM initiation.

In Chapter 7, "Communicating the Need for Change in a Multinational Pharmaceutical Corporation: A Case Study," Giuseppe Raimondi, a division head of an Italian pharmaceutical firm, explores how consultants can effectively communicate the need for a change in a multinational pharmaceutical firm. The author presents a structural solution for improving communication regarding change between the R & D and marketing units in a multinational firm.

In Chapter 8, "Communicating the Need for Shared Responsibility in Nongovernment Joint Venture Projects: Lessons from Years of Experience," Gordon Knowles, a division head of over sixty joint projects throughout the world, explores the need for a shared sense of responsibility in nongovernment joint venture projects. The author discusses how to build esteem, train, reward, and improve communication regarding change.

Part II explores coalignment problems in public sector firms. In Chapter 9, "Communicating Public Sector Performance Messages and Private Sector Management," Ron Cullen, reflecting on his twenty years of experience in turning around governmental units in Australia, discusses a general theory of public sector performance measures for adjusting government units to environmental change.

He maps how action plans and performance measures can bring private sector advances in quality and productivity.

In Chapter 10, "Communicating Health Care Reform: A Change for the Better?," John Johnson draws upon his vast experience as CEO of several hospitals and health care facilities to explore the problems of adjusting communication to change in U.S. health care reform. He then discusses the parallels between health reform and national and organizational reforms in upgrading performance.

In Chapter 11, "Communicating Role Change and Organizational Role Stress in a Government Organization," John Penhallurick, teacher and researcher at the University of Canberra, gathers and analyzes new data examining the relationship between communication, organizational role change, and role stress in a government organization. He finds that trust in the supervisor and the quality of upward and downward communication influences role stress.

Part III explores coalignment problems by organizations in regional cultures. In Chapter 12, "Communicating Change in China," Yanan Ju, drawing upon his experiences as a teacher of communication and marketing in China, discusses the role of communication, cultural business frameworks, and change in the People's Republic of China. He outlines how understanding China's new cultural and business framework structures communication and change.

In Chapter 13, "Communicating Change in Australia," Robyn Johnston, teacher and consultant in Australia, explores organizational change in the Australian public service. She examines how the Australian Council of Trade Union Act of 1987 attempts to restructure communication and thus organizational performance in Australia by redefining educational opportunities and work role categories.

In Chapter 14, "Communication in Asian Job Interviews," Ernest Martin, a college teacher and marketing consultant from Hong Kong, explores the organizational coalignment process in employment interviews in Asia. This discussion of verbal and nonverbal codes in the job interview is revealing of major Western and Asian differences in communication.

In Chapter 15, "Lessons from the Restructuring of Post-Communist Enterprises," Andrzej K. Kozminski, dean of the International School of Business of Warsaw University, examines lessons regarding the relationship of communication and change in the restructuring of post-Communist enterprises. His study indicates what multinationals are missing by not listening to Polish acquisitions by ABB and GE.

This book's excursion into the relationship of communication and change between an organization's stakeholders and its management should prove to be rich in insights and exciting in implications. Enjoy the execution, profit from it, and utilize it.

REFERENCES

Conners, D. (1993). *Managing at the Speed of Change*. New York: Villand Books.

Cushman, D., and King, S. S. (1995). *Communication and High-Speed Management*. Albany: SUNY Press.

Hodgetts, R., Luthans, F., and Lee, Song. (1994). "New Paradigm Organizations: From Total Quality to Leaning to World Class." *Organizational Dynamics:* 5–19.

Powell, T. (1992). "Organizational Alignment as Competitive Advantage." *Strategic Management Journal* 13: 119–134.

Rockart, J., and Short, J. (1989). "IT in the 1990s: Managing Organizational Interdependence." *Sloan Management Review* 30: 7–7.

Young, M., and Post, J. (1994). "Managing to Communicate, Communicating to Manage: How Learning Companies Communicate with Employees." *Organizational Dynamics:* 31–43.

PART 1

Private Sector Organizations

CHAPTER 2

Communicating Change: A High-Speed Management Perspective

Sarah S. King and Donald P. Cushman

High-speed management is a new organizational communication theory being used to competitive advantage by some of the most successful organizations in the world: General Electric, Toyota, Motorolla, NEC, Intel, etc. To examine high-speed management and explore its unique implications from a communication, organization, and market point of view, we are going to (1) survey the philosophic, theoretic, and practical formulation of the original theory (Cushman and King 1988, 1989, 1992, 1993a, 1993b, 1994, 1995) and (2) survey the extensions to this theory as presented in three subsequent publications—a book on high-speed management and teamwork (Ju and Cushman 1995), a book on continuous improvement (Obloj, Cushman, and Kozminski 1995), and a reader in high-speed management with a number of scholars extending the theory in different contexts (King and Cushman 1994b).

HIGH-SPEED MANAGEMENT: THE ORIGINAL THEORY

During the latter half of the 1980s three trends converged which gave rise to the emergence of high-speed management. First, several breakthroughs took place in information and communication technology which dramatically altered how organizational R & D, manufacturing, marketing, and management worked. Second, this information and communication revolution helped facilitate a dramatic increase in world trade, the emergence of a global economy, and the development of three large core markets. Third, the technological breakthroughs and increase in world trade created a volatile business climate, characterized by rapidly changing technology, quick market saturation, and unexpected competition, making success in business difficult.

Rapid environmental change creates organizational problems, but it also creates organizational opportunities. A high-speed management system is a set of philosophic, theoretic, and practical principles for responding to rapid environmental change. More specifically, high-speed management decreases the response time required to get a desired product and/or service to the customer ahead of one's competitors. It does so by employing three separate theories and sets of practices. First, it employs environmental scanning theory to locate the customer's need for new products and/or services and one's competitors' response to that need. Second, it employs value chain theory to identify areas within and across firms where the information and communication processes involved in an organization's integration, coordination, and control system can be improved. Third, it employs a unique continuous improvement theory to reengineer a firm's integration, coordination, control, or communication processes, thus increasing the speed to market of products, thereby creating a competitive advantage. An organization's communication and management systems must have certain specifiable characteristics to respond to the opportunities created by successive, rapid, environmental change. It must be *innovative, adaptive, flexible, efficient, and rapid in response*—a high-speed management system.

Our examination of high-speed management will be divided into three sections. First, we will answer a series of questions regarding the significance of high-speed management to the development of organizational communication theory. Second, we shall examine the three subtheories of high-speed management. Third, we shall explore the three major practical communication processes involved in high-speed management.

THE PHILOSOPHIC PERSPECTIVE UNDERLYING HIGH-SPEED MANAGEMENT

The first question to be asked as we begin our discussion of the philosophic perspective underlying high-speed management is, *Why should students, researchers, scholars, and practitioners in the field of communication be interested in high-speed manage-ment?* The search for theoretic principles capable of yielding signif-icant organizational communication theories has been disappoint-ing. The reason is simple. Up to this point in time, organizational strategy, the prime candidate for locating powerful cross organiza-tional theoretic principles, has had at its core noncommunication activities. For example, consider an organization which pursues a strategy of competitive advantage based on product cost. The cen-tral organizational strategy or process operating must, by necessi-ty, focus on lowering the cost of production or manufacturing activities. Or take an organization which concentrates its efforts on obtaining competitive advantage based on product differentiation. The central organizational strategy or process operating for suc-cess is product uniqueness or R & D activities.

True, human interaction or communication is involved in both organizational manufacturing and R & D activities, but the prima-ry cross-organizational theoretic activities are organizational man-ufacturing and technological innovations, not communication pro-cesses. Communication processes function as second-level support activities and are given their regularities based on the primary organizational activities of production and innovation.

However, when speed of response or time becomes the primary source of competitive advantage, this all changes. Effective com-munication becomes the primary organizational theoretic activity and other organizational processes such as R & D, manufacturing, sales, and servicing products become support activities to the pri-mary process of speed and are adjusted accordingly (Stalk 1988). For those who study the communication process, and in particular those in organizational communication, communication becomes the locus of control in obtaining competitive advantage.

The answer to the first question partially answered our second one: *Why should high-speed management be of value to an organi-zation?* High-end pricing and larger market shares which erode slowly are the driving forces behind the acceptance and practice of a speed-to-market strategy. In addition, when speed to market acts as the perimeter giving an organization x amount of time to get to market to beat the competition, the by-products of such a strategy are affordable quality and marketable productivity, focused on customer pentup demand. This is an additional value-added source of competitive advantage. In the time it takes to get to market before its competition, the organization has as much quality as it can afford, as much productivity as it can sell, based on an accurate estimate of pentup demand. The result is high-end pricing and bigger market shares, with enough profits to initiate the next market adaptation.

More specifically, sustainable competitive advantage in the 1990s will depend upon a corporation's capacity to monitor accurately changes in external economic forces and then reorder a firm's internal and external resources more rapidly than its competitors. To accurately monitor changes in external economic forces and to rapidly orient and reorient a firm's internal and external resources, an organization must have a world class information and communication capability. This capability must provide for a rapid coalignment between product development, purchasing, manufacturing, distribution, sales, and service systems in response to environment change.

Speed to market as a controlling strategy or source of competitive advantage has several unique features which other sources of competitive advantage do not produce. To reduce the time it takes to get a product which customers desire to market before a competitor, a firm must understand what a customer wants and then simplify and reengineer its value chain to rapidly respond to change. Such a strategy first creates a customer focus on pentup and measurable demand in product design, production, and delivery to a well-defined market. Second, such a strategy places product quality within a time frame with a customer focus, creating affordable quality. Third, speed to market seeks to increase productivity but within a price frame that will allow the market to absorb the product, quickly leading to marketable productivity motivating other firms to want to use that as its benchmark or buy the productivity system (Carnevale 1992). Speed to market thus invokes a cluster of variables effecting competitive advantage—a customer focus (what does the customer want?), affordable quality (what is the customer willing to pay?), and marketable productivity (how much can we sell?)—while keeping these sources of competitive advantage within their most effective and efficient range, thus avoiding the problem of providing too little or too much of these qualities.

This brings us to the third question: *How can an organization productively operate in a highly volatile environment?* The global economic environment involves both good and bad news. The good news is that world trade is growing three times faster than gross domestic product in the developed world. The bad news is that environmental volatility in the form of quick market saturation, unexpected competition, and technological breakthroughs are threatening most firms. However, if you have a world class information and communication system which can track in real time changes in the cost of capital, labor, and raw materials as well as consumer taste and competitor response and can quickly realign a firm's internal and external resources through a value chain analysis and continuous improvement processes, then you have an innovative, adaptive, flexible, efficient, and rapid response firm which can profit from environmental volatility—a high-speed management firm.

THE THEORETIC PERSPECTIVE OF HIGH-SPEED MANAGEMENT

To understand the rationale and mechanisms for systematically employing a high-speed management system, we need a theoretic framework to guide the development and maintenance of such a world class information and communication rapid response capability. In decreasing response time required to get a desired product and/or service to the customers ahead of one's competitors, high-speed management as a corporate strategy is based on three separate but interdependent theories and sets of practices. First, environmental scanning theory functions to locate the need for new products and/or services and to ascertain the response of competitors to that need. Second, value chain theory functions to identify areas across and within firms where the information and communication processes involved in an organization's integration, coordination, and control systems must be improved. Third, the unique information and communication continuous improvement theory functions to reengineer a firm's integration, coordination, and control processes, thus increasing the speed to market of products, thereby generating a competitive advantage.

Environmental Scanning

Environments create both problems and opportunities for organizations. Organizations must cope with changes in the cost of capital, labor, raw materials, shifts in consumer taste, government regulations, political stability, and unexpected competition. Similarly organizations depend upon the environment for scarce and valued resources, for market growth, and for acquisitions, joint ventures, coalitions, value added partnerships, and tailored trade agreements. An organization's environment, perhaps more than any other factor, affects its strategy, structure, and performance. However, whether such changes in organizational strategy, structure, and performance lead to positive or negative consequences rests entirely upon the speed, accuracy, and interpretation of the information and communication regarding the significance of the various environmental changes and the rapid reorientation of an organization's strategy, structure, and resources to take advantage of such changes. This process is termed *environmental scanning*.

Environmental scanning is based on the need to know, and the objective of determining what it will take from customers, competitors, and suppliers to get to market first. With customers, there is the need to know what the pentup demand is for products in the area in which you are operating; what the dimensions are by which customers differentiate your product from those of your competitors; and even if the products are identical, what is the perceived differentiation for your customers of your product from others. With competitors, there is the need to know what are their core capabilities and their product life cycle plans; what capabilities differentiate the competition; and what products they intend to bring to market or discontinue. With suppliers, there is the need to know their level of training, their standards, and the price when you suggest a change.

Environmental scanning is at once a simple and complex process. It is simple in that the critical information required to analyze the underlying dynamics of an industry and/or market are frequently shared by all the competitors. It is complex in that the number of areas monitored to affect this dynamic may be large and determining the meaning and implications of information from these diverse areas on each other may be very complex. Environmental scanning allows us to analyze and act on the forces external to an organization which significantly influence its internal relationships.

In regard to each business, as you scan the environment you need to locate the answers to the following questions:

1. What are your business's global market dynamics today and where are they going over the next several years?

2. What actions have your competitors taken in the last three years to upset those global dynamics?

3. What have you done in the last three years to affect those dynamics?

4. What are the most dangerous things your competitors could do in the next three years to offset those dynamics?

5. What are the most effective things you could do to bring about your desired impact on those dynamics? (Tichy and Charan, 1989, 115).

Value Chain Theory Adding Value

Value chain theory allows us the opportunity to focus on the internal relationships which influence an organization's reorientation to external forces. Value chain theory involves the examination of an organization's functional units and process linkages between functions and to evaluate its current and desired level of performance. At the functional business level you take a look internally at the service, design, engineering, purchasing, manufacturing, distribution, and sales units and externally at the suppliers and customers. At the business process level you evaluate linkages between the functional units which make up product development, product delivery, service, and management processes (Rockart and Short 1989; Porter 1986). And in each evaluation, applying high-speed management as a corporate strategy, you take stock of the information and communication coalignment processes that cut across and are at the heart of the operation of each unit in the value chain (see Figure 2.1).

Competitive advantage gained in one functional unit or business process can be added to or cancelled out by an organization's performance in other functional units or business processes. This is what is meant by value-added or value-diminishing chains of activities. When those various sources of competitive advantage are cumulative, then a firm's entire range of functional units and business processes must be linked and configured effectively through the appropriate use of information and communication systems or high-speed management. Once again the appropriate analysis of locating, linking, and configuring of a firm's internal resources is the responsibility of top management as is its reorientation in response to environmental changes.

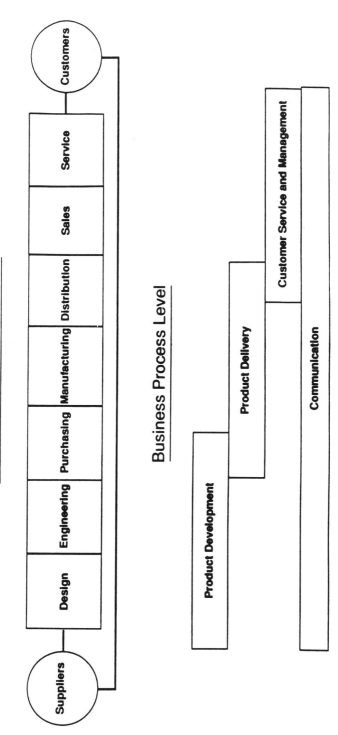

FIGURE 2.1.
An Organization's Value Chain
Source: Revised from J. Rockart and J. Short, "IT in the 1990's," *Sloan Management Review* 30 (1989): 12.

In an organization utilizing value chain theory as a corporate strategy, you compare your findings with those of your competitors to determine the timeline for getting the product to market. You ask yourself (1) what are your organization's and your competitors' core competencies; (2) what do you have to include in a campaign so customers will perceive your core competencies as a controlling concern; (3) what changes in core capabilities must be made to provide your firm with the strongest lead time in getting your product to market before your competitors; (4) what do we do in-house or out-of-house to make the deadline or how quickly can we change if such is necessary; and (5) if we outsource, with whom? In addition to answers to these questions, value chain theory tells you why you must begin a change; how great a tension must be created to motivate employees to abandon old organizational practices for new ones, motivating constructive change; and indicates what skills are involved.

Continuous Improvement

Once we have applied environmental scanning and value chain theory to an organization and have all the data we need to know what we must improve in-house and what we must improve out-of-house, we need to create the tension for and the ability of an organization to continuously improve its effectiveness in managing organizational interdependencies. This continuous improvement process can be enhanced by a self-managed teamwork program, a cross-functional teamwork program, a best practices benchmarking program, and a negotiated linking program.

A *self-managed teamwork program* is created within the organization to implement a workers continuous improvement program within a New England town meeting format. The goal is to improve an organization's productivity, quality, flexibility, adaptability, or response time. These meetings may last from one to three days and include any combination of workers, suppliers, and customers called together by the division head. The division head presents the key market issues, the organization's vision, the competitors' response to that vision, and specific organizational needs and then leaves. Teamwork facilitators generate lists of bad work to be eliminated and good work to be instituted. The group is divided into teams who debate these issues and provide a cost/benefit analysis and action plan for solutions recommended. The division head acts on all high-yield ideas by selecting a team champion, training the team champion in project management, empowering a team to implement the change, setting performance targets, measurement criteria, a time frame, and feedback procedures. The worker improvement team then implements the action plan.

A *cross-functional teamwork program* is created to set up teams whose goals are to map and then improve cross-functional organizational processes. Many of the most significant improvements in organizational performance have come from mapping an important cross-functional organizational process and then asking those involved in the process to simplify and/or improve the functioning of that process. These teams are assigned the task of mapping the decision, implementing it, evaluating, and making improvements in the process mapping. This is established by developing a clear understanding of the process goal; identifying the necessary and critical success factors for achieving that goal; mapping and improving the essential subprocesses to meet these critical success factors; ranking each subprocess and evaluating its productivity, quality, flexibility, and adaptability; outlining a program for improvement; and implementing the change process and fine-tuning its subprocesses. The improvement in organizational process may result from an improvement in skills, from upsizing, from downsizing, or even a change in the functioning of that process.

A *best practices benchmarking program* is instituted in continuous improvement programs when you want to set world class benchmarking standards for productivity, quality, flexibility, adaptability, and response time; when you do not know how to do it so you study those who are; or when you want to track your competitors' progress as you do in environmental scanning. This program usually locates such organizations and arranges a site visit, develops a case study of the processes involved, and trains personnel at its own organization in ways to adapt these innovations. Monitoring and feedback procedures are established for implementing the change.

The primary focus of a *negotiated linking program* is to continuously scan the globe to locate resources in the form of customers, partners, technologies, or consultants capable of enhancing an organization's competitiveness. This program is especially adept when an organization cannot achieve its objectives in the time allotted. The result may be a joint venture, a buyout, or the formation of an alliance. The purpose is to fit your organization with that of another to achieve a benchmark you can afford. If the change is clear, this may not be necessary. If the change is unclear, you may need others to succeed.

The process a negotiated linking program follows is to interact with units holding the potential resources to locate interests, concerns, and contributions to coalignment; to develop the form of coalignment preferred by both units, such as acquisition, joint venture, alliance, partnership coalition, collaboration, licensing technology leasing, transfer, and/or training; and to determine the world class benchmarking targets in market shares, productivity, quality, flexibility, and/or rapid response time to be met before coalignment can take place.

Continuous improvement programs make the changes required for sustainable competitive advantage by improving communication, learning skills, and the application of process to fit within the proscribed time frame. You want to keep your eye on the customers, on the process to be improved, on international benchmarks, and on the competition. Continuous improvement programs aimed at organizational coalignment through (1) a self-managed teamwork program, (2) a cross-functional teamwork program, (3) a best practices benchmark program, and (4) a negotiated linking program are necessary elements in establishing a world class organizational information and communication capability. Continuous improvement programs are essential information and communication processes in high-speed management.

THREE PRACTICAL COMMUNICATION PROCESSES WITHIN AN ORGANIZATION

Once again the question is, *In what sense does communication control all of these processes—environmental scanning, value chain theory, and continuous improvement programs?* The art of high-speed management has as its goals the development of a steady flow of low-cost, high-quality, easily serviced, high-value, and innovative products which meet the needs of the customers and of getting these products to market before one's competitors in an effort to achieve market penetration and large profits. Success in achieving these goals will rest in great part on the appropriate use of information and communicating technology to *integrate, coordinate, and control* the organizational activities involved in achieving these goals. The three organizational coalignment processes are integration, coordination, and control.

Organizational Integration

Organizational integration has as its goal the tieing together, energizing, and creation of a focused collective effort by all of a firm's various stakeholders. Three organizational communication processes converge to make such a collective effort possible: organizational leadership, corporate climate, and teamwork.

Organizational Leadership   If incremental change is required to adapt to market, then the old power, trait, behavioral, and situational theories of leadership can be applied appropriately. However, when volatile and discontinuous change takes place, then a high-speed leader is required. In a turbulent global environment, organizations must develop the capacity to respond rapidly to changes in their environment by dramatically revamping the firm's vision, mission, product mix, value structure, knowledge, alliances, and technological base. A new kind of leadership is required to guide such massive changes. Three trends have converged in the past several years which allow a clear characterization of this new high-speed management leadership pattern. This characterization emerges from the convergence of research and practice on transformational leadership, the management of the network organization, and the management of organizational discontinuities.

Transformational leadership is required to implement massive change and involves five unique skills (Byrd 1987): anticipation of what the change must be, articulation of a vision of the new way to do business, development of value congruence between the old and new organizational practices, empowerment, and self-understanding skills. Those organizations which have been most successful are those which responded rapidly to successive transformational visions by effectively altering and elevating organizational performance. Such responses normally included organizing primarily around processes, not tasks; flattening the hierarchy by minimizing the subdivision of processes; placing middle level managers in charge of processes and process performance; making teams, not individuals, the focus of organizational performance and design; helping to develop employee competencies; combining management and nonmanagement activities; focusing on teams; maximizing supplier and customer contact; rewarding team as well as individual performance (Jacobs 1992).

The research and practice of the network manager adds to our understanding of a high-speed management leader. The emphasis for the network manager is the identification, development, and expansion of a firm's core competencies, which are difficult to imitate and thus a source of sustainable competitive advantage. These include improving knowledge-based competencies, alliance-based competencies, and technology-based competencies. A high-speed management leader thus assumes a new leadership role, that of a coalignment broker. Such a leader functions both within and between firms. He or she must have three skills, that of architect, lead operator, and caretaker of interorganizational coalignment (Snow, Miles, Colman 1993).

Managing organizational discontinuities involves the motivational transformation of a firm from one vision and/or set of core competencies to another. Two skills are paramount: the skill to create a tension for change that is commensurate with the degree of change required and the skill to create a learning environment that shows everyone involved in the change how to change. The transformational leader focuses on anticipating change, articulating a clear vision, empowerment, value congruence, and self-understanding skills for directing and motivating workers involvement. The network leader adds to this the role of coalignment broker who can enhance a firm's core competencies and function through his or her skills as an architect, lead operator in the change, and caretaker of the new linkages. The manager of organizational discontinuity requires skill in creating tension to motivate choice and knowledge of how to change.

The controlling factor for a high-speed management leader is time and speed to market to outperform one's competitors. Time thus controls all other variables. It in turn is controlled through the appropriate use of a firm's information and communication system. A high-speed management leader thus must fulfill at least three new leadership roles: that of transformational leader, manager of organizational networks, and leader of discontinuous change.

Corporate Climate   Human communication in an organizational climate permits a firm's stakeholders to share a common set of values, socialization, monitoring, and operating system capable of motivating, guiding, and providing the satisfactory coalignment of significant collective performance. The goal is a positive corporate performance. Corporate climate is the degree of fit between an organization's culture and the values, interests, and concerns of the individuals as groups of stakeholders upon whom the organization depends for its effective functioning. More specifically, included are the government which regulates an organization, the investors who provide financing, the employees who do the work, and the consumers who buy the products.

In incremental change, old conceptions of corporate culture are satisfactory. In discontinuous change, a new high-speed management conception of values, myths, and social dramas are sought to effect rapid adjustment to massive environmental change. Such corporate values must attempt to create an organization that is lean, agile, creative, learning, and which rewards rapid change. Individual values demand that a leader must be reality oriented, lead rather than manage, and that there be candidness in one's communication, simplicity in one's solutions, and all of these be carried out with dignity and integrity. A firm must have clear rituals that contribute to an organization's strategic goal. These include precise goals on time to market; clear quality, productivity, and customer-focused targets for achieving the goals; and a reward and punishment system for those who do and do not comply.

Teamwork   Rapid change requires commitment and adaptation of change to the skills of workers involved. This is accomplished through teamwork. Successful teamwork is characterized by a mutually constructed, publically agreed to goal which integrates the interests, concerns, and contributions of all of those who contribute to the goal. The four types of teamwork patterns utilized to contribute to the achievement of goals are self-managed teams, cross-functional teams, social-technical teams, and executive teams.

As you may recall from our earlier discussion of high-speed management, the self-managed team functions within the New England Town Meeting format to eliminate the nonessential, nonproductive, or "bad work" and replace it with "good work." The cross-functional team is created to map and then improve organizational performance. The social-technical team combines robots and people to significantly improve quality, productivity, and speed to market. An executive team is composed of top managers and focuses on corporate strategy in outside linkages, such as joint ventures, etc.

Organizational integration relies upon leadership to provide organizational focus, corporate climate to guide organizational motivation, and teamwork to inspire practical action aimed at achieving organizational goals.

Organizational Coordination

Organizational coordination is dependent upon each organizational unit or business process rapidly sharing information through communication and information technology. In any combination— R & D and marketing; R & D, marketing, and manufacturing; R & D, marketing, manufacturing, and MIS—the interface requires new uses of information and communication technology, a strategy for combining people and technology for optimal success, and a brokering at the point of interface of organizational goals and targets. High-speed management provides the corporate strategy topics to be discussed by each unit for coalignment and the case studies for illustrating the most appropriate adaptation of topic in different situations.

The R & D and marketing interface can be best understood through an examination of the information and communication coalignment tools available, which include environmental assessment, product portfolio modeling, and structured innovation. Specific information and communication topics are required for coordination when marketing needs to be involved in the R & D process, when marketing provides information to R & D, and when R & D needs to be involved in the marketing process.

The R & D, marketing, and manufacturing interface utilizes several useful tools in coaligning their organizational functions in the value chain: robots, integrated flexible systems, computer assisted design, computer aided manufacturing, and computer integrated manufacturing systems. Economies of sourcing, scale, focus, scope, and time are the primary strategies for alignment.

The R & D, marketing, manufacturing, and MIS interface find

the useful tools for coalignment to be database management, network management, applications programming, design management, systems support management, and executive information systems, such as the telephone, the pager, electronic mail, voice messaging, mobile communication, FAX, videotext, and teleconferencing. The advent of wireless telecommunication networking capabilities adds a new dimension to the workings of this interface. Strategies for coalignment for this complex interface include business systems planning, critical success factors, applications portfolio, stages approach, value chain approach, and high-speed management approach.

Organizational Control

Successful organizations not only focus their energies and resources through organization integration processes, coalign necessary value chain function through organization coordination processes, but they also plan, monitor, set benchmarks, and correct coalignment functions through organization control processes.

Organizational control takes place at three points in a firm's activities: in the organizational planning and linking stage, in auditing ongoing organizational activities, and in correcting performance by looking to the future. Communication can be used to monitor goal and target achievement, to monitor the relationship between environmental scanning and continuous improvement, and to adjust the organization through continuous improvement programs in differing processes of organizational change. Two new tools of organizational analysis are utilized in high-speed management for organizational control: based on environmental scanning a firm conducts an organizational *high-speed management audit* and employs continuous improvement processes to plan a *reengineering of organizational functions and processes* based on this audit. An information and communication audit explores how an organization can shorten the response time in its ongoing integration, coordination, and control processes through the use of critical success factors to locate activities where turnaround time can be reduced in the coalignment process. The reengineering of organizational processes is executed through continuous improvement programs focused on increasing the speed to market of new products by improving the environmental scanning of industrial competitors, the organization's value chain, and the utilization of new information and communication technologies, resulting in the development and implementation of an organizational information and communication master plan.

To summarize, the critical communication and management processes involved in organizational coalignment are an organization's integration, coordination, and control processes. Organizational integration is achieved by three overlapping subprocesses: leadership, corporate climate, and teamwork. Each has its unique function. Organizational leadership creates a focused set of goals for an organization. An appropriate corporate climate is achieved when an organization's various stakeholders—workers, investors, customers, suppliers, and governments—work together in such a manner as to make these goals achievable. Teamwork functions effectively when separate units, individuals within units, and systems across tasks are coaligned for goal attainment (Barrett 1987).

Organizational coordination is achieved through sharing information in such a manner as to optimize the value-added activities of each of an organization's subunits and environment. This normally involves linking customers, regulators, R & D, marketing, manufacturing, distribution, sales, and service so that the issues, concerns, and contributions of each link in the value chain can be optimized (Bower and Hout 1988).

Organizational control involves the planning, including setting targets for sales, productivity, and quality; monitoring progress toward those targets in real time; and the assessment after the fact of improvements which can be made in performance. These planning, monitoring, and assessment functions, if they are to be realistic, also involve coalignment processes between environmental demands and the value chain which normally takes the form of specific targets or goals and the review of individual and group progress toward these goals, which then form the basis for the organization's recognition and reward system.

EXTENSIONS OF THE ORIGINAL HIGH-SPEED MANAGEMENT THEORY

Researchers have contributed to three major volumes aimed at extending the original theory by Cushman and King on high-speed management. The first volume seeks to expand the work on high-speed management teamwork; the second, on high-speed management continuous improvement programs; and the third is a collection of essays aimed at extending various aspects of the original theory. Let us examine each in turn.

In Yanan Ju and Donald Cushman's book *Teamwork in High-Speed Management* (1994), the authors argue that in the 1990s teamwork has become one of an organization's most important activities for achieving excellence in performance. However, several recent studies indicate that many firms are misusing teamwork and thus failing to achieve their goals. The authors then present a detailed analysis of team members and leaders functioning in self-managed, cross-functional, benchmarking, social-technical, and executive teams within their high-speed management context, which generates high-performance teamwork. The analysis extends our understanding of teamwork within this context in several new directions. More specifically, teamwork can be seen as the magic which makes high-speed management firms work. High-speed management focuses teamwork to generate high-performance, if

1. Its use is appropriately contextualized;
2. Its use is based on a profound understanding of the interdependent nature of modern organizational life;
3. It is used to achieve the goal of speed to market based on international benchmarking;
4. A firm's overlayered structure is simplified and its role, regulations, culture, and role definitions become more fluid and flexible;
5. Team members possess the qualities of intensity, permanent dissatisfaction, and effective and speedy communication;
6. A team and its members know how to anchor and reanchor themselves in organizational life, structurally, culturally, and psychologically; they can develop their skills in a manner so as to help develop mutually constructed and publically agreed to goals, and integrate the unique concerns, interests, and contributions of each team member.

Teamwork magic works only when properly focused and adapted to customer outcomes; appropriately constituted with diversity in skills and knowledge; deeply embedded in a firm's strategy, targets, and culture; and exercises the appropriate communication capabilities. Such a team is a high-performance team because it has a structural, cultural, psychological, and skills anchoring in the firm. If this does not happen, then teamwork degenerates into a management gimmick. The book then details how these positive goals for teamwork are to be achieved and illustrates their appropriate use with examples from such firms as GE, Toyota, and Xerox.

The Ju and Cushman book extends the original high-speed management theory by providing an in-depth development of the philosophic, theoretic, and practical levels of communication within its organizational teamwork context.

In Krzystof Obloj, Donald Cushman, and Andrej Kozminski's book *Winning: Continuous Improvement Theory in High Performance Organizations* (1995), the authors present a detailed analysis of the role played by self-managed, cross-functional, benchmarking, outside linking, and R & D breakthrough teams in adjusting high-speed management firms to rapid environmental change. The introductory chapter traces the relationship of competitive advantage to organizational coalignment and strategic processes. Chapter 2 explores why so many continuous improvement programs fail and why certain modifications are necessary.

Following two now famous studies by Venkatraman and Prescott (1990) and Ernest and Young (1992), the flaws in the previous work on continuous improvement programs are analyzed. The Venkatraman and Prescott's (1990) study demonstrated that in different types of markets, continuous improvement programs are more or less useful. In export, stable, service, and emerging markets, continuous improvement programs are useful. In fragmented, mature, and declining markets, continuous improvement programs are not useful. The Ernest and Young (1992) study indicates that the relative knowledge and skill levels of one's firm strongly influence which firms can use successfully what types of continuous improvement programs. A *novice firm* or a firm with less than 2 percent return on assets (ROA) and/or less than $47,000 value added per employee (VAE) is low in knowledge and skills and should limit itself to learning how to use simple continuous improvement programs like self-managed teamwork to improve within unit performance. A *journeyman firm* or a firm with 2 to 6.9 percent ROA and $47,000 to $73,000 VAE is modest in organizational knowledge and skills and should limit itself to learning how to use cross-functional teamwork to improve basic business processes in performance. A *master firm* or a firm with 7 percent or higher ROA and a VAE of $74,000 and up is high in organizational knowledge and skills and can learn to employ advanced continuous improvement programs like setting benchmarking, outside linking, and a breakthrough R & D programs to improve organizational performance.

Then Chapters 3 through 7 explore in detail the effect these modifications have in each type of teamwork. The major contributions of this work are (1) its analysis of how continuous improvement programs must be modified to succeed; (2) its precise analysis of the role organizational strategy must play in successful continuous improvement programs; (3) its analysis of the nature, function, and scope of self-managed teams, cross-functional teams, benchmarking teams, outside linking teams, and R & D breakthrough teams in successful continuous improvement programs; and (4) its analysis of organizational leadership in each type of teamwork.

A continuous improvement strategy emerges from an environmental scanning analysis of a firm's customer pentup demand, its competitors' product development, the strengths and weaknesses of the firm's value chain, the type of market involved, and the knowledge and skill level of the firm. From such an analysis, a firm must determine which type of continuous improvement to employ. If the change required is an incremental improvement in existing units, then self-managed teamwork is required. If the change is in a firm's business processes, then cross-functional teamwork is required. If the change required is to a new form of production, then setting benchmarking is required. If the change cannot be done within existing skills and/or products, then an outside linking and/or an R & D breakthrough through teams is required. Note that the last two forms of teamwork represent an extension of the traditional continuous improvement literature into new domains, thus extending our understanding of high-speed management.

Obloj, Cushman, and Kozminski provide a complete theory of continuous improvement and its practice within a high-speed management context and in so doing extend our knowledge and understanding of the original theory.

In Sarah S. King and Donald P. Cushman's book *High-Speed Management and Organizational Communication in the 1990's: A Reader* (1994b), the editors present ten essays which seek to extend the original high-speed management theory.

First, Andrzej Kozminski explores the role of high-speed management in global competition. Kozminski finds that the number of industries becoming global is increasing rapidly, a high-speed management strategy is becoming essential for more firms, new pools of economical development are leading to new markets, more and more firms are subject to these economic forces of a global environment, and thus the principles of high-speed management.

Second, Branislav Kovacic explores the relationship between high-speed management, environmental scanning, and coalignment in the forming of strategic alliances. He provides a grid of fifteen cells which indicate the type of information needed to exploit sustainable competitive advantage from outside linkages. He argues that in the development stage of the product life cycle, a firm must obtain information on (1) its own and other firms' product development, (2) product delivery, and (3) product service and management, and then by obtaining each of these types of information for five different types of markets, it can analyze when to form and when not to form a strategic alliance with other firms.

Third, Krzystof Obloj explores the role of leadership in a high-speed management firm. He explores the transcending and energizing role of high-speed management leaders in articulating a new vision, building a long-term strategy, creating momentum, and building a sustainable culture. He then provides examples of this leadership process in two Japanese firms.

Fourth, Ann Nicotera explores high-speed management and the new corporate culture in IBM and GE. In so doing, she contrasts IBM's non-high-speed culture with GE's high-speed culture. She examines differences in linkages with stakeholders, competitors, and allies and the values, rituals, myths, and social dramas involved in each linkage. She then outlines the precise nature of the goals, targets, and monitoring systems in a high-speed management culture.

Fifth, Yanan Ju explores the role of teamwork in two high-speed management firms, GE and Toyota. He concludes that in high-speed management firms, teamwork is focused on speed to market. The organizations employ inter- and intraorganizational teamwork patterns, seek a unique form of team commitment, invigorate a team through a permanent dissatisfaction with current products and service, employ speedy and effective communication, and monitor performance to produce high-quality products.

Sixth, George Tuttle explores high-speed management and new product development and approval process by the Food and Drug Administration at the Merck Drug Company. He demonstrates how the effective use of information technology and communication with the FDA creates a competitive advantage for Merck in reducing the time it takes in getting approval for its new products.

Seventh, Nils Larsen and Pat Joynt explore how high-speed management is employed in the auto industry. They explore in detail how to get new products to market quickly at Ford and Toyota. They analyze the manufacturing breakthroughs that led suppliers and customers to benefit from these changes.

Eighth, Janet Flynn and Francine Carè explore how high-speed management and continuous improvement programs work at the General Electric Corporation. They outline the unique changes made by GE in TQM (total quality management) programs to yield large internal savings and speed products to market. They also explain some of the common problems involved in implementing continuous improvement programs at GE.

Ninth, Rowland Baughman examines the influence of high-speed management on small businesses. He argues that small businesses have always been high-speed management firms par excellence. They utilize high-speed management principles such as staying close to customers and competitors, using quick response to develop new products, employing close coordination within the firm, employing product quality, being user friendly, employing ease of service and competitive pricing for market penetration, scanning the environment for new products, and developing corporate visions that emphasize change and allow for new units with alternative values.

Tenth, Scott Olson explores high-speed management at work in Toyota and GE while observing some of the limitations of the high-speed management process. He discusses the political and social problems which emerge in high-speed management to limit performance, the lag between theory and implementation in some high-speed management firms, and notes the quality of life limitations of high-speed management on workers. He then advocates the transformation of high-speed management into a learning organization as a way to overcome these limitations.

Each of these authors extends and illustrates Cushman and King's original theory in the areas analyzed and provides a practical illustration of the extension provided.

SUMMARY AND CONCLUSIONS

High-speed management is a new approach to organizational communication theory in which firms place a primary emphasis on improving the communication involved in getting a product to market rapidly. Improvements in a firm's rapid response system generate several competitive advantages. Getting to market first allows one to set prices to get high-end pricing. Getting to market first allows a firm to dominate the market, and when competition emerges market shares erode more slowly. In addition, high-speed management tends to generate affordable quality, marketable productivity, and a customer focus. Organizational communication, knowledge or organizational functioning, and organizational performance are all enhanced by the three subtheories of high-speed management: a theory of environmental scanning, a theory of the value chain, a theory of continuous improvement. These three theories put communication at the forefront of all organizational functioning. Finally, improving an organization's communication, its integration, coordination, and control processes allows us to reinterpret the traditional topics of leadership, corporate climate, teamwork, auditing, and so on and various organizational interfaces in way which transforms our understanding and use of these topics by placing communication and rapid response systems at the center of these activities.

We are at the beginning of research on this new theory and several scholars have indicated new ways of extending it, in particular in the areas of teamwork and continuous improvement, as well as various functions within the theory. Limitations of the high-speed management theory are noted in terms of social problems which limit performance, the lag between theory and practice, and the quality of life limitations of employees. This is an exciting development for organizational communication theory at a time when few complete theories of organizational functioning are based on human communication processes.

REFERENCES

Barrett, F. D. (1987). "Teamwork—How to Expand Its Power and Punch." *Business Only* (Winter): 24–31.

Bower, J. L., and Hout, T. M. (1988). "Fast Cycle Capability for Competitive Power." *Harvard Business Review* (November–December): 110–118.

Byrd, R. (1987). "Corporate Leadership Skills: A New Synthesis." *Organizational Business:* 34–43.

Carnevale, A. (1992). *America and the Economy.* Washington, D.C.: U.S. Department of Labor.

Cushman, D. P., and King, S. S. (1988). "High-Technology and the Role of Communication in High-Speed Management." *Informatologia Yugoslavia, separat speciale,* no. 7: 279–284.

———. (1989). "High Technology, High-Speed Communication and Its Implications for International Management." In G. Osborne and M. Midryal (eds.), *International Communication: In Whose Interest?* Canberra, Australia: Center for Communication and Information Research, University of Canberra.

———. (1992). "High-Speed Management: A Revolution in Organizational Communication in the 1990s." In M. Cross and W. Cummings (eds.), *The Proceedings of the Fifth Conference on Corporate Communication.* Reprinted in S. Deetz (ed.), *Communication Yearbook 16* (1993): 209–237; M. Goodman (ed.), *Corporate Communication: Theory and Practice* (Albany: SUNY Press, 1994); and S. S. King and D. P. Cushman, *High-Speed Management and Organizational Communication in the 1990s: A Reader* (Albany: SUNY Press, 1994).

———. (1993a). "Visions of Order: High-Speed Management in the Private Sector of the Global Marketplace." In A. Kozminski and D. P. Cushman (eds.), *Organizational Communication and Management: A Global Perspective.* Albany: SUNY Press.

———. (1993b). "An Eastern and Western European Model of Corporate Communication." In R. Shuter (ed.), *Annual of International and Intercultural Communication,* vol. 18. Beverly Hills, Calif.: Sage, 1993.

———. (1994). "Old Myths and New Realities Regarding Development Communication." In A. Moemeka, *Communication for Development: A Multi-Media Perspective.* Albany: SUNY Press.

———. (1995). *Communication and High-Speed Management.* Albany: SUNY Press.

Cushman, D. P., and Kozminski, A. (1993). "The Rise of Global Communication and Global Management: An Overview." In A. Kozminski and D. Cushman (eds.), *Organizational Communication and Management: A Global Perspective.* Albany: SUNY Press.

Ernest and Young. (1992). Corporate study included in O. Port, J. Cary, K. Kelley, F. Forest, "Quality." *Business Week* (November 30): 66–72.

Jacob, R. (1992). "The Search for the Organization of Tomorrow." *Fortune* 2 (May 18): 91–98.

Ju, Y., and Cushman, D. P. (1995). *Teamwork in High-Speed Management.* Albany: SUNY Press.

King, S. S., and Cushman, D. P. (1989). "The Role of Communication in High Technology Organizations: The Emergence of High-Speed Management." In S. S. King, (ed.), *Human Communication as a Field of Study.* Albany: SUNY Press.

———. (1989). "Technology and Market Forces and Their Application in the International Marketplace." In G. Osborne and M. Midryal (eds.), *International Communication: In Whose Interest?* Canberra, Australia: Center for Communication and Information Research, University of Canberra.

———. (1994a). "High-Speed Management as a Theoretic Principle for Yielding Significant Organizational Behaviors." In B. Kovacic (ed.), *Organizational Communication: New Perspectives.* Albany: SUNY Press.

———. (eds.). (1994b). *High-Speed Management and Organizational Communication in the 1990s: A Reader.* Albany: SUNY Press.

Obloj, K., Cushman, D. P., and Kozminski, A. (1994). *Winning! Continuous Improvement Theory in High Performance Organizations.* Albany: SUNY Press.

Porter, M. E. (1986). "Changing Patterns of International Competition." *California Management Review* 27, no. 2 (Winter): 9–39.

Rockart, J., and Short, J. (1989). "IT in the 1990s: Managing Organizational Interdependence." *Sloan Management Review* 30: 7–17.

Snow, C., Miles, R., and Colman, H. (1993). "Managing Twenty-first Century Network Organizations." *Organizational Dynamics:* 5–19.

Stalk, G., Jr. (1988). "Time—The Next Source of Competitive Advantage." *Harvard Business Review* (July–August): 41–51.

Tichy, H., and Charzon, R. (1989). "Speed, Simplicity, and Self-

Confidence: An Interview with Jack Welch." *Harvard Business Review:* 112–120.

Venkatraman, N., and Prescott, J. (1990). "Environment Strategy Coalignment: An Empirical Test of Its Performance Implications." *Strategic Management Journal* 11: 1023.

CHAPTER 3

Leading Organizational Change: A High-Speed Management Perspective

Donald P. Cushman and Sarah S. King

Today is an age of global competition, rapid technological change, and too much productive capacity. Chief executives are beginning to march to a set of standards they never dreamed of embracing in the past.

The new order eschews loyalty to workers, products, corporate structure, businesses, factories, communities and nations. All such allegiances are viewed as expendable under the new rules. With survival at stake, only market leadership, strong profits, and high stock prices can be allowed to matter.

(Prokesch 1987, 1)

A tight fit between market opportunities, corporate strategy, and the internal integrative system of an organization is the hallmark of a successful corporation. The strong test of organizational leadership is maintaining such a tight fit in a turbulent environment. The task of managing incremental change in a stable environment is relatively simple and straightforward. The leadership merely fine tunes existing policies within the organization's integration processes. But turbulent change requires a leadership to undertake frame-breaking change. Frame-breaking change requires the creation of a new vision, and the significant realignment of existing organizational integration processes to implement that vision.

In a turbulent global economic environment, organizations must develop the capacity to respond rapidly to changes in their environment by dramatically revamping a firm's vision, mission,

product mix, value structure, knowledge, alliance, and technological base; that is, its core capabilities. A new kind of leadership is
required to guide these activities. Three trends have converged in the
past several years that allow a rather clear characterization of this
new high-speed management leadership pattern. This characterization emerges from the convergence of the research on (1) transformational leadership, (2) network leadership, and (3) leading an
organization through discontinuous change. Let us explore each of
these trends in turn and characterize the emergent outcome.

TRANSFORMATIONAL LEADERSHIP

The most effective leaders in a volatile economic climate recognize
the need for frame-breaking change through scanning the environment for opportunities for and threats to organizational success.
They then construct and implement a new vision aimed at changing the direction and repositioning their firms for short-term success. However, as Tushman, Newman, and Romanell (1986) indicate, such visionary leadership is rare. In their study of forty
instances of frame-breaking change, over 80 percent were precipitated by a financial crises in which the CEO was replaced, whereas
only 20 percent were existing CEOs who recognized the need for
discontinuous change. In a turbulent global environment, change
is the only constant, and leaders must be capable of responding
transformationally to environmental change. "What is required of
this kind of leadership is an ability to help the organization develop a vision of what it can be, to mobilize the organization to accept
and work towards achieving the new visions, and to institutionalize the change that must last over time" (Tichy and Ulrich 1987,
59). Transformational leaders thus have a core set of responsibilities to provide an organization with a new vision, mobilize
commitment to that vision, and institutionalize the changes needed
to implement the vision. In meeting these core responsibilities,
such a leader must (a) exercise a unique set of skills, (b) focus a
firm's goals and means for achieving these goals, and (c) restructure the firm to facilitate rapid change.

Transformational Leadership Skills

Byrd (1987) argues that transformational leadership requires five
unique skills: (1) anticipating skills, (2) visioning skills, (3) value-

congruence skills, (4) empowerment skills, and (5) self-understanding skills.

Anticipatory skills, according to Byrd (1987, 36), entail "projecting consequences, risks and trade-offs (having foresight), actively seeking to be informed and to inform (scanning and communicating), and proactively establishing relationships (building trust and influence)." Anticipatory skills include the ability to see and understand patterns of environmental forces, to know when to reassess or challenge assumptions, to see the value and limitations of alternatives, to recognize "hybrid" behaviors, and to balance human and technical interest (Hunsicker 1985).

Visioning skills involve those processes of communication which lead people to want to be a part of an exciting and involving vision. When effectively internalized, such a vision provides inspiration and a direction to behavior. However, commitment to a vision occurs only when people feel they are actively involved in creating it. The skills associated with vision entail creating mental and verbal pictures of desirable future states in which others can participate and feel they have a necessary part to play.

Value-congruence skills involve those processes involved in articulating values that can give appropriate direction to organizational activities. Values are often internalized so deeply that they define personality and behavior. Transformational leaders must be in touch with workers, investors, and consumer values and be able to articulate and appreciate the congruence between them. Value-congruence skills entail knowing, understanding, articulating, and integrating these values into a workable system.

Empowering skills involve allowing the stakeholders of an organization to share the achievement and responsibilities of the organization. It involves decentralization of power and status to achieve commitment and flexibility. The skills associated with empowerment entail being willing to share power, rewards, control, and visions with the others in an organization. It means the creating of a team, not just a leader and a group of followers.

Self-understanding skills involve a recognition of one's own strengths and weaknesses and the location of others who can synergize the strengths and compensate for the weaknesses. Self-understanding skills entails the use of a variety of tools to recognize one's strengths and weaknesses, realizing that ego strength is a requirement of leadership but must be moderated by help from others.

Refocus a Firm's Goals and Means for Achieving These Goals

Such transformational changes require the revamping of an organization's mission and values, power and status relationships, and the leadership team. *Frame-breaking change always involves a new definition of corporate mission and a reformulation of an organization's values to support the change in mission.* AT&T changed its corporate mission and had to modify its corporate value system to become more competitive, aggressive, and responsive to consumer demands. Similarly shifts took place in corporate mission and values of GE and Apple Computer.

Frame-breaking change involves altered power, status, and interaction patterns. Some individuals and groups lose and some gain in this process. What is important is that the organization's integration, coordination, and control processes be adjusted to reflect these changes. Decentralization at AT&T and GE required a new conception of who has what power, status, and need for communicating with whom.

Frame-breaking change may involve the use of a new leadership team. Change is always a high energy activity. To proceed rapidly and minimize disruptions and maximize benefits, the CEO must install trusted leaders at key points in the change process to lead the change. This requires a leadership team with synergy, to overcome pockets of resistance, risk, and uncertainty. The leadership team must direct frame-breaking change and provide the energy, vision, resources, and role models for a new corporate order.

Restructuring the Firm's Goals to Achieve These Goals

Ostroff and Smith (1992), two consultants with McKinsey and Company, found that those organizations that responded rapidly to successive transformational visions by effectively altering and elevating organizational performance had several common operational features across firms, industries, and economic environments.

1. *Organize primarily around process, not task.* Base performance objectives on customer needs, such as low cost or fast service. Identify the processes that meet (or don't meet) those needs—order generation and fulfillment, say, or new-product development.

2. *Flatten the hierarchy by minimizing subdivision of processes.* It's better to arrange teams in parallel, with each doing lots of

steps in a process, than to have a series of teams, each doing fewer steps.

3. *Give senior leaders change of processes and process performance.*

4. *Link performance objectives and evaluation of all activities to customer satisfaction.*

5. *Make teams, not individuals, the focus of organization performance and design.* Individuals acting alone don't have the capacity to continuously improve work flows.

6. *Combine managerial and nonmanagerial activities as often as possible.* Let workers' teams take on hiring, evaluating, and scheduling.

7. *Emphasize that each employee should develop several competencies.* You need only a few specialists.

8. *Inform and train people on a just-in-time, need-to-perform basis.* Raw numbers go straight to those who need them in their jobs, with no managerial spin, because you have trained front-line workers—salesmen, machinists—how to use them.

9. *Maximize supplier and customer contact.* That means field trips and slots on joint problem-solving teams for all employees all the time.

10. *Reward individual skill development . . . instead of individual performance alone.* (Jacob 1992, 96)

The research on transformational leadership provides a clear outline of the initial skills, uniqueness, and operational features of a high-speed management leader who must respond rapidly to successive transformational change. Research on managing the network organization adds to this outline.

NETWORK LEADERSHIP

As Snow, Miles, and Coleman (1992, 6) argue, firms that are to be competitive in the 1990s need a leader who can

- Search globally for opportunities and resources;
- Maximize returns on all the assets dedicated to business whether owned by the managers's firm or by other firms;

- Perform only those functions for which the company has or can develop expert skills;
- Outsource those activities that can be performed quicker, more effectively, or at lower cost by others.

To meet these leadership imperatives, a network leader must expand and strengthen a firm's core competencies and assume the role of coalignment broker.

Expand and Strengthen a Firm's Core Competencies

In the dynamic and competitive global environment facing most leaders today, the only real source of sustainable competitive advantage, as we have seen, is the ability to respond rapidly and transformationally to the changes in market forces. A leader can achieve this ongoing renewal only by identifying, developing, and expanding a firm's core competencies. The term *core capabilities* refers to those portions of a firm's value chain "which allow it to consistently distinguish itself along dimensions that are important to its customers" (Bartmess and Cerney 1993, 81). Leaders interested in success in today's globally competitive environment must focus on locating and then continuously improving such capabilities. However, core capabilities create no competitive advantage if they are easy to imitate by one's competitors. Core capabilities that are difficult to imitate and continuously improve are what effective leaders seek to create. We believe that there are at least three separate and always combinable means for converting value added organizational functions and/or business processes into strategic capabilities that are difficult to imitate and thus a course of products with a sustainable competitive advantage. These are (1) knowledge-based competencies, (2) alliance-based competencies, and (3) technology-based competencies (Obloj, Cushman, and Kozminski 1994).

Knowledge-based competencies arise when in comparing a firm's value chain with the value chain of all of the firm's competitors, one locates some single or combination of value-added organizational functions and/or business processes in which one excels in comparison to one's competitors. The question will then arise as to how the firm should strategically link and configure those value-added activities with its customers to produce a product that has a sustainable competitive advantage. In such cases, it is one's own firm's unique knowledge in the form of value-added activities which when grouped into capabilities in linking with the customers, yields a competitive advantage (Barton 1992).

②   Alliance-based competencies reside in comparing a firm's value chain with a firm's competitors and finding that, although some aspects of a firm's value chain can produce value added activities, some portions of the firm's value chain of most concern to the customer are not present or not functioning at an appropriate level. Under such conditions, an organization may choose to form one or more linking arrangements with other firms that are performing well in these customer sensitive areas to obtain sustainable competitive advantage. Such linkages may take the form of mergers, acquisitions, equity partnerships, consortia, joint ventures, development agreements, supply agreements, or marketing agreements (Nohria and Garcia-Pont 1991, 105; Prahalad and Haimal 1990).

③   Technology-based capabilities reside in comparing a firm's value chain with a firm's competitors and finding that, although some aspects of a firm's value chain can produce value added activities, some portions of a firm's value chain of most concern to the customer cannot function without the addition of some new technology. Under such conditions, the firm's entire value chain may be in need of modification to reap the benefits of the addition of this new technology. The knowledge necessary to obtain this value-added advantage resides in the innovative and appropriate use of these new technologies (Stalk, Evans, and Schulman 1992).

The Toyota automobile corporation combined their three types of core competencies when it created the Toyota Production System (TPS), sometimes called *lean production management,* in its automobile manufacturing. They employed alliance-based core competencies in developing just-in-time production, knowledge-based core competencies in the form of new manufacturing materials, and technology-based core competencies in automating their production lines in a unique manner to eliminate defects. Toyota's lean manufacturing system has for the past twenty years built cars for the world market on an average faster, with higher quality, more unique features, and at a lower cost than any of its competitors. Customers have responded to this knowledge-based capability by increasing Toyota's market shares, ranking these cars top in quality, and demanding that other producers provide similar standard features (Womack, Jones, and Roos 1990).

The Role of Coalignment Broker

Successful leaders in network organizations must proceed through several operational steps in developing a firm's core competencies in a in-imitable manner. Such a leader must (1) understand pent-up customer demand; (2) be aware of competitors core competencies; (3) identify one's own core competencies; (4) decide how one's own core competencies can be strengthened through outside linkages; (5) develop a vision, set of priorities, and operations for forging a strong set of inimitable process-oriented linkages; and (6) then continuously improve these linkages and core capabilities through teamwork, setting benchmarking, and further linkages (Bartlett and Goshal 1993).

The organizational network management literature thus gave rise to a new leadership role, namely, that of a coalignment broker, which functions both within and between firms and which must be added to our transformational leadership role and skills to make clear the characteristics of high-speed management leadership. In a network organization a leader does not plan, organize, and control resources that are held in-house; rather such a leader serves as a coalignment broker across firms, many of which are not under a single firm's control. Such a coalignment broker must have three skills—those of architect, lead operator, and caretaker of inter-organizational coalignment (Snow, Miles, Coleman 1993).

Leaders who act as architects facilitate the emergence of specific operating networks that can function at given levels of quality and productivity within a specific high-speed management time frame. Leaders who act as lead operators must establish the correct coalignment between functional units and firms giving them a clear vision, specific missions, and performance targets for assisting in fulfilling both firms' goals. Then a monitoring, reward, and adjudication system for conflicts must be put in place to guarantee high performance. Finally, network leadership requires constant caretaking; namely, coaching, resource enhancement, and fine tuning to maintain a high performance. Here the tools of continuous improvement teams, setting benchmarking, and new external linkages come into play. In addition to the top management team, each firm, according to Bartlett and Goshal (1992, 124–129), must develop three additional levels of leadership: the business mana-ger who is a strategist, architect, and coordinator; the country manager who is an environmental scanner, builder, and contrac-tor; and the functional or process manager who is a monitor, cross-pollinator, and champion.

Whereas the research on transformational leadership yields a focus on anticipating change, visioning, empowerment, and value congruence skills for directing and motivating worker involve-ment, the research on network leadership adds to this the role of coalignment broker who has the skills to create outside linkages with firms, who can enhance one's own firms core competencies and function as an architect, lead operator, and caretaker of these linkages. We are now in a position to explore the contributions of the literature on managing organizational discontinuities to our characterization of a high-speed management broker.

LEADING DISCONTINUOUS ORGANIZATIONAL CHANGE

The research literature on managing organizational discontinuities focuses on the roles and skills involved in transforming a firm from one vision or set of core competencies to another. This literature yields two rather specific sets of insights for the high-speed man-agement leader: (1) organizations will go through periods of rapid and dramatic change during which the vision and core competen-cies to be acquired are *known,* and on other occasions the vision and core competencies to be acquired are *unknown;* and (2) the leaders who will successfully guide change must employ some roles and skills that are unique to and some common to each of these types of change (Burdett 1993, 10).

Unique Change Skills

Differential roles and skills are involved in leading a change and setting performance targets where the vision or core competen-cies are known (stable change) and those where they are un-known (unstable change). Table 3.1 contains a list of these differ-ences.

Common Change Skills

Common to both types of change is the need to create a positive learning environment in which a firm's employees are guided

TABLE 3.1.
Types of Change Skills

Known	Unknown
Single vision communicated	Multiple visions communicated
Clear performance targets	Flex performance targets
Manage organizational change	Manage organizational constraints
Improve core competencies	Outservice multiple core competencies
Empower decision making	Centralize decision making
Follow a fixed time frame	Follow multiple time frames
Flex time performance, ahead of competition	Flex performance against competition
Create tension and release it	Minimize tension
Bring core skills in-house	Leave core skills out-of-house
Limit outside linkages	Increase outside linkages
Set benchmarks	Make suppliers use benchmarks
Employ teams	Make suppliers employ teams
Boundaryed organizational system	Boundaryless organizational system

on a journey of organizational renewal in which they redefine the assumptions underpinning the meaning and measures of (a) performance, (b) work, and (c) the organization itself. The first of these transformations, performance, requires a redefinition of a firm's critical success factors. The second, work, requires a redefinition of empowerment. The third, a redefinition of the firm, requires a knowledge of outside linking or networking possibilities (Burdett 1993).

To understand the pattern of possibilities for success in such a transformation, a high-speed management leader must have an estimate of the time available to get a product to market ahead of its competitors and some knowledge and skill in expanding or contracting a firm's span of attention for meeting these deadlines. The major leadership skills involved in meeting these deadlines are (a) creating an organizational tension sufficient for motivating a firm's leadership and workers to leave their old core competencies and move to a new set; (b) creating a learning framework to guide the change in core competencies; and (c) targeting objective critical success factors, empowerment goals, and networking links to be established within the prescribed time frame (Burdett 1993, 13–14).

A leader must be careful in attempting to create the tension necessary for change to create a positive learning environment as well. If one creates too much tension without guiding the productive channeling of that tension into positive learning situations, emotion renders the employees motionless and work halts. If one creates too little tension then employees hold on to old habits and resist change. Methods are available to leaders for creating a positive tension which can lead to the appropriate level of learning and implementation of new core competencies. Among these are benchmarking with both the best in the industry and the best, period; moving from seniority to meritocracy; improving the quality and openness of performance feedback by including peers and subordinates in the process; removing those, especially those at senior levels, who represent poor role models; encouraging risk; taking nondecision-making levels out of hierarchy; rewarding success; discouraging concepts of turf; striving for synergies; and focusing on output (Burdett 1993, 16).

Two examples will serve to illustrate the use of all these skills and tools for creating a known and unknown transformational change. In the mid-1980s the Chrysler Automotive firm was having trouble designing and producing cars in a short enough time span to compete with Ford and Toyota, the leading U.S. and Japanese firms. The CEO Lee Iacocoa decided to discontinue the firm's old core competencies in design, engineering, and producing and transform the firm's core competencies to Ford and Toyota's lean production model. The firm made a commitment of $1 billion over five years to construct and implement a new R&D and production center. To create a strong and positive tension for the acquisition and implementation of these new knowledge, technology, and parts alliance competencies, all the old competency units were closed and Chrysler outsourced the design, engineering, and production of its new car models from Japanese firms (Levin 1992).

During the first three years of new competency acquisitions, all the tools for extending a firm's span of attention were employed and during the final two years of new competency implementation, all the tools for shortening a firm's span of attention were employed to produce new models within a two-year time frame. In addition, the implementation process set Chrysler's performance benchmarks against the best Ford and Toyota facilities in the world. The work force was downsized by cutting both managers and workers who could not learn and implement the new skills, and all the types of change tools for known competencies were exploited to create a world-class R&D and production center. By 1991 the Chrysler auto division had been completely restructured, new core competencies were in place, and a steady flow of new products were on the way to market, expanding Chrysler's market shares, and the types of cars offered from a single platform. Chrysler's stock went up and the firm was in an excellent competitive position to turn the firm over to a new management team upon Iaccoca's retirement (Schonfeld 1992, 56–57; A. Taylor 1992:82).

In the early 1990s the American Telephone and Telegraph Company faced a crisis and an opportunity of unknown proportions on two fronts (Andrews 1993b, 1). First, new developments in cellular technology were beginning to reveal the broad outline of a revolution in long distance phone, computer, and visual transmission services. Motorola had began a program to launch sixty-eight low-level satellites that could create a global wireless telephone revolution (Lewyn 1992, 25–29). Second, new developments in electronic games, radio, and multimedia technology were indicating the broad outline of a revolution in centralizing TV, telephones, radio, and computer communication in a single unit. AT&T was heavily involved in computer and long distance communication through wire cable and high-level satellites. To protect itself from becoming knowledge and technologically outdated, AT&T CEO Robert Allen embarked on a broad acquisition and alliance program in both of these areas. AT&T paid $12.6 billion to acquire McGraw Cellular giving them control of a vast wireless network and bringing the core knowledge and technology involved in-house. Next, it invested heavily in ten firms involved in the multimedia research and development and set up alliances with these firms while keeping them outside AT&T primary core competencies. Finally, AT&T embarked on a strong set of alliances with local cable television and telephone companies to supply either cable or wireless service (Andrews 1993b, 1). The results have been an increase in sales, profits, and stock prices and AT&T is now poised to transform its firm in any or all of these directions (Kirkpatrick 1993, 35–66).

A high-speed management leader has as a controlling interest time, speed to market to outperform one's competitors. A high-speed management leader also must fulfill at least three new leadership roles: transformational leader, network leader, and leader of discontinuous change.

AN EXAMPLE OF HIGH-SPEED MANAGEMENT
LEADERSHIP IN A WORLD-CLASS FIRM

The search for internal synergies, the development of strategic alliances, and the push for new ventures, all emphasize the political side of a leader's work. Executives must be able to juggle a set of constituencies rather than control a set of subordinates. They have to bargain, negotiate, and sell instead of making unilateral decisions and issuing commands. The leader's task, as Chester Barnard recognized long ago, is to develop a network of cooperative relationships among all the people, groups, and organizations that have something to contribute to an economic enterprise.

(Kanter 1989, 90)

In attempting to locate an example of a high-speed management leader to analyze, we turn to Jack Welch, the CEO of the General Electric Company (GE). He was selected for three reasons.

First, his thirteen year reign as CEO of General Electric has produced rather dramatic results. GE's sales rose from $27.9 billion to $62.2 billion, profits rose from $2.9 billion to $4.7 billion, stock appreciation went from $31 per share to $93 per share with stockholder equity reaching $73.9 billion. GE thus became the fifth largest industrial corporation in America, the third largest in profits, and the second largest in stockholder equity (*Fortune* April 9, 1993, 185).

Second, GE is one of only eight U.S. multinational firms to make a profit in each of the last twenty years. In addition, each of GE's fourteen businesses are ranked number one or two in market shares in the world with a thirteen-year increase in productivity of over 110 percent and average increases in quality and response time of over 300 percent.

Third, Jack Welch has won *Foreign World Magazine*'s outstanding leader in the world, *Fortune* magazine's Leadership Hall of Fame Award, and numerous other leadership awards. In addition, over twenty of GE's former top executives have become successful CEOs of such global firms as GTE, Allied Signal, Goodyear Tire, Owens-Corning, Ryland Group, General Dynamics, Wang Laboratories, Sundstrand, Rubbermaid, M/A Communications, USF&G, Zorn Industries, Clean Harbor, and Systems Computer Technology (*New York Times* March 9, 1992, D1).

Let us examine briefly Jack Welch as a high-speed management leader (i.e., transformational, network, and discontinuities leader) across three of his anticipated needs for a transformation in the General Electric Corporation.

Transformation 1. To The Most Competitive and Valuable Firm in the World

In 1981, Jack Welch became CEO of the General Electric Corporation and anticipated his first need for a transformational change. Welch (1988, 12) recalls his thoughts: "At the beginning of the decade . . . we faced a world economy that would be characterized by slower growth with stronger global competitors going after a smaller pie. In the context of that environment we had one clear-cut major competitor: Japan, Inc. . . . powerful . . . innovative . . . and moving aggressively into many of our markets."

In an attempt to create and operationalize a transformational vision, Welch set two clear and simple goals for his firm and outlined the operational targets for reaching these goals.

To Become the Most Competitive Corporation in the World   This principle is currently operationalized to mean that each of GE's thirteen businesses should (1) invest only in businesses with high growth potential where GE can become the number 1 or 2 in market shares in the world; (2) increase productivity and grow 6 percent per year; (3) decentralize power and responsibility downward to make each business unit as fast and flexible as possible in responding to global competition; (4) develop low-cost, high-quality, easily serviced products that are customer oriented to yield increased market shares in order to fund the R&D and acquisitions necessary to remain number 1 or 2; (5) monitor carefully the ability of each business to meet productivity and financial targets; and (6) intervene when necessary to make each business become a "win-aholic."

To Become the Nation's Most Valuable Corporation   This principle is currently operationalized to mean the "most valuable" in terms of market capitalization. This principle manifests itself in a number of specific ways at GE: (1) keep earnings rising at 5 to 10 percent per year; (2) keep stock appreciation and yield at about 15 to 20 percent per year; (3) shift earning mix so 50 percent can come from a high-growth area; (4) keep supplier productivity rising at about 5 to 10 percent per year; (5) maintain exports as percent of sales at about 50 percent; and (6) maintain management's reputation as an entrepreneurial, agile, knowledgeable, aggressive, and effective competitor.

Jack Welch created an organizational tension in 1981 by redefining his firm's goals and targets. He then released the tension in a series of dramatic and now famous moves. First, he cut GEs 150 independent business units down to 14, each positioned in a high-growth industry in which GE ranked number 1 or 2 in market shares in the world. These businesses were aircraft engines, broadcasting, circuit breakers, defense electronics, electric motors, engineering, plastics, factory automation, industrial power systems, lighting, locomotives, major appliances, medical diagnostics, financial service and communications (Sherman 1989, 40). Second, between 1981 and 1993, Welch sold over 200 of GE's business units worth $10 billion while acquiring and combining over 300 business worth $20 billion into 14. He closed 78 production facilities, invested $25 billion in automating the remaining 200 U.S. units and the 130 abroad in twenty-four countries, making them world-class manufacturing facilities. Third, Welch shed over 150,000 workers, one out of every four workers. He reduced nine layers of management to five, releasing one out of every four managers. Fourth, he decentralized power, expanded his managers' span of control, built an all new executive team, and restructured every business, replacing thirteen of fourteen business leaders.

Welch realized that GE would have to undertake framebreaking changes if it were to meet this challenge and become a world-class competitive organization. Welch (1988, 2) sketched his vision and described its roots.

> Our experience during the late '70's in grappling with world competition etched very clearly on our minds the belief that companies that held on to marginal businesses—or less than world-competitive operations of any sort—wouldn't be around

for very long. That analysis led us to a strategy that said we had to be number one or number two in each one of our businesses . . . or we had to see a way to get there . . . or exit if we couldn't. The product businesses had to achieve global leadership positions in cost, quality and technology. Our services businesses had to define and attain leading niche positions in the broad spectrum of markets they served. That was—that is—our strategy: simple, even stark.

In 1988, Welch stood back and reflected on this effort: "Now, how we went at this can be described from two totally different perspectives. One perspective would use words like 'downsizing,' 'reducing,' 'cutting.' We think that view misses the point. We see our task as a totally different one aimed at liberating, facilitating, unleashing the human energy and initiative of our people." At the heart of this change and institutionalization process was Welch's (1988, 3) use of empowerment.

> Sure we saved. Simply by eliminating the company's top operating level, the sectors, we saved $40 million. But that was just a bonus that pales in importance to the sudden release of talent and energy that poured out after all the dampers, valves and baffles of the sectors had been removed. We can say without hesitation that almost every single good thing that has happened within this company over the past few years can be traced to the liberation of some individual, some team, some business.
>
> So we reduced the number of management layers in the company to get closer to the individual—the source of that creative energy we needed.
>
> In reducing these layers, we are trying to get the people in the organization to understand that they can't do everything they used to do. They have to set priorities. The less important tasks have to be left undone. Trying to do the same number of tasks with fewer people would be the antithesis of what we set out to achieve: a faster, more focused, more purposeful company.
>
> As we became leaner, we found ourselves communicating better, with fewer interpreters and fewer filters.
>
> We found that with fewer layers we had wider spans of management. We weren't managing better. We were managing less, and that was better.

Finally, Welch and his new GE management team demonstrated self-understanding in what the institutionalization of change had done for the organization. Welch (1988, 3) continues:

> We found that the leaders—people with a vision and a passion—soon began to stand out. And when they did, we found our own self-confidence growing to the point that we began to delegate authority further and further down into the company. Businesses were allowed to develop their own pay plans and incentives that made sense for *their* marketplaces. They were given the freedom to spend significant sums on plant and equipment on their own, based on *their* needs, *their* judgement, *their* view of their marketplace. Freeing people to move rapidly and without hesitation makes all the difference in the world . . . we have found what we believe is the distilled essence of competitiveness—the reservoir of talent and creativity and energy that can be found in each of our people. That essence is liberated when we make people believe that what they think and do is important . . . and then get out of their way while they do it.

Transformation 2. To Speed Simplicity and Self-Confidence

In April 1988 (Welch 1988, 4) this first massive reengineering was all but complete and Welch began to anticipate the need for a second transformation in GE. Welch reflects:

> . . . today the world is even tougher and more crowded. Korea and Taiwan have become world-class competitors, as hungry and aggressive as Japan was in 1981. Europe is on fire with a new entrepreneurial spirit and leadership that is among the world's best. Many of its most aggressive companies, like Electrolux and ASEA of Sweden, Philips of Holland, and Siemens and Bayer of Germany, are after our markets through acquisitions and joint ventures—just as we are going after theirs.
>
> At the same time, the Japanese are more sophisticated and aggressive than ever—building servicing plants outside Japan, including dozens just over the Mexican border.

By 1988, Ge's challenges were internal and even larger than in 1981. Welch (1988, 1–2) reflects: "We had to find a way to combine the power, resources, and reach of a *big* company with the hunger, the agility, the spirit, and fire of a small company." The rationale for this change was simple, that only the most productive, high-quality, and rapid response firms were going to win in the 1990s. If you cannot produce a top quality product at the world's lowest price and get it to market in less time than your competitors, you are going to be out of the game. In such an environment, 5 percent annual increase in productivity and quality will not be enough, more will be needed. Welch argued that now a firm must (1) define its vision in broad, simple, and strategic terms; (2) maximize its productivity, quality, and speed to market; and (3) be organizationally and culturally innovative, flexible, and rapid in responding to shifting customer demand for low-price, high-value products. He then called for GE to reorient its internal vision to "speed, simplicity and self-confidence." To meet this internal vision, two new goals and sets of targets were put in place.

To Develop a Skilled, Self-Actualizing, Productive, and Aggressive Work Force Capable of Generating and Employing Practical and Technical Knowledge   This principle is operationalized currently to mean GE wants to create an environment in which GE will be viewed as a challenging place to work and that will significantly enhance worker skills so that they can find another job if the company no longer needs them—a place where employees are ready to go but eager to stay. To actualize this goal (1) develop employee awareness that the only road to job security is increasing market shares; (2) develop employees who are more action oriented, more risk oriented, and more people oriented; (3) develop employees who relentlessly pursue individual and group goals; (4) develop employee skills and performance through timely and high-quality education programs; (5) hold employees responsible for meeting productivity and financial targets; and (6) reward high performance and deal effectively with low performance.

To Develop Open Communication Based on Candor and Trust   This principle is operationalized to mean sharing with all employees the corporation's vision, goals, and values; opening up each employee to discussion regarding his or her strengths, weaknesses, and the possibility for change. This is accomplished by speaking openly and listening carefully to discussions aimed at preparing, articulating, refining, and gaining acceptance for unit visions; showing candor and trust in sharing and evaluating personal and business plans; motivating employees to become more open, more self-confident, more energized individuals in generating and employing practical and technical knowledge (Cushman and King 1994).

Two new mechanisms were put forward to create a tension capable of meeting these new goals—reengineering GE's corporate culture and creating of a continuous improvement program. A new corporate culture was devised and put in place by GE stakeholders to aid in the development of speed, simplicity, and self-confidence. This new culture focused on improving organizational productivity, quality, and response time.

Next GE put in place a continuous improvement program aimed at reengineering GE's organizational processes by increasing the firm's productivity and quality while decreasing its response time. The program included a self-managed team program called *workout,* a cross-functional team program called *process mapping,* a benchmark *best practices* program, and an aggressive outside linking program.

(1) *A New England Town Meeting.* A unit or function is created within the organization to implement a worker continuous improvement program within a New England town meeting format. Its goal is to improve an organization's productivity, quality, flexibility, adaptability, or response time. It is an attempt to eliminate nonessential, nonproductive, or "bad" work and replace it with "good" work. These New England-style town meetings last from one to three days. They begin with the division head calling together 20–100 workers, suppliers, or customers.

The meeting then proceeds in the following manner:

- The division head opens the meeting with a presentation of key market issues, the organization's vision in responding to these issues, how the organization and its competitors are responding to this vision, and specific organizational needs for increased productivity, quality, flexibility, adaptability, and rapid response time. The division head leaves at this point in the meeting.

- Teamwork facilitators take over and generate a list of bad work to be eliminated and good work to be undertaken in responding to the various areas of concern.

- The group is then divided into teams of five to ten members to analyze, discuss, and debate potential areas for improvement.

- Each team then provides a cost-benefit analysis and action plan for the solutions recommended.

- The division head then returns and listens to a cost-benefit analysis and action plan from each group.

The division head acts on all high-yield ideas by selecting a team champion, training the team champion in project management, empowering a team to implement the change, setting performance targets, measurement criteria, time frame, and feedback procedures. The worker improvement team then implements the action plan. New England town meetings create practical knowledge within a unit.

(2) *A Cross-Functional Teamwork Program.* A unit or function is created to set up cross-functional teams whose goals are to map and then improve cross-functional organizational processes. Many of the most significant improvements in organizational performance have come from mapping important cross-functional organizational processes and then asking those involved in the process to simplify or improve the functioning of that process. This approach has been very profitable for organizations because many of these processes have developed and expanded over time without anyone examining the entire process and exploring its improvement.

Here cross-functional teams are set up and assigned the task of mapping the decision, implementation, and review levels of important organizational processes. The cross-functional team is then asked to evaluate and make improvements in the process mappings. This is accomplished in four steps:

- Developing a clear understanding of the process goal.
- Identifying the necessary and sufficient critical success factors for achieving that goal.
- Mapping and improving the essential subprocesses to meet these critical success factors.
- Ranking each subprocess and evaluating its productivity, quality, flexibility, adaptability, and how to make improvements.

The unit or function then implements the change process and fine tunes its subprocesses. Cross-functional teams create across unit or process practical knowledge.

(3) *A Best Practices Benchmarking Program.* A unit or function is created to scan one's own organization and the globe for

world-class competitors and to study how various parts of these organizations succeeded in setting world-class benchmarking standards in regard to productivity, quality, flexibility, adaptability, and response time. This unit usually locates such organizations and makes a site visit, develops a case study of the processes involved, and trains personnel at its own organization in ways to adapt these innovations to its organization. This unit then sets up monitoring and feedback procedures for and implements the change. A best practices program disseminates practical knowledge.

(4) *A Negotiated Linking Program.* A unit or function is created within an organization whose purpose is to continuously scan the globe to locate resources in the form of customers, partners, technologies, and consultants capable of enhancing an organization's competitiveness. Such resources may include land, labor, capital, market entry, distribution channels, technology, or training, etc. This unit then

- Interacts with the unit holding the potential resource to locate its interests, concerns, and contributions to coalignment.
- Develops the form of coalignment preferred by both units, establishes a network of over 200 alliances, acquisitions, joint ventures, partnership coalitions, collaboration, licensing technology leasing, transfer, and training.
- Determines the world-class benchmark targets in market shares, productivity, quality, flexibility, or rapid response time to be met before coalignment can take place.

The organizational negotiated-linking program then formulates the negotiated coalignment agreement aimed at mobilizing external practical knowledge for organizational usage.

The practical objective of workout was to

> get rid of thousands of bad habits accumulated since the creation of GE 112 years ago. The intellectual goal was to put the leaders of each business in front of 100 or so employees, eight to ten times a year to let them know what their people think about how the company can be improved and then make the leaders respond to those changes. Ultimately we are restructuring the leader-subordinate relationship to challenge both to make GE a better place to work. It will force leaders and workers to combine

in creating a vision, articulating the vision, passionately owning the vision, and relentlessly driving it to completion. (Tichy and Charon 1989, 113)

By the end of 1993, over 70,000 employees will have participated in three-day workout town meetings with remarkable results. In GE's plastic division alone, over thirty workout teams have been empowered to make changes. One team saved GE Plastics $2 million by modifying one production process, another enhanced productivity fourfold, and a third reduced product delivery time 400 percent (*Workout,* September 1991, 1–2). Another business, NBC, used workout to halt the use of report forms that totaled more than 2 million pieces of paper a year (Stewart 1991, 44). GE Credit Services used workout to tie its cash registers directly to the mainframe, cutting the time for opening a new account from 30 minutes to 90 seconds. Similar results have been reported from workout projects in GE's other businesses demonstrating a remarkable companywide reorientation of coalignment processes between worker capabilities and organizational needs.

While this internal transformation of GE's value chain was taking place, Jack Welch also realized that some other global organizations were achieving greater productivity, quality control, flexibility, adaptability, and rapid response time than GE, even with the workout program in place. In the summer of 1988, GE began its best practices program aimed at locating those organizations that had outperformed GE in a given area, developing a case study of how they did it, and then employing these case studies as world-class benchmarks for improving GE's performance.

GE scanned the globe and located twenty-four corporations that had in some area outperformed GE. They then screened out direct competitors and companies which would not be credible to GE employees. Welch then invited each corporation to come to GE to learn about its best practices and in return to allow GE to come to their companies and study their best practices. About one half of the companies agreed. They included AMP, Chapparral Steel, Ford, Hewlett Packard, Xerox, and three Japanese companies. GE sent observers to develop case studies and ask questions. These best practices case studies have been turned into a course at Crotonville, GE's leadership training center, and is offered to a new class of managers from each of GE's fourteen businesses each month (Stewart 1991, 44–45).

Finally, as GE's top management team reviewed the projects that had been successful from both their workout and best practices programs, it noticed a difference in the types of product which saved up to $1 million and those which saved $100 million. The latter always involved changes in organizational processes which spanned the entire value chain. They cut across departments and involved linking with suppliers and customers. All emphasized managing processes, not functions. This led GE to establish its cross-functional teamwork program aimed at mapping and then improving key organizational processes. Such process maps frequently allowed employees for the first time to see and understand organizational processes from beginning to end. They demonstrated also the need for a new type of manager, a process manager who could coalign an organization's total assets. It allowed employees to spot bottlenecks, time binds and inventory shortages, and overflows.

Since implementing such a cross-functional teamwork program, GE appliances has cut its sixteen-week manufacturing cycle in half, while increasing product availability 6 percent and decreasing inventory costs 20 percent. The program has cost less than $3 million to implement and has already returned profits 100 times that (Stewart 1991, 48). Product mapping programs have provided also an empirical basis for changing how GE measures its management and workers' performance. GE now employs world-class cross-functional process benchmarking standards to evaluate its various business performances and award its bonuses and merit awards for process improvement practical knowledge (Cushman and King 1993).

The 1990s, according to Jack Welch (1988, 4), will be a "white-knuckle decade for global business . . . fast . . . exhilarating," with many winners and losers. But according to Welch GE is ready. His transformational vision, mobilization, and institutionalization in the 1980s has put GE in position to meet these new threats head on with minimal stress, and with the communication, speed, flexibility, and efficiency of a creative firm. Welch forsaw this development in 1988 (page 4):

> We approach the '90's with a business system, a method of operating, that allows us to routinely position each business for the short- and long-term so that while one or more are weathering

difficult markets, the totality is always growing faster than the world economy.

No one in the world has a set of powerful businesses like ours. They've never been stronger. And big, bold moves are enhancing their global competitiveness: . . . Plastics by expansion in the U.S., Europe and the Far East . . . GE's numerous domestic acquisitions . . . Aircraft Engine with its European partnership . . . Factory Automation's worldwide venture with Fanue of Japan . . . Medical Systems' French and Japanese acquisitions . . . NBC's new station and programming initiatives . . . joint ventures by Lighting in the Far East and most recently, Roper's acquisition by Major Appliance. The list of moves goes on and on and will continue at an even faster pace. Our business strategy, grounded in reality has become real. Our businesses are number one or two in their marketplaces.

To go with our business strategy, we've got a management system now in place and functioning that supports that strategy—one that is lean, liberating, fast-moving—an organization that facilitates and frees and, above all, understands that the fountainhead of success is the individual, not the system.

Transformation 3. The Push to Become a Major Player in the Pacific Rim Markets

In 1992 Jack Welch began to reflect on the need for a third transformation in GE. He believed that the slow 3 percent projected growth rate for European, U.S., and Japanese core markets over the next several years would limit GE's growth. He believed that if GE were to remain a global leader, it must take steps to position itself in the major emerging markets of the Pacific Rim: China, India, Mexico, and Southeast Asia. These markets are growing and will continue to grow at 8 to 12 percent per year for the next ten to twenty years. In addition, GE's growth in revenue from these areas had gone from $10 to $20 billion in the last three years (Smart, Engadino, and Smith 1993, 64–70). Welch believed that to remain a global leader, GE had to shift its center of gravity from the U.S.-Europe relationship to the U.S.-Pacific Rim markets. This was to be accomplished through a two-pronged strategy with specific performance targets for each.

GE Must Become a Multipolar, Multicultural Firm   This principle is operationalized currently to mean that, although GE's fourteen businesses are currently number 1 or 2 in Europe and the United States and should defend this status, they must now become number 1 or 2 in the major markets of the Pacific Rim: China, India, Mexico, and Southeast Asia. To actualize this goal, GE must (1) develop profit centers in each of these markets; (2) develop a multicultural pool of business leaders and employees; (3) integrate Pacific Rim nations into their R&D, manufacturing, sales, and service systems; (4) extend GE's management system into these major markets; and (5) increase investment in GE from the region.

To Employ GE's Strong Infrastructure in Technology Transfer Management Training, and Financial Services to Broadly and Deeply Penetrate These Markets   To do this GE is (1) developing joint ventures in technology transfer with firms in the region, (2) training foreign nationals in the United States and then sending them back to Asia to head GE units, (3) exporting GE's training programs to the region, (4) using GE financial services to fund projects in the region which use GE products, and (5) making small $10 million investments throughout the region to hedge against foreign currency fluctuations and other forms of economic instability.

Thus far, the results of these strategies have been promising. GE's reality-based action training programs have taken managers from Asian cultures and trained them in management skills in the United States. Next these managers were shipped to the Pacific Rim's major markets to interview old, new, and potential GE customers, competitors, and business managers. Finally, GE asked these managers to develop market penetration plans and a value chain, engineering plans to better position the firm's business in the region. Similarly GE's middle management training programs are rotating promising multicultural leaders through different businesses and markets in Asia to create a truly global multipolar, multicultural leader.

GE has invested over $100 million in factories to produce medical imaging equipment, plastics, appliances, and lamps in India. GE sales in India will go from $400 million to $1 billion by the year 2000. GE has moved boldly into China where the government plans to add $100 billion in power generators, 100 jet engines, 1,000 medical imagers, and over 200 locomotives in the next four years. GE Capital has been creative in helping the Chinese government set up a new development bank to fund these activities. In Indonesia GE is part of a $2 billion power plant project and offered an array of technology transfer projects to help upgrade Indonesia's industrial capacities.

In Malaysia, GE now owns a 49 percent interest in UMW Corporation. In Mexico, GE has over twenty factories with 21,000 employees who have upheld GE appliances as a household name. GE will have over $1.5 billion in sales this year, up from $900 million last year. GE broadcasting has joined with Rupert Murdoch's Star TV system to launch a new business and news channel throughout the Asian region. Finally GE Capital, a $155 billion per year financial arm, has made $200 million in funds available for loans to small business in Asia. In short, GE is on the move again, transforming its firm, people, and resources to fit the needs of customers in the Pacific Rim (Stewart 1993, 64–70). In so doing, it brings GE's unique brand of management to Asia. GE's blend of entrepreneurial spirit with a hard driving and intensely competitive focus transfers into an obsession with performance, an ability to shift strategy rapidly to take advantage of change, an appetite for risk taking and deal making, and an engineer's yen to run productive, high-quality, and rapid-response operations. In addition GE's CEO Jack Welch, may be one of the world's best transformational, network, and discontinuities leaders. He is looking to position GE as a dominant player in the Pacific Rim region while maintaining a dominant position in Europe and the Americas.

CRITICAL SUCCESS FACTORS OF A HIGH-SPEED MANAGEMENT LEADER

> The basic function of [leadership] appears to be the coalignment not merely of people in coalitions but of institutional action—of technology and task environment into a viable domain, and of organizational design and structure appropriate to it. Leadership functions well when it keeps the organization at the nexus of several necessary streams of action.
>
> (Thompson 1967, 21)

We began our investigation of corporate leadership with a review of the literature covering four decades of research. Beginning with power perspectives and proceeding through trait, behavioral, and contingency perspectives, we traced the role of leadership in corporations from charismatic leadership through situational leadership. We then noted that these perspectives all presupposed a relatively stable business environment based on incremental change. However, with the advent of a turbulent global economic environment and the need to deal with discontinuous change, a new high-speed management leader has emerged. This type of leader focuses on transformations, network management, and managing organizational discontinuities. The critical success factors for this final type of leader are these:

1. A leader must have accurate information on customer pentup demand, competitor core capabilities, and product life-cycle timelines and one's own core capabilities.

2. A leader must effectively anticipate and communicate a vision of the next transformation, goals, targets, and a time frame for implementing the known or unknown change.

3. A leader must select the non-imitable core competencies to be acquired and adjust the firm's span of attention and tension levels to motivate this enhancement within the time frame required.

4. A leader must act as a broker of these new coalignment patterns both within and outside the firm.

5. A leader must institutionalize a monitoring and reward program for the transformed performance target in following known and unknown patterns of change.

REFERENCES

Andrews, E. (1993a). "AT&T Paying $12.6 billion for McCaw Cellular." *New York Times* (August 17): A-1.

———. (1993b). "AT&T Reaches Out and Grabs Everyone." *New York Times* (August 8): Section 3, p. 1.

Bartlett, C., and S. Goshal. (1993). "What Is a Global Manager?" *Harvard Business Review* (October–September): 124–132.

Bartmess, A., and K. Cerney. (1993). "Building Competitive Adventure Through a Global Network Capability." *California Management Review* (Winter): 78–123.

Barton, D. (1992). "Core Capabilities and Core Rigidities: A Paradox in Managing New Product Development." *Strategic Management Journal* 13: 111–128.

Blake, Robert, and Jane Mouton. (1978). *The New Management Grid.* Houston: Gulf Publishing.

Bray, D. W., R. J. Campbell, and D. L. Grant. (1974). *Formative Years in Business: A Long Term AT&T Study of Managerial Lives.* New York: John Wiley & Sons.

Burdett, J. (1993). "Managing in the Age of Discontinuity." *Management Decisions* 31: 10–17.

Byrd, Richard. (1987). "Corporate Leadership Skill: 'A new Synthesis'." *Organizational Dynamics:* 34–43.

Cohn, R. (1992). "The Very Model of Efficiency." *New York Times* (March 2): D1–D8.

Cushman, D., and S. King. (1994). *High-Speed Management and Organizational Communication in the 1990s: A Reader.* Albany: SUNY Press.

———. (1993). "High-Speed Management: A Revolution in Organizational Communication in the 1990s." In S. Deetz, *Communication Yearbook 16,* pp. 209–236. Newbury Park, Calif.: Sage Publications.

Dumaine, B. (1993). "The New Non-Manager Managers." *Fortune* (February 22): 36–112.

Fortune. (1991). "General Electric as CEO Boot Camp." (April 8): 12.

French, J., and B. Raven. (1959). "The Bases of Social Power." In D. Cartwright (ed.), *Studies of Social Power,* pp. 150–167. Ann Arbor, Mich.: Institute of Social Research.

Harris, G. (1993). "The Post-Capitalist Executive: An Interview with Peter Drucker." *Harvard Business Review,* (May–June): 115–122.

Hersey, P., and K. H. Blanchard. (1977). *Management of Organizational Behavior.* Englewood Cliffs, N.J.: Prentice-Hall.

Hunsicker, J. Quincy. (1985). "Vision, Leadership and Europe's Business Future." *European Management Journal* 3 no. 3: 22–38.

Jacob, R. (1992). "The Search for the Organization of Tomorrow." *Fortune* 2: 91–98.

Kerr, S., and J. M. Jarmier. (1978). "Substitutes for Leadership: Their Meaning and Measurement." *Organizational Behavior and Human Performance* 22: 375–403.

Kanter, R. (1989). "The New Managerial Work." *Harvard Business Review* (November–December): 85–92.

Kirkpatrick, D. (1993). "Could AT&T Rule the World?" *Fortune* (May 17): 55–64.

Levin, D. (1992). "New L/H as in Last Hope." *New York Times* (July 12): Section 3, p. 1.

Lewyn, M. (1992). "AT&T's Bold Bet." *Business Week* (August 30): 27–32.

Liberson, S., and J. F. O'Conner. (1972). "Leadership and Organizational Performance: A Study of Large Corporations." *American Sociological Review* 37: 117–130.

Likert, Rensis. (1961). *New Patterns of Management.* New York: McGraw-Hill.

Miner, J. B. (1978). "Twenty Years of Research on Role Motivation Theory of Managerial Effectiveness." *Personnel Psychology* 31: 739–760.

Mintzberg, H. (1973). *The Nature of Management Work.* New York: Harper and Row.

Nohria, N., and C. Garcia-Pont. (1991). "Global Strategies, Linkages, and Industrial Structure." *Strategic Management* 6: 105–124.

Obloj, K., D. P. Cushman, and A. Kozminski. (1994). *Winning: A Continuous Improvement Theory and Practice.* Albany: SUNY Press.

Ostroff, F., and D. Smith. (1992). "Redesigning the Corporation: The Horizontal Organization." *The McKinsey Quarterly* 1: 148–168.

Prahalad, C. K., and G. Haimal. (1990). "The Core Competencies of the Corporation." *Harvard Business Review* (May–June): 74–91.

Prokesch, Steven. (1987). "Remaking the American C.E.O." *New York Times* (January 25): Section 3, 1 and 8.

Schonfeld, E. (1992). "Iacoca, Lee's Parting Shot." *Fortune* (September 7): 56–57.

Sherman, D. (1989). "The Mind of Jack Welch." *Fortune* (March 27): 39–50.

Smart, T., P. Engadino, and G. A. Smith. (1993). "GE's Brave New World." *Business Week* (November 8): 64–70.

Snow, C., R. Miles, and H. Coleman. (1992). "Managing Twenty-first Century Network Organizations." *Organizational Dynamics:* 5–19.

Stalk, G., P. Evans, and L. Schulman. (1992). "Competing on Capabilities: The New Rules of Corporate Strategy." *Harvard Business Review* (March–April): 57–69.

Stewart, T. (1991). "GE Keeps Those Ideas Coming." *Fortune* (August 12): 118–122.

———. (1992). "The Firm of Tomorrow." *Fortune* (May 18): 93–98.

———. (1993). "Reengineering: The Hot New Managing Tool." *Fortune* (August 23): 41–48.

Stogdill, R. M. (1974). *Handbook of Leadership: A Survey of Theory and Research.* New York: The Free Press.

Taylor, A. (1992). "Chrysler's Next Boss Speaks." *Fortune* (July 27): 82–83.

Taylor, W. (1991). "The Logic of Global Business: An Interview with ABB's Percy Barnevik, *Harvard Business Review* (March/April), 91–105.

Thompson, J. D. (1967). *Organizations in Action: Social Science of Administration Theory.* New York: McGraw-Hill.

Tichy, N. M. (1989). "GE's Crotonville: A Staging Ground for Corporate Revolution." *Academy of Management Excellence* 3: 99–106.

——— and P. Charon. (1989). "Speed, Simplicity, and Self-Confidence: An Interview with Jack Welch." *Harvard Business Review* (September–October): 112–120.

——— and Devanno M. (1986). "The Transformational Leader." *Training and Development Journal* 40, no. 7 (July): 27–32.

——— and Ulrich B. (1984). "SMR Forum: The Leadership Challenge—A Call for the Transformational Leaders." *Sloan Management Review* (Fall): 59–68.

Tushman, M., Newman, B., and Romanelli E. (1986). "Convergence and Upheaval: Managing the Unsteady Pace of Organizational Evolution." *California Management Review* 29 no. 1 (Fall): 29–44.

Welch, J. (1988). "Managing for the Nineties." *GE Speech Reprint* (April 27).

Womack, J., D. Jones, and M. Roos. (1990). "How Lean Production Can Change the World." *New York Times Magazine* (September 23): 22–37.

Yukl, G. (1981). *Leadership in Organizations.* Englewood Cliffs, N.J.: Prentice-Hall, 1981.

Zaleznick, A. (1977). "Managers and Leaders: Are They Different?" *Harvard Business Review* (May–June): 67–78.

CHAPTER 4

Improving Community Service: Strategic Cooperation Through Communication

Rodney G. Miller

Many managers and supervisors have difficulty if the desired way of managing is not spelt out to them. Positive behaviour is much more likely to occur if it is specifically requested of people.

Emphasis needs to be placed on the importance of staying close to the people and operations of the organisation, being out and about, knowing what is going on, responding quickly, spending time talking and listening to people, involving them in developing better ways of operating, and most importantly setting a good example by their own behaviour, consistently, day after day.

James Strong, Chief Executive, QANTAS
The Australian Way (December 1993), p. 4

What a leader does communicates best. Leaders earn credibility by achieving results. Typical challenges for a leader now are (1) high-speed organizational change; (2) limited authority for wider responsibility; (3) adding value to the organization by helping others achieve results, while also adding value to the organization in the leader's specialization. This chapter describes the application of leadership and high-speed management principles to improve the community-service-based fund raising of a nonprofit organization. An organization achieves competitive advantage in this area by delivering high-speed community service. Let me illustrate the importance of "getting there" first.

Woody Allen is hardly an authority on leadership, yet he is credited with pointing out that the world should not be so preoccupied with invaders from outer space whose technology is hundreds of years ahead of ours. He claims it is not advanced technologies supported by plans for world domination that will win such a struggle. He worries about the invading force that is equipped to be anywhere fifteen minutes ahead of us (Burnet 1993). The fifteen-minute advantage would allow them each morning to eat all the breakfast cereal, use all the toothpaste, and catch all the taxis in New York, or anywhere else. They would paralyse whole cities. More seriously, these invaders could use even traditional weapons fifteen minutes before we have thought of targeting ours. The same point is evident when my son's soccer team plays. The competitive advantage when seven-year-olds chase goals is the split second that decides which team's foot gets to the ball first.

In order that an organization might develop a competitive advantage, it needs futuristic thinking as well as strategic planning to anticipate and then capitalize on future paradigm shifts (Jones 1993, 54). Mega-trends in the community that relate to service organizations include projected years of peak focus in leisure and tourism to be about 2020 AD and outer space about 2050 AD (p. 66). The popularized warnings of Alvin Toffler and others since the 1970s about the information age and the related impact on employment have translated with massive effects on people, organizations, and communities. Some might say what society experienced as a result in the early 1990s was the beginning of structured unemployment. Learning from this lesson of recent history, the valued member of an organization engineers all plans with consideration of such global trends. We need to

- stay close to customers and competitors;
- think constantly about new products and their development;
- speed up delivery by close coordination among design through delivery/servicing systems;
- ensure quality, easy access, and competitive pricing;
- prepare for flexible shifts, perhaps totally out of large product sectors;
- develop a culture that emphasizes change;

- scan the globe for potential takeovers or partnerships to improve competitiveness (Cushman and King 1993, 71–72).

We now need to integrate principles of leadership (Doyle and Kraus 1982, Bennis and Nanus 1985, Bennis 1989, Batten 1989, Thayer in press) and high-speed management (Cushman and King 1993, Jones 1993). Important shifts of emphasis in management have emerged during the last decade. Focus has increased on the global economy, visions for the future, a coach-cum-coordinator role for managers, access to different management tools such as total quality management, reengineering (Hall, Rosenthal, and Wade 1993; Stewart 1993), and EVA (economic value added) (Tully 1993), along with principles of best practice to help with the achievement of high performance in organizations.

Amid these often complementary perspectives, the special values of high-speed management theory are its employment of three separate theories and sets of practices and its focus on "getting there" first. As King and Cushman show (1994, 2), high-speed management is especially valuable in the turbulent times of the 1990s, which require flexibility in services, systems, and people to recognize and meet the expectations of customers and the challenge of competitors. High-speed management emphasizes speed of delivery of services and of the communication process changes so necessary to scan the environment; to locate areas where an organization's integration, coordination, and control system can be improved; and to employ a unique continuous improvement theory to increase the speed to market of products (pp. 2–3).

The purpose in this chapter is to describe how one organization, Queensland University of Technology, set out to improve its performance in community service. The chapter describes a process to improve delivery of community service, by outlining

- Environmental scanning processes developed to identify the values and services a community expects to see delivered;
- Interventions used to locate communication processes and the information which required improved integration, coordination, and control for better internal cooperation;
- Extension of the continuous improvement process by using the agreement of service standards and detailed checklists to improve goal alignment and increase the speed of service delivery.

The chapter comments on the dynamics of managing communications for timely impact. For an organization to deliver high-speed community service, everyone must learn to lead. Ideally, everyone thinks and acts as high-speed coordinators and looks for ways to get closer to customers and the competition. Everyone can think up better ways to get ahead of the community's expectations. The real challenge is creating a basis for more members of an organization to do this better.

THE ORGANIZATION

Queensland University of Technology (QUT) was reconstituted in January 1989 from its predecessor, Queensland Institute of Technology, formed in 1965. In May 1990, a major structural change followed because QUT amalgamated with an institution of approximately similar size. The new organization is one of Australia's largest universities, with 24,000 students and 2,600 staff members. In 1993, the *Independent Monthly's Good Universities Guide* made the inaugural award of the title "Australia's University of the Year" to QUT.

Since the 1970s QUT was a leader among Australian tertiary education institutions in emphasizing the integration of theory and practice in its teaching programs. It supported this value by providing services to business, government, and the professions, initially by encouraging individual staff members to provide consultancies and continuing education courses. More recently, it also provided a lead in offering places to privately funded students and in contract research. These services are part of the university's commercial activities. The total QUT budget in 1993 was $230 million, of which $30 million resulted from research/consulting, business, and resource development activities.

The university strengthens its link with the community through a coordinated alumni relations and fund raising program. As in North American universities, this development program secures resources which are at least partly philanthropic and usually for the university infrastructure. Fund raising is a relatively new activity for Australian universities, which are largely government funded. In the six years following QUT's first effort at fund raising in 1987, its annual income was increased from less than $0.5 million in 1987 to

$1.9 million in 1993 (showing a 55 percent increase over the previous year's result). This positioned QUT well to secure substantial resources locally and internationally to fund initiatives that benefit the community it serves. For this to occur, however, many more members of the organization (especially managers of operational areas) needed to see the value of focused community service. It required agreement on what community needs were best served, which community leaders had a mutual interest in seeing these needs served, and what long-term commitment each operating manager would make to build relationships with these leaders.

QUT's experience might apply widely to public sector organizations that are being "privatized" or "corporatized." On the extent to which it might apply to the organizations in Eastern Europe now seeking to compete in a global economy, I will be interested to hear from others who are experienced in such organizations. The chapter has application in third sector organizations. Many continue with mixed success to grapple with the challenge of deciding best practices to empower leadership and staff, particularly in the area of community service and fund raising. In the difficult economic times of the early 1990s, some nonprofit organizations continued to secure increased income from fund raising. These organizations focused on strengthening relationships in the community.

Opportunities to improve the strategic cooperation inside the organization and with the community coincide almost exactly with the processes for substantial resource development. Fund raising does more than test organizational relationship building. The process of making, renewing, or upgrading a gift is the process by which an organization gives meaning to the life of the investor (Rosso 1991, 7). Nonprofit organizations capable of involving and tracking the involvement of people are sophisticated managers of person-to-organization relations. The real "horsepower" in community service is for people within the organization to develop sophisticated leadership skills to use this capability.

Typically, as priorities shift away from routine line management of people, equipment, and budgets toward the leadership of community linkage, the importance of organized interpersonal (especially face-to-face) communication increases. At QUT, the valued work associate (whether carrying the title of manager or not) recognized the importance, stated so well by James Strong at the beginning of this chapter, of involving others to develop better ways of operating. When the value of any position is determined by what the incumbent brings to the changing organization, anyone who coordinates others has tremendous opportunity and challenge. Briefly, the opportunity is to achieve more with less and the challenge is to engage work associates more completely in processes to improve results, "consistently, day after day."

COMMUNICATION AS A VALUE

The organizational values that pertain at a particular time will influence what improvement is possible. A core organizational value that QUT council adopted as part of the mission and goals statement at the time of amalgamation was the need to cultivate effective communication at all levels of the organization (Dixon 1990, 52). Emphasis on communication in an organization implies that, the first building block of high-speed management, "environmental scanning" would be well established. As "communication" found expression as an organizational value at QUT, however, two ideas about service permeated the organization.

One idea was based in bureaucracy and another was enterprise-oriented. The first focused on internal service mainly. Work groups here had trouble overcoming their past. Internal clients and "important" internal processes filled the agenda and the working week with internal issues. Value was measured against the reinforcement of comfortable internal values. Sometimes advocates of this idea of service would clothe arguments for conservation of the bureaucracy, its committees, reports, "due process" and peer-assessment in politically correct language that sounded community oriented. Typically asserted were the virtues of learning from others, openness and cooperation, but listening to the community was undeveloped.

In the enterprise outlook, focus was on service through building relationships. People internal and external to the organization jointly identified what the future would likely pertain. A leader can draw on this group to design a vision to equip the organization to meet that future. The real work of the leader then begins, for the key value in the enterprising organization is to achieve or exceed the community's expectations.

Operating units, to address the community's expectations, must grow. Instead of being cost centers or profit centers, they need to struggle with becoming centers to improve relationship with the community. As are many organizations, QUT is still working through the tension between the bureaucratic and enterprise outlooks. How effectively members of the organization listen to community leaders about the needs the community would like served is the key to the future.

WHAT THE COMMUNITY EXPECTS

The idea of a university as an ivory tower of intellects opposes what the community expects from today's university. Community linkage is a measure of strength, which QUT's CEO drew to the organization's attention about a decade ago. What the community would like is for universities to listen to it. The university that masters this skill will do best.

Accordingly, the first step in installing high-speed management principles for a university requires refinement of environmental scanning systems, initially around the CEO. The community-centered organization invites community leaders to comment on every strategic move. When it reviews its mission, marketing plan, quality system, or major programs, listening is the first step. Learning how to listen and how to integrate listening into operations challenges organizations. For effective fund raising, both are daily requirements.

At QUT, the need to secure better market information while strengthening linkages for fund raising and alumni relations led to regular briefings with community leaders and breakfasts with graduates. Let me illustrate how the community leader briefings served the dual role of environmental scanning and strengthening of linkages between the university and community leaders. Senior management were host to a series of two or three briefings with selected investors, prospects, and "hot suspects." The CEO briefly outlined the recent achievements, called on an operating manager to outline recent goals and achievements of the operating area, and then invited attendees to say what issues and community needs the university should address. For a second event, we provided a summary of "what we thought we heard" and invited further comment—finishing after all this at the second or a third meeting with a summary of possible responses that the university might make to these needs, if proper resources were available. Invitees were followed up individually, with the visiting team from QUT seeking always to listen for possible matching of the person's key interests and concerns with the organization's capability.

The least understood area of major funds solicitation was the level of listening and involvement needed before making an "ask." It might require coordinated involvement over at least six to twelve face-to-face contacts over many months or even years. A high-speed challenge, of course, is to shorten this time to negotiate how best to direct information, identify interest, secure involvement, select appropriate invitations, and shape the "ask" for investment earlier. Increased involvement of management in these community leader briefings identified real investment opportunities. Managers materially helped increase the availability of relevant prospects for investment. Equally important, organizational managers projected themselves as members of a "listening organization."

From environmental scanning during day-to-day interaction with community leaders, four other expectations were evident. These were return on investment, usefulness to the community, liking of and by constituents, and reputation for ethical relationships.

1. *Return on investment.* Investors provided funds because they believed in the leadership and the cause of the organization. Keeping focus on the achievement of results that benefit investors was the key. How well a leader communicated this focus with a compelling image of a desired state of affairs (Bennis and Nanus 1985, 28) is shown by whether everyone is talking and doing something about how to get better returns for investors.

2. *Usefulness to the community.* The organization that defines its mission in terms of the benefits it brings to the community must go on to state what use the community wants to make of it. The uses can be economic, cultural, social, professional, or global, or all these. Through delivery of higher quality educational services, a university might prove its usefulness in different ways to each of its stakeholder groups. Students define

usefulness differently to a supplier of its banking services. Leaders relentlessly ask questions to help members of the organization focus on activity that is useful to these different community stakeholders now or in the future.

3. *Liking of and by constituents.* Liking others and showing it provides powerful entry to being liked by others. So, too, the organization that tells its community through a simple, visible action what the community *needs* to hear from it will stand out. Drucker illustrated this well with a hospital. He said that, on any objective evaluation, it was the poorest of three competing hospitals in an area, and yet the community was full of praise for this one hospital (1990, 125). What made it so visible was that two weeks after a patient was discharged, somebody from the hospital called to find out how the patient was. If the report was that recovery was slow, the hospital called again three weeks later. At the end of the year the patient received a calendar as a memento. Although such activity was known to be routine, it said loudly that the organization remembered its constituents (p. 125). Commitment to sustained action in this area is available to all.

4. *Reputation for ethical relationships.* Both inside and outside the organization, no value is more important. There are no degrees of honesty. Many religions fortunately also allow for lapses and so provide for forgiveness as a basis for continued growth. People in the organization needed to understand accepted standards of courtesy, timeliness, relevance, clarity, or other expectations of performance. Assurance of their fulfillment builds the trust which constituents should feel in the organization.

For competitive advantage, these values must be grown quickly. QUT senior management's ongoing community leader briefings, graduate breakfasts, and day-to-day interaction with community leaders provided a wealth of information and useful follow-up opportunities for fund raising. In order that this system be adapted and used by operational areas, high-speed management theory was also used to organize the second-stage development which was to locate where and how to improve the integration, coordination, and control systems for community service delivery. QUT needed coordinated interventions for this.

COORDINATED INTERVENTIONS

The most effective nonprofit organizations charge three groups with the securing of resources from the community and delivery of accountability to the community: the governing board and CEO; senior management; and development professionals, whose role is to coordinate and support the fund raising and accountability activities of first two groups. A development board might supplement the governing board and would consist of community leaders with the "wallop" to reach community wealth. At QUT, its foundation's finance council served this function. It was decided that, to move forward, coordinated interventions with the cooperation of the CEO and other organizational leaders would be necessary. Few senior managers at QUT were yet focused on a regular program of community outreach.

More seriously, the first intervention, a development operations audit commissioned by the development manager (McGoldrick and Osborne, 1993), noted serious misunderstandings about fund raising among some managers. Some even held the sincere but mistaken belief that the federal government would cut funding or that the CEO would cut budgets as funds were raised. As the auditors recommended, organizational effectiveness required direct address of such concerns. Some managers were more experienced in fund raising than others, and each would need to be worked with differently (Duck 1993, 112).

The second intervention commenced after development liaison people established working relations with their respective areas of responsibility. The chair of the university's governing board, the president of the QUT Foundation, and the development manager met with heads of area individually. These meetings, held in an informal setting, discussed priorities for fund raising within the area. The conversations located the objectives, the process, and the next steps for fund raising. Actions were confirmed in writing. These included objective-setting meetings with selected managers who reported to them, invitations to submit descriptions of projects requiring funding, commitment to identify at least three CEO or board-level community leaders for each head and their managers to work with, an audit of capabilities for fund raising, and the establishment of a special board of community leaders to help fund raising. Emphasis centered on the tremendous cooperative effort required to extend QUT's community relationships, to secure substantial income regularly to the area.

In parallel with these, the third intervention involved the QUT Foundation in restating its vision. QUT had set its primary function to bring the benefits of teaching, research, technology, and service to the community. The QUT Foundation then tied together the university and the community by helping areas to secure funds that would equip the university to better serve the community's needs. The resources raised ensured high-quality teaching, research, and service through the development of partnerships with areas, which in turn added value to the operations of business, government, and the professions.

The three interventions (audit, senior-level meetings, and a vision statement) were used not only to locate areas for improving communication and information systems but also to commence agreement of the way forward. The wide range of understandings and limited development of community service capabilities required the development unit itself to restructure operations to be able to assist areas to deliver high-speed service. The basis for development staff to be credible coordinators would be the use of their close knowledge of customers and competitors to secure successful partnerships with the community. The third challenge in implementing high-speed management principles therefore was to commence a unique continuous improvement process for the development unit, first, and then to extend this with managers of operational areas. The development staff coordinated the fund raising of the operational managers and so the development unit needed to change its systems to increase the speed of getting community services to market.

DEVELOPMENT SERVICE STANDARDS

In the development unit's quarterly review sessions, customers regularly had their say to the unit staff. Internal customers, not surprisingly, said they most looked for "creative ideas" and "access to people with money." The unit met both these expectations, but the customers showed little understanding of the capabilities of the fund raising staff. Following these discussions, the development unit met to set quality standards for its own service. These directed the unit to add value and were informed by the perspective of high-speed management, in particular in respect of the unit's value-adding role to bring operational managers and community leaders closer to one another.

Focus:

1. Emphasize the *benefits to others*, in terms of the difference made to the customer.
2. Affirm the *access* the unit provides to internal/external leaders in decision-making positions.
3. State your *knowledge of the customer's business* by showing how stronger operations will result for the customer.

Meet or exceed expectations:

4. Agree to the time to the next action and look for ways to *speed* the offering of new services, decision making, or closing to ask for funds.
5. Suggest actions that are *useful* to solve problems now or to rethink services or to reengineer processes to better meet customers' needs.
6. Be *simple and clear* in all contacts, providing brief verbal or written summary as needed.

Cost competitiveness:

7. Create ideas and insights that visibly enhance a project's attractiveness to a funding source.
8. Increase income to the internal customer so the *revenue to cost ratio* improves.
9. Build *strategic teams* (by linking three community leaders to each internal customer) which will produce income.

Having agreed on these standards within the development unit, the development manager had to work with each fund raising coordinator to negotiate their use. Taking guidance from a sales vice-president who decided that her regional directors should run their operations independently, the manager of the unit set up a one-on-one meeting with each coordinator to find out what his or her plans were and how each wanted to interact with him. During this round of conversations, he reached explicit agreements about what kinds of decisions or problems each would like help with, how each would update him, and how the coordinators would keep each other informed (Duck 1993, 112). This resulted in the development manager adopting a tailor-made role as coach, which each coordinator would in turn also need to learn. It was a role not greatly different from what the fund raising coordinators would need to adopt to establish similar working relationships with the operational managers—except that differences in power relations and lack of reporting line in these relationships would require the visible presence of the development manager from time to time.

CHECKLIST FOR "CONTRACTED" RELATIONS

Relationships never fit exactly with service standards. Performance in building community relationships consistently rises when leaders are aligned in their goals, objectives, and standards for action. Our view of what is timely, useful, and clear differs according to whether we are the customers or the service deliverers. Accordingly, to test how the unit's customer-service standards might work in practice, the development team met as a group with several heads of area, who responded to the presentation of plans for the year ahead. The team used a checklist for Critical Step Contracts in these presentations. This required specific agreement on action, time, and person responsible for the critical steps to involve individuals or groups more closely in QUT. This checklist follows:

who/what/when

1. Search out QUT projects
    - "walkabout,"
    - talk with area executives,
    - invite project proposals.

2. Set objectives for
    - project focus to benefit community,

- access to funding sources,
- cost/timelines,
- area of development,
- making the project relevant to the community,
- assistance with writing or editing project statement.

3. Identify prospects
    - match prospects and Finance Council/QUT staff,
    - set strategy for briefings about projects.
4. Record involvement steps for prospects
    - draft correspondence for signature,
    - liaise with key invitees and public affairs for media and functions.
5. Ask
6. Follow up
    - draft and review agreements,
    - report activities to one another and the office database,
    - obtain QUT approvals,
    - chase, receive and acknowledge investment,
    - establish QUT accounts.
7. Stewardship
    - arrange thank-you or acceptance event,
    - liaise regularly between QUT and investor,
    - invoice and chase commitments,
    - secure regular reports to investors,
    - coordinate copy for brochures and relevant publications,
    - revise planning, implementation, and evaluation of what we do,
    - celebrate and tell others about our success.

Emphasis was placed on using this "contract" openly between the development professional and the heads of area to help build understanding of each other's expectations. It was also used to review expectations with the development manager. More, rather than minimal communication is encouraged to move toward the exchange enjoyed between friends: "treat others as we would like our friends to treat us." Support of the specific targets within the development process in this way means performance rises against predetermined targets.

THE WAY AHEAD

As leadership sets new targets for QUT's community service, the continuous use of the processes described allows a common language, increased alignment, and greater confidence among people at various levels to suggest how best to achieve community service targets. Cooperation, communication, and coordination remain core requirements for doing so. The continuing value of the high-speed management perspective will be found not only in the issues drawn on here, but also in the characteristics of leadership (especially transformational leadership) articulated within it (Cushman and King 1994, 2–4). Coordinators of the community service function will achieve much when, chameleonlike, they pull the process along through the internal volunteers' actions. This professional coordinator, to become a leader, must work selflessly to give glory to others when the job is well done—and to share the defeat of others. Lao Tzu's well-known wisdom pertains that a leader is best when people barely know that he or she exists. Leaders develop opportunities for celebration and making others aware of achievements in ways that do not distract from the value of the ego of the customer.

It takes special qualities for people to be effective and enjoy this professional activity. The real challenges of high-speed management and adding value as leaders require improved integration of staff responsibilities with professional development and reward systems. The single piece of learning from the past twenty years about how to manage customer service is sobering: that an employee treats customers exactly the same way a manager treats the employee (Kiechel 1993, 35). This realization underscores the importance for leaders of community service to become high-speed management leaders. In this context, the essential personal qualities for anyone leading community service are the ability to focus, organized interpersonal skills, initiative taking with competitors and customers, quick follow-up and response, tough accountability to and from others, candor about problems, speedy decisions, and flexibility. Largely through the development of these qualities in its people will an organization advance.

REFERENCES

Batten, J. D. (1989). *Tough-Minded Leadership*. New York: American Management Association.

Bennis, W. G. (1989). *On Becoming a Leader*. Reading, Mass.: Addison-Wesley.

———— and Nanus, B. (1985). *Leaders: The Strategies for Taking Charge*. New York: Harper and Row.

Burnet, K. (1993). "Relationship Fund Raising." Address to Fundraising Institute Australia. Brisbane.

Cushman, D. P., and King, S. S. (1994). "The Nature, Function, and Scope of High-Speed Management Leadership." Paper at Inter-University Center Conference on Organizational Communication; Sydney, Australia.

————. (1993). "Visions of Order: High-Speed Management in the Private Sector of the Global Marketplace." In *Organizational Communication and Management: A Global Perspective*, ed. A. K. Kozminski and D. P. Cushman, pp. 69–83. Albany: SUNY Press.

Dixon, T. C. (1990). "Reorganising a University." *Australian Journal of Communication* 17, no. 3: 38–63.

Doyle, M., and Kraus, W. A. (1982). "Senior Management Briefing: Improving Quality, Productivity, Harmony and Profitability." Unpublished paper.

Drucker, P. F. (1990). *Managing the Non-Profit Organization: Practices and Principles*. Oxford: Butterworth-Heinemann.

Duck, J. D. (1993). "Managing Change: The Art of Balancing." *Harvard Business Review* (November–December): 109–118.

Hall, G., Rosenthal, J., and Wade, J. (1993). "How to Make Reengineering Really Work." *Harvard Business Review* (November–December): 119–131.

Jones, J. W. (1993). *High-Speed Management: Time-Based Strategies for Managers and Organizations*. San Francisco: Jossey-Bass.

Kiechel, W. (1993). "How We Will Work in the Year 2000." *Fortune* (May 17): 30–37.

King, S. S., and Cushman, D. P. (1994). "High-Speed Management and Organizational Communication: Cushman, King, and Associates." Paper at Inter-University Center Conference on Organizational Communication; Sydney, Australia.

McGoldrick, W. P., and Osborne, K. E. (1993). "An Audit of the Development Program: Queensland University of Technology." Unpublished paper.

Rosso, H. A. (1991). *Achieving Excellence in Fund Raising: A Comprehensive Guide to Principles, Strategies, and Methods.* San Francisco: Jossey-Bass.

Stewart, T. A. (1993). "Reengineering: The Hot New Managing Tool." *Fortune* (August 23): 25–29.

Strong, J. (1993). "Chief Executive Comment." *The Australian Way* (December): 4.

Thayer, L. (In Press). *Making High-Performance Organizations: The Logic of Virtuosity.*

Tully, S. (1993). "The Real Key to Creating Wealth." *Fortune* (September 20): 34–42.

CHAPTER 5

Lessons from Mergers and Acquisitions of Multinational Corporations in Post-Communist Countries

Krzysztof Obloj

INTRODUCTION

Every business goes through several stages of growth and change. Skillful management of the organizational evolution maintains a workable fit between an organization and its environment by constant and usually incremental refinements. This approach is the essence of the Japanese *Kaizen* movement, aimed at maintaining and improving organizations. Japanese continuous improvement consists of literally millions of small, constant, mundane improvements developed and implemented by all organizational members each year (Imai 1986).

My conviction however, well-documented by research on organizational successes (Peters and Waterman 1982), failures (Meyer and Zucker 1989), and transitions (Nelson and Clutterbuck 1988) is that such an approach is particularly suitable in relatively stable environments. It is profoundly functional and productive as long as the organizational environment evolves in a similar, piecemeal fashion. In the turbulent environment that most business organizations face today, dramatic and rapid breakthroughs are necessary to shake up and restructure an organization. Therefore, long periods of improvements and alignments should be punctuated with discontinuous reorientation, to maintain an overall momentum of change and build new ones (Tushman, Newman, and Romanelli 1986).

A rather special case of such a transition occurs nowadays in Poland and other countries of the Eastern bloc. The privatization process of the enterprises in Poland triggered three common scenarios for the privatized enterprises. In scenario one, a foreign company acquires a Polish firm for strategic reasons. The second scenario involves Polish investors buying the company. The final scenario occurs when the company is purchased by its own employees or managers. As empirical research shows (Chelminski, Czynczyk, and Sterniczuk 1993) the frame-breaking, revitalization process occurs only in the first case, whereas in the second and third cases lack of capital, know-how, and will is common.

It is the purpose of this chapter to illustrate the stereotypes, symbolism, and real action during high-speed revitalization of a company in Poland. More specifically I shall

1   Define the concept of revitalization and explicate its major pattern according to the theory and research;
2. Explore main strategies of revitalization in terms of scope, thrust, and nature of the changes in a major case of revitalization of a Polish company acquired by European multinational;
3. Discuss how stereotypes, symbolism, and real action interplay during the revitalization effort.

I hope that because of the rather clinical conditions of revitalization processes in Poland this analysis can shed some light on the symbolism and key factors of successful revitalization.

THE CONCEPT OF REVITALIZATION

Abundant company histories, case studies, and research show the evolutionary patterns of organizational life cycles. One of the first was Chandler's (1962) seminal study of strategy and structure relations in big American firms; for example, duPont, General Motors, and Sears. Tracking the evolution of several firms, Chandler concludes persuasively that successful companies are able at an important moment of their history (e.g., in the time of crisis) to come up with a significant strategic change that enables them to catch up to or even dominate their respective industries for years.

The importance of creative revitalizations was confirmed in other research. Miller and Friesen (1984) report on a series of studies that covered "quantum changes" in more than forty firms in diverse industries and a joint research program of Columbia, Duke, and Cornell Universities that tracks the history of large sample of firms in different industries finds that most successful firms have a similar evolutionary pattern: long periods of incremental improvements punctuated by major changes (Tushman, Newman, and Romanelli 1986). In the United Kingdom an analysis of a large sample of case studies reported by Slatter (1986) indicates that corporate recovery is a mix of incremental changes and marketing, financial, organizational breakthroughs. Specifically the generic recovery moves include change of management, strong central financial control, organizational change and decentralization, product-market reorientation, improved marketing, growth via acquisitions, asset reduction, investment, debt restructuring, and other financial strategies.

The extensive study of twenty revitalization and turnaround processes presented by Nelson and Clutterbuck (1988) indicated that most followed a similar pattern. They started with a mixture of "quick and dirty" assessment and action by a new chief executive, communication of crisis situation and severe cutbacks. The new management team was developed as was a program of medium- and long-term investments and expansion. Then the implementation stage started, during which each of the companies searched for a special, critical element on which it focused (e.g., customer care, innovation, specialization).

A rather interesting and complex study of six revitalization efforts was completed by Harvard researchers with a general conclusion that "corporate revitalization rests on the capacity of leaders to develop an organizational context that will influence people—managers, workers, and union leaders alike—to change behaviors and attitudes" (Beer, Eisenstat, and Spector 1990, 223).

This area of research offers three types of insights. First, successful revitalization starts with a good diagnosis of the causes of crisis, both external (environmentally driven) and internal. Second, there is a pattern in successful revitalization, a kind of a critical path that smart organizations follow (Slatter 1984, Nelson and

Clutterbuck 1988, Beer, Eisenstat, and Spector 1990). Successful revitalization starts with quick diagnosis and cutbacks and then small, isolated, even peripheral operations are targeted for a quick improvement. Only after experiencing the positive effects of these efforts do the organizations continue with implementation of a long-term program of core operations improvement. Third, for the revitalization to be successful and sustainable in the long run, top management must confront its own behavior and redefine major assumptions underpinning organization and management. A shift from survival toward empowerment, innovation, and focus on adaptation is necessary (Burdett 1993).

However, what is most striking in this line of research (especially made in the United States) is a powerful, even if invisible, assumption that the revitalization is an almost totally rational process.

Revitalization (in spite of its complexity) is described as an orderly and rational process with organizational leaders in full control, despite an abundant literature that indicates the importance of symbolism and the presence of irrationationality in the management process (for a good review, see Czarniawska-Joerges 1993). Let us now turn to an analysis of major corporate revitalization efforts in Poland and confront it with research results.

AFTER THE ACQUISITION: REVITALIZATION OF A COMPANY

A unique situation that enabled researchers to monitor adaptive behaviors of firms occurred in the beginning of 1990s. In the post-communist countries in the Eastern and Central Europe, a dramatic shift of the business environment occurred, from planned to free-market economies. State owned firms scrambled to adapt to this new situation. Research shows that most of the state-owned firms in Poland and Hungary were unable to adapt because they have followed the incremental improvement mode. This approach does not fit the dramatic shift in the environment, which demands high-speed revitalization of the companies (Obloj and Davis 1991, Kozminski 1993). However, Chelminski, Czynczyk, and Sterniczuk (1993) reported that some of the revitalizations performed by the multinationals were very successful (e.g., ABB bought the Polish turbine producer Zamech, Unilever bought the detergent plant Pollena). Therefore I performed clinical research on a 1992 Polish acquisition by the major European company XXY. (The description is based upon a clinical case study of the revitalization developed by K. Obloj in 1993 and 1994. The management of the company demanded confidentiality and so the name of the company has been disguised.) The target company specialized in the production of railroad equipment and employed about 1,500 people. Because of the dramatic contraction of the demand in the traditional Eastern European market, the acquired firm was losing money. The acquirer was one of the largest European multinationals and had already acquired and successfully revitalized several companies in Eastern Europe, including Poland. The firms acquired in Poland were managed from Polish national headquarters of the XXY company by a mix of Polish and foreign executives.

My research, performed in October and November, started with unstructured interviews with the middle management of the newly acquired company during the training program. I followed this by structured and unstructured interviews with top and middle management of the acquired company, analysis of documentation, and on-site observation of the performance of one division of the company. The general picture that my research revealed is a striking mix of three elements: stereotypes, "real, down-to-the earth" action programs, and symbolism. These combined to create a much more complex and chaotic picture of revitalization than the typical portrayal in previous research. Let us examine these three major elements in turn and explain their functions and relations.

Stereotypes as a Guide for Action

The managers of the XYZ company started preparation for the restructuring of the company with three major stereotypes in mind: (1) Polish managers do not know too much about production, quality, marketing, finance, and accounting. (2) Foreign consultants are the best solution to the problems arising at the beginning of the acquisition. (3) Restructuring comes first, vision and strategy follow.

The first stereotype is an outcome of the general view of the Eastern European firms and is generally correct. Managers in the acquired firm were not exposed to modern accounting and finance. In addition marketing remained underdeveloped and was not considered necessary. These managers were generally good at production because they had extremely important *practical knowledge* of management on the shop floor in this particular firm and with this particular equipment. However, the stereotype did perform a useful function in this respect because most managers lacked enough will and drive to improve production management techniques. Therefore, the acquirer decided during the first stage of revitalization to move marketing activities to one of its own divisions abroad and concentrate on training Polish managers in modern accounting, finance, organizational behavior, strategy, and production techniques. Also, the Polish managers were supported and in some cases directed by outside consultants. The flip side of this stereotype is that it stops consultants and foreign managers from listening carefully to local managers.

The second stereotype is an almost natural extension of the first one. To quickly implement new ways of management, the acquirer brought in an army of foreign consultants, some of them Polish-speaking expatriates. The consultants made diagnoses and offered recommendations. Managers of the company were asked by Polish headquarters to implement these suggestions immediately. Even when the best Polish managers of the company questioned the wisdom of recommended changes they were told to proceed. As I shall discuss later, from time to time consultants were not only nonprofessional but they implemented dummy solutions to rationalize their presence and heavy fees.

The third stereotype is probably an outcome of the previous two. Because it was assumed that Polish managers were not competent and the enterprise was mismanaged, the central thrust was on restructuring the whole firm at the same time. A new divisional structure was introduced, a new financial system and budgeting were put in place, one third of the employees were laid off, a new evaluation system was implemented, and production was reorganized in the relays division. Two important drawbacks of this situation were as follows. First, too many restructuring programs in the same time period created a chaotic situation. Second, because of so many things happening in such short time, nobody explained to the managers why the changes were being implemented and what final outcomes were expected. Therefore, it is easy to understand why the major complaint voiced during interviews with managers was that they did not know or understand the overall strategy of change and restructuring.

Revitalization Program: Real and Symbolic Importance

The revitalization effort was massive and therefore somewhat chaotic. Many changes were introduced simultaneously: total structural reorganization, new financial and accounting systems, layoffs, a new evaluation system, substantial training program (including obligatory English classes for all top and middle managers), new production management methods based on teamwork, just in time deliveries, and time management. At the same time new offices and renewed production facilities were being built. At the surface the program appeared to be perfectly rational and pragmatic. However, deep, clinical interviews; short questionnaires with open-ended questions; and observation revealed that the whole revitalization process had several interesting unintended and intended symbolic elements that interplayed with rational programs.

A New Structure   The structural changes led to the introduction of a typical divisional structure that replaced an old, functional one. Six product divisions were created with a responsibility for procurement, production, and partial marketing (in Poland, because total exports were controlled by foreign subsidiary of XXY). Budgeting was implemented—each division had to develop and negotiate a budget within the top management budget and work according to its premises. Investment decisions remained centralized at the top management level. Divisions were created in accordance with management theory and practice to decentralize decision making and achieve managerial accountability. Foreign consultants stressed the novelty of the structure and the symbolic implications that every division and its management were now responsible for results. However, the new structure has had an unexpected drawback. Before its implementation a main buyer—the Polish railroad—had only one counterpartner—the selling office at the firm. With the introduction of a divisional structure, a complex purchase required the buyer to deal with at least five sellers. A form of chaos followed as divisions were not very willing to accommodate the demands of each other. The CEO responded by establishing a new post, coordinator, at the top level. At the time of research it was not obvious how this coordinator should enforce cooperation of the independent divisions.

A New Financial System   Consultants recommended implementation of new, heavily computerized, Western financial and accounting systems. Despite many warnings by managers of the financial and accounting department of the firm, these systems were implemented. The pragmatic rationale was simple—to make the accounting system transparent and on-line. The symbolic rationale was less openly acknowledged but also obvious—to indicate the introduction of novel, different solutions. Only after six months of implementation efforts, consultants arrived at the conclusion that it was a mistake. The choice was ill-suited to Polish conditions because of a different accounting and tax system in Poland, something that was known from the very beginning. Because of all the effort and investment already undertaken, the decision was made to continue to struggle and adapt the system.

Layoffs   Layoffs followed immediately after the acquisition. More than one third of the personnel was laid off during 1992 and the first few months of 1993. A minority of the employees retired or left. Most were shed off according to the revitalization plan, as all but core activities were shut down or spun off.

The layoffs were necessary as the company was overstaffed. However, they also sent a symbolic message: "Cut cost regardless" and "spin off all noncore activities." One activity that was discontinued was the assembly of equipment at the railroad sites. This activity demanded extensive practical knowledge about company equipment, conditions at different railroad stations, and an extensive network of contacts among railroad maintenance brigades. Against the advice of Polish managers, consultants recommended the spinoff due to the "peripheral nature" of this activity. The problem that almost immediately surfaced was unreliable, costly, and late assembly at the railroad sites. At the time of this research, reestablishment of the former teams was being discussed.

The second interesting symbolic aspect of the layoffs is the fact that as long as the layoffs lasted, the CEO was a Pole. After the first two major waves of layoffs ended, the Polish CEO was asked to resign and a foreign manager, with "clean hands," was put in charge.

Training   The managers of the divisions and the managers of the finance, accounting, and human resource departments were trained extensively in their respective functions. Special training sessions exposing them to the principles of management in XXY were also performed. English-language classes were obligatory for all top and middle managers. Middle managers were trained primarily in communication, problem solving, negotiation, and leadership, as well as in finance, accounting, and production management using games, lectures, and case studies.

Both the pragmatic and symbolic value of the training is obvious. The pragmatic importance is in upgrading management skills and achieving better efficiency. Symbolically, training became a way to differentiate between good managers and employees (ones that company decided to invest in) from bad ones (that were not offered training, the first warning signal that they might be laid off).

Production Changes   One of the divisions (the relay division) was chosen as a target for far-reaching changes in its production system. First, it was moved to new premises. The management of the division and the production facilities were put on the same floor. The production facilities (mainly assembly of relays) were completely remodeled and equipped with new tables and ergonomic chairs. New production systems based upon the principles of cost and time reduction, just-in-time deliveries, and flexibility were introduced.

The cost and time reduction was achieved by shortening, simplifying, and limiting material and documents flows. Introduction of a simple two-bin system combined with teamwork at the assembly line replaced complex and unreliable production planning and the traditional assembly line, where every employee performed one, well-designed operation. The quality controllers were replaced by self-control performed by team members.

Just-in-time deliveries were achieved by minimizing the number of suppliers and forcing them to adapt to new delivery schedules based on the principle of small batches delivered to order.

Flexibility was achieved mainly by teamwork and increasing universality of the skills of employees as they rotated within teams.

The division quickly became a benchmark for other divisions of the company and also other firms acquired by XXY. It was frequently visited by XXY managers from all over the world and used as a showcase of good work.

This division exemplifies two interesting examples of symbolism. The first one is the process of moving production facilities and staff departments, shifting them from one building to another as well as from one floor to other. Research showed that several departments and production facilities were constantly moved without any clear rationale. One possible explanation is that such reorganization created an illusion of constant, high-speed change and progress. They symbolically indicate that the revitalization process is constant and far-reaching.

The second example relates to the constant need for consultants and foreign managers to introduce novel solutions even if these solutions are harmful or a mere smokescreen. I already mentioned the heavily computerized financial system that did not perform. In the production department in the relay division foreign consultants in charge of designing and monitoring the revitalization process faced a visit from XXY headquarters. To prove the reach of their revitalization the consultants put a fax machine at the main table in the assembly room and claimed that the restructuring process had reached so far that orders from buyers came directly to the shop floor and were immediately executed. They also claimed that thanks to the computerization the assembly teams could check at any moment on the number of parts in stock. There were two problems with these claims. First, there was no way to connect the fax so they tied the cable under the table. The delegation of top managers of XXY and accompanying journalists were so impressed that the fax machine became a well-known and heavily publicized symbol of progress. Every time official delegations visited the factory, the fax was brought in to perform its dummy role. There was no real need nor possibility for the orders to come directly to the relay assembly floor, bypassing the marketing department.

Second, there was no computer program for monitoring the stock at this time. Therefore whenever high-ranking managers from XXY visited the factory, shift managers checked through the computer. They compared the quantity of parts with the stock at the warehouse and warned the warehouse by phone to adapt real quantity of parts to the "dummy" figures in the computer program.

CONCLUSIONS

Despite the limited scope of our research (case study) it offers some interesting insight into the turnaround process.

First, as most models indicate, successful turnaround follows a pattern composed of several strategies applied sequentially or laterally. In our case this is also true, and almost all strategies described by Slatter (1986) were used; that is, change of management, strong central financial control, organizational change and decentralization, product-market reorientation, improved marketing, asset reduction, investment, debt restructuring, and other financial strategies.

Second, despite many programs performed at the same time one program, the revitalization of the relays division, lead the way. However it definitely was not a small, isolated, or peripheral operation. On the contrary, a very important, visible operation was revitalized at high-speed and quickly became a benchmark for all other divisions.

Third, our analysis shows an interplay of stereotypes and symbolism, and their important implications for the process of company turnaround. The whole process was guided more by stereotypes than diagnosis of the situation. In this way consultants and foreign managers minimized the time and effort necessary for understanding the situation. Also each of the introduced strategies has its pragmatic and symbolic components. Therefore the whole process of revitalization has an aura of dramatic endeavor. Finally politics, irrational mistakes, stupidities and even smokescreens were revealed by our research as a organic component of the revitalization process.

REFERENCES

Beer, M., Eisenstat, R. A., and Spector B. (1990). *The Critical Path to Corporate Renewal.* Boston: Harvard Business School Press.

Burdett, J. O. (1993). "Managing in the Age of Discontinuity." *Management Decision* 31, no. 1: 10–17.

Chandler, A. (1962). *Strategy and Structure.* Cambridge Mass.: MIT Press.

Chelminski, D., Czynczyk, A., and Sterniczuk, H. (1993). *First Experiences with Privatization* [in Polish]. Warsaw: Center for Privatization.

Czarniawska-Joerges, B. (1993). *The Three Dimensional Organization.* Lund: Chartwel Bratt.

Imai, M. (1986). *Kaizen: The Key to Japan's Competitive Success.* New York: Random House.

Kozminski, A. (1993). *Catching Up.* Albany: SUNY Press.

Meyer, M. W., and Zucker, L. G. (1989). *Permanently Failing Organizations.* London: Sage Publications.

Miller, D., and Friesen, P. (1984). *Organizations: A Quantum View,* Englewood Cliffs, N.J.: Prentice-Hall.

Nelson, R., and Clutterbuck, R. (eds.). (1988). *Turnaround.* London: Mercury Books.

Obloj, K., and Davis, A. S. (1991). "Innovation Without Change: The Contradiction Between Theories-Espoused and Theories-in-Use." *Journal of Management Studies* 28, n. 4: 323–338.

Peters, T. J., and Waterman, R. H. (1982). *In Search of Excellence.* New York: Harper and Row.

Slatter, S. (1986). *Corporate Recovery.* Harmondsworth, Middlesex: Penguin Books.

Tushman, M. L., Newman, W. H., and Romanelli, E. (1986). "Convergence and Upheaval: Managing the Unsteady Pace of Organizational Evolution." *California Management Review* 29, no. 1: 29–44.

CHAPTER 6

Organizational Inertia or Corporate Culture Momentum

Michael B. Goodman

[handwritten: showing us so many orgs are stuck classical in]

C-17 Put on Final Notice as Pentagon Mulls Options, (*Aviation Week and Space Technology*, May 17, 1993)

Station Foul-ups Spur Calls for Radical Change at NASA, (*Aviation Week and Space Technology*, March 8, 1993)

McDonnell Probed on Bills Charged to U.S.: Costs of defense Contractor to Receive Scrutiny In House Panel Hearing (*The Wall Street Journal*, October 13, 1993)

Rude Awakening: Quake Jars Assumptions blared the headline in the Sunday, January 23, 1994, *New York Times*. Even though the text of the article explores assumptions about the practice of architecture, its structural reference to life in Southern California may also be an appropriate metaphor for the future of corporate communication. To inherit the future, corporations have to survive today.

no matter how good a company's vision is, no matter how excellent the company is, no matter how much quality it puts into its products, no matter how much team effort it directs toward its customers, many companies may not survive into the next century, *no matter what they do.*

What does a corporation need to survive? Sometimes nothing more than what John David Rockefeller said of his wealth, that he just happened to be close by as an enormous door to opportunity opened, and he was lucky: *chance and timing.* The present and the future are dynamic, constantly changing, adapting, and moving forward. Yes, being at the right place at the right time and being smart enough to recognize the opportunity that changes bring—it certainly worked for Rockefeller.

Business is in the middle of an uncomfortable, often painful period of change brought on by enormous political, financial, social, and technological forces. One can look at the process of change as linear or historical; events happen in a unique sequence. Or one can see the events as cyclical, happening with predictable repetition, as the seasons of the year. A third view puts the two together in a state of uneasy compatibility—seasons come and go, but no season is exactly the same as the last.

Often external forces can help an organization achieve its vision or speed its demise. Such power must be understood to either work with it, or to determine if it can, like a force of nature, be harnessed and at what cost.

Vision is the future we want to happen. And according to the William Bridges (*Transitions* 1980), vision is the third and last phase of change. It follows (1) the beginning phase—the *end* of the old; (2) the neutral—neither old or new—a rite of passage like the Vision Quest of the Plains Indians or *ma,* Japanese for full of nothingness.

One way to create the future—the vision or third phase—has been through the eyes of visionaries: artists, prophets, seers, yes, even madmen. So it is not without surprise that corporations occupy a special place in artistic concepts of the future. Future corporate and municipal concepts tend to be utopian: no dirt, no disease, no dissent. Of course, every realist knows that such static states are undesirable, at least, and destructive at best. *Stasis* is by definition an absence of movement, in short, intellectual and physical death.

Movies supply some popular visions of the corporate future: the mining village in the movie *Outland* with Sean Connery; or the black, dark urbanscapes of *Blade Runner* with Harrison Ford; and the same overpowering images in both *Batman* movies; the intellectual hell of Bradbury's *Fahrenheit 451* and Orwell's *1984;* even the technological hell of *2001: A Space Odyssey* remains powerful for those who have a long attention span. However, these images of the corporate future seem out of focus, not a useful map to get from here and now, to there and tomorrow. An antitechnology subtext informs them—a longing for the good old days, which never were. Memory miraculously washes away the grime of the past; and prediction can numb the labor pains for the future.

In addition to being the future we want to happen, vision implies a dream; and that in itself is enough to fuel the drive for the future. In a similar time of turbulence (born in 1865 the end of the Civil War and died in 1939 the year Hitler invaded Poland) Irish senator, statesman, poet, essayist, playwright, Nobel Prize winner William Butler Yeats wrote a complex and mystical book called *A Vision,* in which he attempted to explain the progress of history, as well as the creative spirit. Part mysticism, part meditation, part mumbo-jumbo, Yeats *did* articulate a concept that serves as a map of ideas and events, or at the very least he attempted to conceptualize the apparent chaos of events. Figure 6.1 describes his notion of the progress of events as a conical helix:

His concept shows the progress of time as a line following the surface of a cone. It appears linear up close, but from afar it moves in cycles, a curve. Without getting into conflicting theories of physics, Yeats was on to something. Of course, Albert Einstein's concept was more successful and caught on; nevertheless, Yeats gave us a metaphor to explain the progress of change, and the apparent acceleration of change.

Like following the line on the cone, the participants in events are so close to the present that they cannot see that what appears to

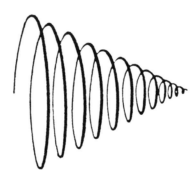

FIGURE 6.1.
In *A Vision* Yeats saw the movement of events as a dynamic "gyre" or conical helix, rather than as linear movement that prevailed at the time.

be a line, is actually a curve. It is as if we are all fifteenth century Europeans before Columbus sailed West, to go East. To move involves risk and probable loss, as well as opportunity and possible gain; not to move at all is to wither and die. We must give up the "old" world for the "new." Our lack of metaphors may blind us to forces in the organization that are very strong; forces like gravity or the tide, which often go unnoticed.

A look at some events may help. Business faces enormous changes as the population of America grows increasingly diverse; race relations are a major social and political concern; integrating technological advances in communication and transportation into current business practices is essential to productivity and competitiveness; major shifts in the population and mass illiteracy provide an enormous challenge to American business; and competition is fierce in a world market.

Sound familiar? The description is of America at the end of the nineteenth century, not contemporary business issues. Yet these similar events represent a cycle, not history repeating itself. Occurrences have come around again, however, they are not repeating the past; more like an echo—the event occurs again, familiar, but changed by time, people, and context.

Whether the business environment is in a state of evolution or revolution, the flood of books and articles that try to make sense of the upheaval all use some verb with a *re-* prefix: *re*invent, *re*engineer, *re*think, *re*structure. These verbs imply that something can be done to *re*verse a downward trend or to keep those organizations that are not on a destructive course from drifting into one. Indeed, people and their organizations and technologies can have substantial impact on the world. But often powerful, yet subtle forces have an enormity that must be understood to use them productively, or one is overwhelmed by them. These forces can stop change and threaten the survival of the corporation.

Organizational inertia and *corporate culture momentum* are such forces. In corporations we can observe the effects of these forces either propelling the organization into the vision of the future it desires or derailing it into oblivion. These two terms borrowed from physics might help to provide a metaphor or an analogy to help describe the motion to the future. *Inertia* is the tendency of a body to resist acceleration; or it is the tendency of a body in motion to stay in motion in a straight line unless disturbed by an external force. That is physics, but it is also the resistance to motion, action, or change. And organizations have inertia.

Momentum is the force of motion, impetus, or impetus in human affairs; an impelling force, an impulse, something that incites, a stimulus; loosely a force or energy associated with a moving body. Because it is associated with a body already moving, the implication is that the force of inertia has been overcome. It is a positive force that like the tide or the wind, we sense the subtle power. In a big sporting event we sense which team has momentum and which does not. We cannot measure it or see it, but we know it is there nevertheless.

These two forces of an organization can be thought of as part of the culture of the organization. In an environment of change, understanding how these forces work can determine actions and outcomes of change programs.

In that spirit this discussion of the cases treats momentum as a positive force in the perpetuation of a corporate culture, hence corporate culture momentum. Ott's concept of the organizational culture perspective deals with change as the force to perpetuate the organization (Ott 1989).

In attempting to understand the organizational behavior of corporations in transition or under stress, the tools of cultural anthropology can prove powerful in illuminating the forces at work in these situations. The forces of culture at work drive one company, such as Johnson & Johnson in the Tylenol poisonings, to react quickly and responsibly and another to be slow and unresponsive.

BACKGROUND ON ORGANIZATIONAL INERTIA AND MOMENTUM

The examination of change in organizations has been large and focused on the understanding the nature of change (Watzalawick 1978, Miller and Friesen 1984, Hinings and Greenwood 1988), the need for change (Child and Kieser 1981, Meyer 1982, Bartunek 1984, Dutton and Duncan 1987, Milliken 1990), the process of change (Kanter 1983), and the use of change as a strategic tool (Quinn 1980).

Inertia appears in the literature of change as part of the understanding of change. Hannan and Freeman (1984) developed a structural inertia theory in which organizational reliability and accountability give formal organizations an advantage over loose collectives. Reliable performance means timeliness and quality to customers. Accountability is of value to customers of products and services that have some risk, such as medical care or air travel. To provide reliability and accountability an organization must be stable over time and capable of reproducing itself. Such organizations use institutionalization and standardized practices to achieve these goals. The ability for the organization to change is sacrificed to stability. The irony for many organizations is that the very processes that created success, often eventually lead to failure (Hammer and Champy 1993).

Change represents a threat to such organizations. Inertia exists in an organization when its core features are changing less rapidly than the changes taking place in its environment. Organizational inertia then for many organizations, particularly older and larger ones, increases the chance of failure.

Momentum in organizational change is relatively undiscussed, much less studied. Kelly and Amburgey (1991) have discussed the concept. In their study of change in the U.S. certified air carrier industry 1962–1985, they mention the concept of momentum: "We definitely saw momentum in organizational change processes. These organizations were significantly more likely to repeat changes that they had experienced in the past. We suggest that the concept of momentum is complementary to inertia theory and that a useful way to think about inertia is that environmental change" (Kelly and Amburgey 1991, 608–609). They go on to suggest that the issue is important and needs further investigation because it is related to internal characteristics such as culture, power, decision making, communication, and leadership.

Instead of conceiving momentum as "complementary" to the negative connotations in inertia, the meaning of momentum is positive and implies that inertia has been overcome to produce or change movement. Its use in the discussion of change in organizations should be positive as well.

ORGANIZATIONAL INERTIA AND CORPORATE CULTURE MOMENTUM INSTANCES

A revealing way to discuss these forces is to look at some familiar business examples and see how inertia and momentum have acted to determine the outcome. Some useful examples of organizational inertia include the NASA Challenger accident, the McDonnell Douglas DC-10 door blowouts, and the C-17 TQM initiatives that almost ended the program. In the context of these phases of change we will end with a beginning and mention examples of corporate culture momentum: the Tylenol poisonings, J. Steven Ott's concept of perpetuating culture in organizations, and the Dallas Cowboys and the Buffalo Bills.

ORGANIZATIONAL INERTIA

NASA Challenger Accident

Most Americans over forty know exactly what they were doing on November 22, 1963, when President Kennedy was assassinated in Dallas, and most over twenty know exactly what they were doing on January 28, 1986, when the launch of the twenty-fifth shuttle, Mission 51-L, exploded 72 seconds after liftoff from the Kennedy Space Center at 11:38 *a.m.* EST. In the mountain of information about the incident, most periodicals followed the detailed technical coverage by *Aviation Week and Space Technology* because the issues were so technically daunting to anyone not involved ("Shuttle 51-L Loss" 1986a–d). After all, this *was* rocket science. The accident sliced to the heart of contemporary American culture, because the shuttle had become a symbol of American dominance in science and technology. This was more than the loss of the lives of the crew, it was a body blow to the American spirit. The nation grieved and asked why. Why, after all the assurances that NASA had given that space travel was routine, why had such a catastrophic failure occurred?

The technical answers came in the Report of the Presidential Commission on the Space Shuttle Challenger Accident [the Rogers Commission] (Presidential Commission 1986; Fallows, 1986) as well as in thoughtful analyses from technical journals (Bell and Esch, 1987). Most adhered to the information in the Rogers Commission Report because it was thorough, thoughtful, clear, candid, and concise. Two findings of the commission became part of the nine recommendations. The two that most concern this discussion of organizational inertia are Recommendation II, shuttle management structure and Recommendation V, improved communications.

These two items indicate the symptoms of organizational inertia taking place within NASA. Tompkins (1993) has detailed the organizational communication imperatives of NASA and the tendency of the organization to fall back on the processes that gained it success. What he calls imperatives can be seen as inertia at work, the culture of the organization moving relentlessly in spite of efforts to change. At the time of the disaster, to procure funding, NASA needed to demonstrate to Congress that the shuttle was moving from a test and development stage to an operational stage. That political and financial pressure led the agency to speak of the shuttle missions almost in terms of commercial air transport, the shuttle being described as a glorified truck launching satellites and bringing materials into orbit to build the space station. A recent General Accounting Office report reinforces the inertia at work in the NASA culture. It could just as well have been written in the period before Challenger exploded, reflecting pressures on the program that led up to the 1986 disaster: "NASA has recognized the need to reduce the cost of its most expensive program—the space shuttle . . . over 30 percent of NASA's total budget. NASA wants to lower this proportion and has established a goal to reduce shuttle operating costs by 25 percent by fiscal year 1997. Accomplishing a reduction of this magnitude will require the streamlining or elimination of many flight processing procedures and related documentation requirements. In doing so, special care will be required to see that these efforts do not compromise safety, either on the ground or in flight" (NASA 1993). A similar effort to streamline space shuttle processing had taken place at both Kennedy and Johnson Space Centers in the years before 1986.

Nobel Prize winner and Rogers Commission member Professor Richard Feynman, noted for his wit as well as his physicist's integrity and candor, explained the communication and organizational management situation NASA was in after the Apollo Program was completed:

> But then, when the moon project was over, NASA had all these people together: there's a big organization in Houston and a big organization in Huntsville [Alabama site of the Marshall Space Flight Center which was responsible for the solid rocket boosters and O-rings], not to mention at Kennedy, in Florida. You don't want to fire people and send them out in the street

when you're done with a big project, so the problem is what to do?

You have to convince Congress that there exists a project that only NASA can do. In order to do so, it is necessary—at least it was *apparently* necessary in this case—to exaggerate: to exaggerate how economical the shuttle would be, to exaggerate how often it would fly, to exaggerate how safe it would be, to exaggerate the big scientific facts that would be discovered. "The shuttle can make so-and-so many flights and it'll cost such-and-such; we went to the moon, so we can *do* it!"

Meanwhile, I would guess, the engineers at the bottom are saying, "No, no! We can't make that many flights. If we had to make that many flights, it would mean such-and-such!" And, "No, we can't do it for that amount of money, because that would mean we'd have to do thus-and-so!"

Well, the guys who are trying to get Congress to okay their projects don't want to hear such talk. It's better if they don't hear, so they can be more "honest"—they don't want to be in the position of lying to Congress! So pretty soon the attitudes begin to change; information from the bottom which is disagreeable— "We're having a problem with the seals; we should fix it before we fly again"—is suppressed by big cheeses and middle managers who say, "If you tell me about the seals problems, we'll have to ground the shuttle and fix it." Or, "No, no keep on flying, because otherwise, it'll look bad," or "Don't tell me: I don't want to hear about it."

Maybe they don't say explicitly "Don't tell me," but they discourage communication, which amounts to the same thing. It's not a question of what has been written down, or who should tell what to whom; it's a question of whether, when you *do* tell somebody about some problem, they're *delighted* to hear about it and they say "Tell me more" and "Have you tried such-and-such?" or they say "Well, see what you can do about it"—which is a completely different atmosphere. If you try once or twice to communicate and get pushed back, pretty soon you decide, "To hell with it."

So that's my theory: because of the exaggeration at the top being inconsistent with the reality at the bottom, communication got slowed up and ultimately jammed. That's how it's possible that the higher-ups didn't know. (Feynman 1988, 214–215)

And of course the Nobel laureate has described the inertia that gripped the NASA culture and was one contributing factor to the events that surrounded the decision to launch in the face of information that suggested to wait for better conditions.

McDonnell Douglas and the DC-10 and C-17

Although the DC-10 and C-17 events are not etched in American culture, they share with the NASA Challenger accident similar organizational inertia issues. The Douglas Company had always led the commercial aircraft industry, as did McDonnell Aircraft lead in military aircraft, until Boeing captured the commercial market in the 1950s with the 707. Douglas saw a wide-bodied "airbus" as key to its recapture of the industry lead. By the time Douglas was taken over by McDonnell in 1967, Boeing's 747 was flying. The pressure to develop its DC-10 to compete with the Boeing craft was strong. The DC-10 was certified by the FAA in July 1971 and received positive reviews of its performance. "But on June 12, 1972, an aft bulk cargo door of a DC-10 in flight from Los Angeles to New York separated from the body of the aircraft at about 11,750 feet over Windsor, Ontario. Rapid cabin decompression occurred as a result, causing structural damage to the cabin floor immediately above the cargo compartment. Nine passengers and two stewardesses were injured. A National Transportation Safety Board (NTSB) investigation found that the probable cause of the malfunction was the latching mechanism in the cargo door and recommended changes in the locking system" (Beauchamp 1989, 43). Beauchamp reports that before the in-flight failure, the problem with the doors had appeared in July 1970 during tests and was reported by a design engineer at Convair, the subcontractor to Douglas for the cargo doors. The subcontractor's warnings were heeded with a "band-aid fix" rather than a complete redesign, because the locking system that Douglas had specified, electric over hydraulic, was cheaper. The financial and schedule forces present were similar to the ones NASA experienced.

The combination of McDonnell and Douglas had created a large hierarchical organization that had become set in its ways by the 1980s. Changes in the U.S. Department of Defense (DOD) strategic and budget priorities precipitated a wave of change among defense contractors. McDonnell Douglas as the largest contractor to the DOD followed the dictates of the Pentagon and began to implement a total quality management (TQM) program in February 1989. A year later the effort was described this way in *The Wall Street Journal:*

> It has been a year since McDonnell Douglas Corp.'s Monday Morning Massacre, and still the blood drips.
>
> In fact, last year's sudden shake-up at the giant transport-aircraft facility here [in Long Beach, California where the C-17 military cargo plane is assembled]—in which four of nine management levels vanished, and all managers were forced to reapply for their own jobs—remains perhaps two years away from bearing fruit. And that assumes the effort doesn't simply rot first. (Wartzman 1990)

A company official noted that the transition had not been easy. They had not paid enough attention to training and communication (Scott 1990). But the TQM program did not bear fruit. By December 1991, *Aviation Week and Space Technology* reported: "A hard-headed management philosophy—described by some as 'repressive' and 'militaristic'—prevails today at Douglas following the collapse of the 'empowered' production line teams and a host of management problems that surfaced following the reorganization" (Douglas Boosts . . ." 1991). Employees complained that the company went halfway and stopped. It did not prepare them adequately for such broad-based and revolutionary change. Officials admitted they had not provided the necessary foundation to grow the program in an orderly way. The flat organizational chart that was in place in 1989 had been replaced by a more hierarchical one by the end of 1991 ("Douglas Boosts . . ." 1991).

By May 1993 the misdirected effort and management detours had a negative impact on the C-17 program: "The C-17 program faces termination this August unless the Pentagon gets concrete assurances from the Air Force, McDonnell Douglas and an independent review team that schedule, cost and technical problems are manageable" (Morrocco 1993). Eventually, the Air Force reduced the performance—range and payload—specifications for the transport in January 1994, explaining that the changes did not pose a threat to the operational requirements for the aircraft. The end of the Cold War had made some of the specifications less critical. "Canceling the C-17 program was a 'very tempting' option, [then Defense Secretary] Aspin said. But it was rejected because of the urgent requirement for airlift" (Morrocco 1994).

Organizational inertia had played an important role in thwarting the changes McDonnell Douglas attempted to make through its total quality management efforts on the C-17 program, and inertia brought the Department of Defense to the brink of canceling the program. It might well be argued that the inertia in the Department of Defense itself contributed not only to the confrontation, but also to the agreement that saved the C-17 program for McDonnell Douglas.

Though organizations may be extremely innovative and on the cutting edge of technology, such as the aerospace and high technology organizations NASA and McDonnell Douglas, a hierarchical management structure and culture allows organizational inertia to continue and strengthen, making change difficult. Organizational inertia suggests that old, big, hierarchical organizations foster inertia. And organizational inertia resists change.

CORPORATE CULTURE MOMENTUM

Tylenol Poisonings

Nowhere in organizational behavior is the concept of inertia or momentum as evident as it is during a corporate crisis. Organizations with inertia as their mode of behavior tend to have difficulty in handling crises; those with momentum usually hope for the best, but they also plan for the worst. "Planning for a crisis as a fact of corporate life is the first step in its resolution, and a subsequent return to normal operations. No one can predict when the event will occur, only that sometime in the life of an organization a product will fail, your market will evaporate because of a new invention, the stock will fall, an employee may be caught doing something illegal, the CEO will retire, the workforce will go on strike, a terrorist will plant a bomb" (Goodman 1994). The tylenol poisonings have become a textbook example for how a corporation should behave in a crisis. David Collins, executive at Schering-Plough, was vice president at Johnson and Johnson at the time of the tylenol crisis. During an panel discussion on crisis in March 1990, Collins was asked about his role in the event and why he thought the corporation was able to respond so successfully. He said that everyone in the corporation "just knew what to do" even though they had policies and a handbook for the contingency. In his own modest way David Collins was describing in symbolic terms the culture of Johnson and Johnson. The beliefs and values that propeled the behavior is set down in the one-page company statement called simply "Our Credo":

> We believe our first responsibility is to the doctors, nurses and
> patients, to mothers and all others who use our products
> and services. In meeting their needs everything we do must
> be of high quality. . . .
> We are responsible to the communities in which we live and
> work and to the world community as well. We must be
> good citizens . . .

Between September 29 and October 1, 1982, seven people died after taking cyanide-contaminated extra-strength tylenol, More than a decade later the magnitude of the actions Johnson and Johnson took continues to define the relationship of the corporation to the society at large. Society of course lost the sense of safety as well as the lives of those poisoned. And financially, the price the company paid was staggering: an undisclosed settlement with the families of the victims in May 1991; $100 million charge for recalled product in 1982; costs related to the recall; advertising messages during and after the poisonings. Barton estimates the corporation "incurred about $500 million in costs due to the Tylenol crises," and Mark Mitchell of the University of Chicago "estimates that the loss in brand value has been about $1 billion since the first crisis occurred" (Barton 1993). Despite the tremendous financial burden and potential to destroy the company image and good will, "there is no question that their management's superb handling of the incident is the standard against which most other major incidents have been measured" (Barton 1993).

Perpetuating Organizational Culture

The momentum of its corporate culture drove Johnson and Johnson to behave ethically and responsibly. Its company credo is an artifact symbolic of its underlying assumptions. Other companies in similar circumstances have acted less heroically. Why are some organizations so different even in the same industry? How can a culture be identified, perpetuated, or changed? Why are organizational cultures so difficult to change?

J. Steven Ott offers an explanation:

Culture

Organizational culture originates in the general culture, the nature of the business; and the beliefs and values (or the *script*) of the founder and/or early dominant leader(s). It develops and is refined through the learning members share from experiences encountered while solving problems of organizational (or organizational identity) survival . . . organization members through combinations of processes:

- Preselection and hiring of new members.
- Socialization or enculturation of new and older members who are in the process of crossing (or are preparing to cross) organizational boundaries
- Removal of members who deviate from the culture, either physically from the organization or from positions of influence.
- Reinforcing or changing members behaviors.
- Altering or reinforcing peoples' beliefs, values, and ideologies—their perceptions of truth and reality.
- Communication through verbal, behavioral, and material symbols. (Ott 1989)

An organization's culture is extremely powerful and difficult to develop, perpetuate, and change. If the movement of a culture is constructive, consider it momentum; and inertia, if negative. Johnson and Johnson met the challenge of a potentially devastating crisis because the people who made its culture were equipped to act together.

THE COWBOYS AND THE BILLS

Sports offers a convenient language to discuss organizational behavior, interesting analogies for business actions, and a dramatic demonstration of the concept of corporate culture momentum. Teams need momentum to win, particularly professional teams. To win consistently, year after year, is no accident. Two contemporary examples of sports teams with cultures that exhibit momentum are the Dallas Cowboys and the Buffalo Bills.

The Cowboys amassed an impressive record for winning under their original coach Tom Landry. But as he, the team, and the owners aged, the number of victories and championship did also. The team was sold, and the new owner fired Landry, a culture hero to the team, the city, and to the entire sport. To move forward, to change the old and reach for the new, Landry had to go. In a few years the team was back in the Superbowl, winning in 1993 and in 1994. During an individual game it is easy to sense the "momentum" of one team over the other. For the Cowboys, the momentum was palpable.

The same can be said of the Buffalo Bills. Any team that wins consistently over time exhibits momentum, and has mastered the art of perpetuating a winning culture. Buffalo won its division four years in a row—1991, 1992, 1993, 1994—and went on to play in the Superbowl in each of those four years. It matters little that in each of the four appearances they lost. The fact that they were there in the first place demonstrates the momentum in the organization.

Sports allows a convenient analogy for organizations since the measure of performance boils down ultimately to winners and losers. Winners have momentum. Consistent winners have mastered the art of developing a culture in which momentum rather than inertia is dominant.

LAST THOUGHTS

As corporations begin to reengineer, reinvent, rethink, restructure, or start their "journey" of change, considering the culture of the organization is a critical step in becoming ready for change. If an organization prepares inadequately for change, resistance emerges, organizational inertia thrives, and the efforts to change fail. The vision of the future flickers as forces slow, deflect, and eventually stop its progress.

An organization that uses its cultural momentum to overcome the forces of inertia moves toward its vision. It has a much stronger chance to attain the reality of its vision: *What is driving your organization to its vision—inertia or momentum?*

REFERENCES

Barton, Laurence. (1993). *Crisis in Organizations: Managing and Communicating in the Heat of Chaos.* Cincinnati: South-Western Publishing Co.

Bartunek, J. M. (1984). "Changing Interpretive Schemes and Organizational Restructuring." *Administrative Science Quarterly* 29: 355–372.

Beauchamp, Tom. (1989). *Case Studies in Business, Society, and Ethics,* 2nd ed., pp. 40–47. Englewood Cliffs, N.J.: Prentice-Hall.

Bell, Trudy E., and Esch, Karl. (1987). "The Fatal Flaw in Flight 51-L." *IEEE Spectrum* (February): 36–51.

Bridges, William. (1980). *Transitions: Making Sense of Life's Changes.* Reading, Mass.: Addison-Wesley.

Child, J., and Kieser, J. (1981). "Development of Organizations over Time." In *Handbook of Organizational Design,* pp. 28–64. Oxford: Oxford University Press.

Deal, Terrence, and Kennedy, Allan. (1982). *Corporate Cultures: The Rites and Rituals of Corporate Life.* Reading, Mass.: Addison-Wesley.

"Douglas Boosts Production Without Key TQM Provision." (1991). *Aviation Week and Space Technology* (December 9): 61–63.

Dutton, J., and Duncan, R. B. (1987). "The Creation of Momentum for Change Through the Process of Strategic Issue Diagnosis." *Strategic Management Journal* 8: 279–295.

Esch, Karl. (1986). "How NASA Prepared to Cope with Disaster." *IEEE Spectrum* (March): 32–36.

Fallows, James. (1986). "The Americans in Space," *New York Review of Books* (December 18): 34–48.

Feynman, Richard P. (1988). *"What Do You Care What Other People Think?"—Further Adventures of a Curious Character.* New York: W. W. Norton.

Goodman, Michael B. (1994). *Corporate Communication: Theory and Practice.* Albany: SUNY Press.

Hammer, M. and Champy, J. (1993). *Reengineering the Corporation.* New York: Harper Business.

Hannan, M. T., and Freeman, J. (1984). Structural, Inertial, and Organizational Change, *American Sociological Review,* 49: 149–164.

Hinings, C. R., and Greenwood, R. (1988). *The Dynamics of Strategic Change.* Oxford: Basil Blackwell.

Kanter, Rosabeth Moss. (1983). *The Change Masters.* New York: Simon and Schuster.

Kelly, Dawn, and Amburgey, Terry. (1991). "Organizational Inertia and Momentum: A Dynamic Model of Strategic Change." *Academy of Management Journal* no. 34, 3: 591–612.

Lenorovitz, Jeffrey. (1993). "Station Foul-ups Spur Calls for Radical Change at NASA." *Aviation Week and Space Technology* (March 8): 58–59.

Meyer, A. D. (1982). "Adapting to Environmental Jolts." *Administrative Science Quarterly* 27: 515–537.

Miller, D., and Friesen, P. H. (1984). *Organizations: A Quantum View.* Englewood Cliffs, N.J.: Prentice-Hall.

Milliken, F. J. (1990). "Perceiving and Interpreting Environmental Change." *Academy of Management Journal* 33: 42–63.

Morrocco, John D. (1993). "C-17 Put on Final Notice as Pentagon Mulls Options." *Aviation Week and Space Technology* (May 17): 62–63.

———. (1994). "Easing C-17 Specs No Threat to AMC." *Aviation Week and Space Technology* (January 3): 26–27.

National Aeronautics and Space Administration (1993). "NASA: Major Challenges for Management: Testimony Before the Legislation and National Security Subcommittee, Committee on Government Operations, House of Representatives." Washington, D.C.: United States General Accounting Office (GAO/T-NSIAD-94-18), October 6.

———. (1986). *Report to the President: Actions to Implement the Recommendations of the Presidential Commission on the Space Shuttle Challenger Accident—Executive Summary.* Washington, D.C.: NASA, July 14.

North, David M. (1993). "C-17 Should Fulfill USAF Airlift Mission." *Aviation Week and Space Technology* (May 10): 42–47.

Ott, J. Steven. (1989). *The Organizational Culture Perspective.* Pacific Grove, Calif.: Brooks/Cole Publishers.

Pasztor, Andy. (1993). "McDonnell Probed on Bills Charged to U.S.: Costs of Defense Contractor to Receive Scrutiny in House Panel Hearing," *The Wall Street Journal* (October 13): A4.

Presidential Commission on the Space Shuttle Challenger Accident [The Rogers Commission]. (1986). *Report to the President: Report at a Glance.* Washington, D.C.: U.S. Government Printing Office, O-157-336.

Quinn, J. B. (1980). *Strategies for Change: Logical Incrementalism.* Homewood, Ill.: Richard D. Irwin.

"Rude Awakening: Quake Jars Assumptions." (1994). *New York Times,* (January 24).

Scott, William B. (1990). "Aerospace/Defense Firms See Preliminary Results from Application of TQM Concepts." *Aviation Week and Space Technology* (January 8): 61–62.

"Shuttle 51-L Loss" [special section with numerous articles]. (1986a). *Aviation Week and Space Technology* (February 3): 16–29.

———. (1986b). *Aviation Week and Space Technology* (February 10): 18–24, 53–65.

———. (1986c). *Aviation Week and Space Technology* (February 17): 18–27, 100–107.

———. (1986d). *Aviation Week and Space Technology* (February 24): 22–30.

"Space Shuttle: Status of Advanced Solid Rocket Motor Program: Report to the Chair, Subcommittee on Government Activities and Transportation, Committee on Government Operations, House of Representatives."

(1992). Washington, D.C.: United States General Accounting Office (GAO/NSIAD-93-26), November.

"Status of C-17 Software: Testimony Before the Legislation and National Security Subcommittee, Committee on Government Operations, House of Representatives." (1993a). Washington, D.C.: United States General Accounting Office (GAO/T-NSIAD-93-2), March 18.

"Status of the C-17 Development Program: Testimony Before the Subcommittees on Military Acquisition and on Oversight and Investigations, Committee on Armed Services, House of Representatives." (1993b). Washington, D.C.: United States General Accounting Office (GAO/T-NSIAD-93-6), March 10.

"Status of the C-17 Development Program: Testimony Before the Legislation and National Security Subcommittee, Committee on Government Operations, House of Representatives." (1993c). Washington, D.C.: United States General Accounting Office (GAO/T-NSIAD-93-8), March 18.

Steinberg, Jacques. (1993a). "Connecticut Store Owner Sentenced in Tax Fraud," *New York Times* (October 21): B1 and B6.

———. (1993b). "Papers Show Greed, Calculation and Betrayal in Stew Leonard Case," *New York Times* (October 22): B5.

Tompkins, Phillip. (1993). *Organizational Communication Imperatives: Lessons of the Space Program.* Los Angeles: Roxbury Publishing Company.

"U.S. Seeks to Ease Friction in Companies: A Conference Looks for Ways to Create More Jobs and Lift Efficiency." (1993). *New York Times* (July 27).

Wartzman, Rick. (1990). "McDonnell's Shake-up Still Reverberates: Year-old Restructuring Remains Far from Bearing Fruit," *The Wall Street Journal* (February 7): A8.

Watzalawick, P. (1978). *The Language of Change.* New York: Basic Books.

Yeats, W. B. (1937, 1966). *A Vision.* New York: Collier Books.

CHAPTER 7

Communicating the Need for Change in a Multinational Pharmaceutical Corporation: A Case Study

Giuseppe Raimondi

INTRODUCTION: THE EUROPEAN PHARMACEUTICAL INDUSTRY

With 320 million consumers, the European Economic Community (EEC) is the second marketplace for drug chemicals, with an estimate of $40.7 billion in 1990, just behind the United States ($44.5 billion), and quite a bit before Japan ($31.2 billion).

Europe is also a first class supplier of drugs. The value of production constitutes a real challenge for the main competitor, the United States. Such production is made by over 1,500 companies located in Europe, which may be classified as

1. Major multinational groups, leaders in the world market;
2. Medium-sized companies operating in more than two countries in the EEC, keeping most of their research and production facilities in their own mother countries and whose main ambition is to enter the former class;
3. Small companies, operating with few drugs, which constitutes the 5 percent of the European national markets.

Although big multinationals from all over the world are consistently present over the market (20 percent), drug production is primarily an European affair.

The opening of the common market in 1993 has been seen by European pharmaceutical firms as a great opportunity to further develop their hegemony over their internal market. However, with companies reporting that only 2 percent of their sales growth comes from price rises, the way to maintain such a pace of growth is mainly dependent on their ability to create new portfolio products; promote mergers, alliances, and cooperations; and stay close to the market needs.

BOEHRINGER INGELHEIM CORPORATION: THE INTERNATIONAL CONGLOMERATE AND THE FRENCH BRANCH

Boehringer Ingelheim (BI) is a German-based multinational group involved mainly in researching, manufacturing, and marketing pharmaceutical compounds all over the world. The Human Pharmaceuticals business unit, at 80 percent, makes the largest contribution to net sales within the BI Corporation. This unit comprises the field of prescription drugs, self-medication, and the hospital market. The Human Pharmaceutical strategy concentrates in Europe, North America, and Japan, even though domestic branches are located in almost every corner of the world.

Beyond pharmaceuticals, the Industrial and Special Products business units research and produce in the fields of chemicals, animal health, bakery products and human nutrition. Global sales rose from DM 4.2 billion in 1991 to DM 5.2 billion in 1992, testifying to the great effort of the entire group toward entering the exclusive club of first class corporations. BI ranked 479 among the first 500 companies in the world in 1992.

Boehringer Ingelheim France is the French branch of the international conglomerate. Even in France, the core of BIF is constituted by pharmaceutical activities. However, all the activities of the group are coordinated by the BIF headquarters located in Paris, where the president, and the Board of Directors operate within few departments that have been decentralized for strategic reasons.

Almost all pharmaceutical activities are concentrated in Reims, a middle-size town in the Champagne region, where the main pharmaceutical plant is located. This plays a key role in the whole range of pharmaceutical activities of the French group, because more than 80 percent of the total amount of pharmaceutical compounds is produced in Reims.

It follows logically that all other activities deeply related to the production of drugs have their headquarters in Reims; namely, the Medical department (in charge of developing new compounds), the Sales department, and the Marketing department. As may be easily noticed, these three departments form a fundamental chain between production and the market and, as a consequence, cover a basic function directly related to their degree of integration.

We will focus our attention upon the Marketing department located in Reims, a newly established one, because it was created for strategic reasons only few years ago. Here I performed an internship for more than three months.

PREREQUISITES FOR CREATING A NEW MARKETING DEPARTMENT

It is hard to believe how successful companies over the entire world market are able to crystallize their configuration, becoming, as a consequence, almost totally impermeable to any kind of structural change. Indeed, this is the case of Boehringer Ingelheim France, which was forced in the mid-1980s by a too evident market decline to create an independent unit to cope with the complexity of the so-called surrounding environment. This was a radical move in BI's corporate philosophy, which is based on a static approach, according to which organizational structures had to be perpetuated, because *any* change could cause a process of progressive disintegration.

Before the decision to implement a brand new department, the marketing activities were incorporated into the sales department, which was in charge of deciding strategies and plans. In other words, marketing had to be subordinated to the sales functions and ways of thinking, because the Sales department was considered the real force of the company. However, at the end of the 1970s, sales at BIF began declining in a palpable way, while the pharmaceutical field in France as a whole was experiencing an euphoric positive trend.

Despite contingent efforts constituted by massive ads and promotional campaigns, the negative tendency persisted up to the early 1980s, revealing a wrong strategic position. As research clearly pointed out, almost all BIF drugs were considered obsolete by physicians and, as a consequence, were not prescribed to patients. The emergence of such a problem was a real shock for the entire company, forcing the German headquarters to

1. Promote agreements with major corporations in the field to acquire innovative research to be transformed into marketable drugs (however, this was a long-term plan, because it takes twelve or thirteen years to bring a drug to market in Europe—and France is no exception);

2. Establish a new alignment with the market via the creation of an independent unit to cope with the customer needs, accelerating, at the same time, the speed in response to the market.

THE MARKETING DEPARTMENT

Cloned by the Sales department, the Marketing department was, from the very beginning of its life, formed by very young managers, maybe to demonstrate the "new deal" undertaken by the French strategic apex of the company. In fact, the Marketing department was headed by a young general manager, who directly supervised all product managers in the structure. Nevertheless, the new structure was considered by the "old guard," the Sales and Medical general managers, as the price to pay to modernization, because no beneficial effect would have come for the "real" operative units, from the Production to the Medical and Sales.

Such a mental attitude was sealed by the fact that the Marketing general manager was a former assistant of the Sales general manager. Their relationships remained anchored in the past, perpetuating a sort of "father-son" dependence. Of course, this pattern of interpersonal behavior had deep consequencies for the BIF structure in itself, because the Marketing department was mentally configurated as "the little son" of Sales. In sum, nothing really changed with the creation of the new department. The process of interdepartmental subjugation was perpetuated and *this was revealed by the pattern of interdepartmental communication.*

Who suffered the most in such a situation was the group of product managers belonging to the Marketing department, in charge of elaborating market strategies to improve the image and the penetration of the entire BIF set of products. What our informal speeches discovered was a process of progressive isolation in crucial moments, that is, when all product managers had to conform their data to the experiences "from the field" before elaborating their marketing plans to the General Pharmaceuticals director.

THE MINTZBERG ANALYSIS

Even though what we have described up to this point was almost overtly stated in the departments mentioned, we used the Mintzberg analysis to furnish an "objective" base to our analysis, because we had to periodically report to the Human Resources general manager. The so-called objectivity, in fact, is a medium that legitimates and substantiates what is merely under the nose of general managers, who, at the same time, do hesitate to deny the evidence because "external observations" belong to the realm of personal opinions and, therefore, have no validity in resembling the "external reality."

According to Henry Mintzberg, there is a precise correlation between the type of environment into which an organization is rooted and its structure in terms of organigram. The theoretical assumption is that every kind of environment requires a typical organizational structure and vice versa, organizations have to have a specific structure to cope with *their own environment*. Because there is a privileged pattern of communication for every single organizational structure, it syllogistically follows that the environment and organizational communication are deeply interrelated.

Therefore, we asked all the product managers to define their own environments according to two main sets of variables formed by the BIF's products they were in charge of (independent variables) and by the most important difficulties they had to cope with in elaborating their marketing plan (dependent variables).

The combination of these two sets of variables defined four environmental facets expressing the environmental degree of difficulties.

1. Stability,
2. Complexity,
3. Diversity,
4. Hostility

The Independent variables were BIF' products:

1. Caldine,
2. Bronchodual,
3. Atrovent UDV,

4. Surbronc,
5. Frubiose,
6. Actilyse.

The Dependent variables were environmental difficulties. Some were related to stability:

- *Governmental regulations* (all laws rules and procedures related with BIF products),
- *Sources of supply* (the degree of supplier reliability),
- *Customers demand* (all unpredictable changes in the demand),
- *Expectation for novelty* (the degree of expectation for new products expressed by customers),
- *Rapidly changing technology* (unpredictable technological changes in the products' segment).

Some were related to complexity:

- *Collecting and analyzing data* (the process of gathering, comparing, and elaborating all kind of data),
- *Addressing scientific questions* (replying to scientific questions asked by physicians),
- *Contacting opinion leaders* (keeping in touch with the most influential scholars and physicians in specific fields of medicine),
- *Choosing a market strategy* (finding out the most effective marketing strategy related to specific products),
- *Implementing a marketing strategy* (realizing, step by step, the appropriate marketing strategy).

Some were related to diversity:

- *Range of customers* (how many different targets with whom to keep in touch),
- *Range of products* (how many products in the same market segment),
- *Range of suppliers* (how many suppliers with whom to cope),
- *Number of geographical areas* (how many regions, districts, and so on involved in the process of commercialization),

- *Number of sales representative* (how many reps were engaged in this process).

And some were related to Hostility:

- *Competition* (how hard is competing with similar products in the same market segment),
- *Governmental reimbursement* (the process of governmental reimbursement of drug price),
- *Gross margin* (the company's gross profit for specific products),
- *Customers' knowledge* (the main targets' knowledge of the product).
- *Customers' receptivity* (the main targets' potential or effective receptivity of the product).

We asked the product managers to rank the products they were in charge of on a three-point scale, expressing the degree of difficulty in relation with each of the four environmental facets mentioned. The result of this process of "environmental interpretation" was translated in twenty-four specific charts which, in turn, were grouped together to get an overview for each environmental dimension. Figures 7.1 to 7.4 illustrate the main four areas of environmental difficulty with which the Marketing department must cope. At the end, the charts were assembled into a single one (Figure 7.5), representing a global view of environmental difficulty.

What is pretty clear from the "objectivity" of the Mintzberg analysis is the sense of isolation felt by *all* product managers in the department. The very fact that, by their own definition, the environment was seen as "very difficult" testifies the degree of "disconnection" from the other two departments (Sales and Medical) from which they could gather vital information for their daily job.

Undoubtably, such was the lack of intracommunication in the horizontal dimension of the company that no internal interdepartmental meeting could compensate for it. The pragmatic result of the product manager's discomfort was a dangerous stagnation in sales, even though a cardiovascular product belonging to

FIGURE 7.1.
Environmental Stability, Aggregated Figures

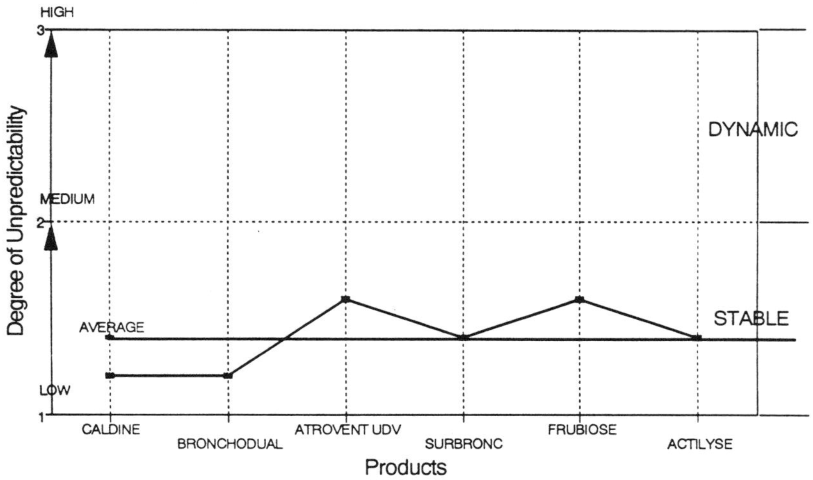

Degree of Stability,* from Stable to Dynamic (1.40)

Variables Involved	Caldi	Bronc	Atrou	Surbr	Frubio	Actily
Governmental Regulations	1 S	1 S	2 M	3 D	1 S	1 S
Sources of Supply	1 S	1 S	2 M	1 S	1 S	1 S
Customers Demand	1 S	2 M	2 M	1 S	3 D	2 M
Expectation for Novelty	2 M	1 S	1 S	1 S	2 M	2 M
Rapidly Changing Technology	1 S	1 S	1 S	1 S	1 S	1 S
Average	1.2	1.2	1.6	1.4	1.6	1.4

* Correlated with job unpredictability

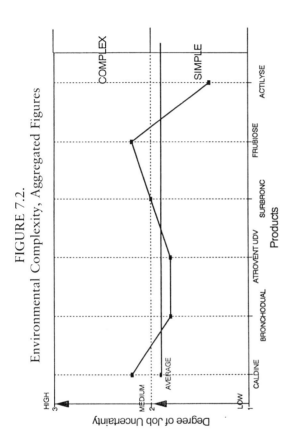

FIGURE 7.2.
Environmental Complexity, Aggregated Figures

Degree of Complexity,* from Simple to Complex (1.90)

Variables Involved	Caldi	Bronc	Atrou	Surbr	Frubio	Actily
Collecting and Analyzing Data	1 S	1 S	1 S	1 S	1 S	1 S
Addressing Scientific Questions	2 M	1 S	1 S	2 M	2 M	1 S
Contacting Opinion Leaders	3 C	2 M	3 C	3 C	3 C	1 S
Choosing a Market Strategy	2 M	3 C	2 M	3 C	3 C	2 M
Implementing a Marketing Strategy	3 C	2 M	2 M	1 M	2 M	2 M
Average	2.2	1.8	1.8	2.0	2.2	1.4

* Correlated with job uncertainty

121

FIGURE 7.3.
Environmental Diversity, Aggregated Figures

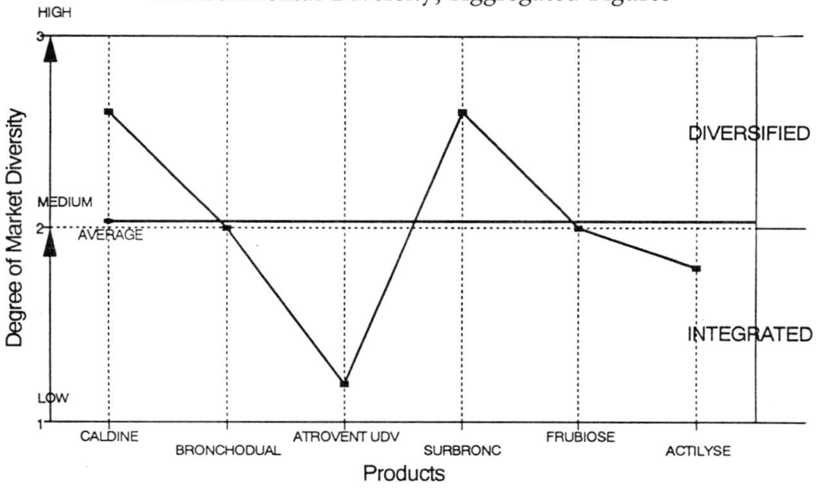

Degree of Diversity,* from Integrated to Diversified (2.03)

Variables Involved	Caldi	Bronc	Atrou	Surbr	Frubio	Actily
Range of Customers	3 D	3 D	1 I	3 D	2 M	2 M
Range of Products	3 D	2 M	1 I	3 D	3 D	1 I
Range of Suppliers	1 I	1 I	1 I	1 I	1 I	1 I
Number of Geographical Areas	3 D	2 M	2 M	3 D	3 D	3 D
Number of Representatives	3 D	2 M	1 I	3 D	1 I	2 M
Average	2.6	2.0	1.2	2.6	2.0	1.8

* Correlated with market diversity

FIGURE 7.4.
Environmental Hostility, Aggregated Figures

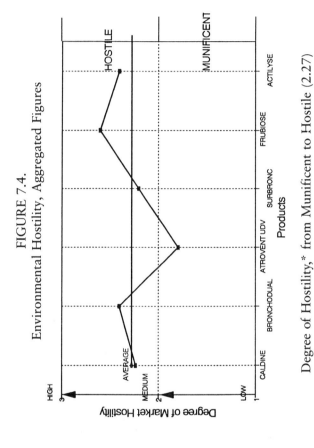

Degree of Hostility,* from Munificent to Hostile (2.27)

Variables Involved	Caldi		Bronc		Atrou		Surbr		Frubio		Actily	
Competition	3	H	3	H	2	M	3	H	3	H	3	H
Gov Reimbursement	1	M	1	M	2	M	3	H	3	H	2	M
Gross Margin	1	M	2	M	1	M	2	M	3	H	2	M
Customers' Knowledge	3	H	3	H	3	H	1	M	1	M	3	H
Customers' Receptivity	2	M	3	H	1	M	2	M	3	H	2	M
Average	2.2		2.4		1.8		2.2		2.6		2.4	

* Correlated with market hostility

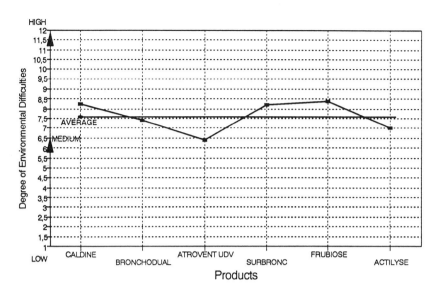

FIGURE 7.5.
Global Environmental Difficulties (Stability + Complexity + Diversity + Hostility)

the newest generation of drugs was launched in its domestic market.

It is not too hazardous to affirm that the reason for this quasi-failure is a deficiency in pragmatism that could not be compensated for by any experience, because every pattern of inter-departmental communication was considered superficial and inappropriate.

SUGGESTIONS FOR A BETTER COALIGNMENT OF THE MARKETING DEPARTMENT

From the Figure 7.5 depicting the global degree of environmental difficulty can be easily inferred that the marketing department needed better horizontal coordination, especially among those departments whose tasks and jobs were related with the main product manager's activities; namely, Sales and Medical. Product managers, in fact, voiced their discomfort stressing the environmental difficulties they had to cope with.

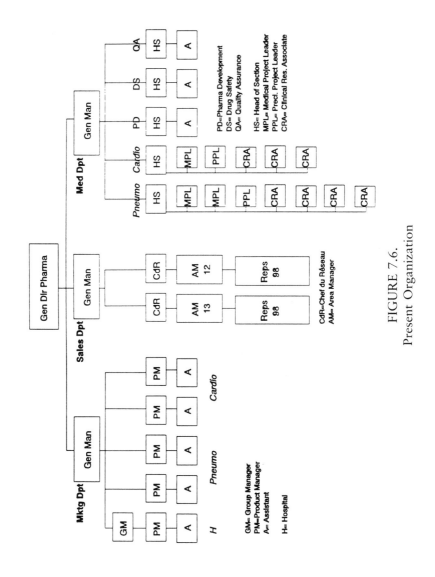

FIGURE 7.6.
Present Organization

The present structure is shown in Figure 7.6. However, to us, a better horizontal coordination could be achieved via a *self-managed team* involving the middle layers of these three departments to assure better and strategic speed in response to those tasks product managers pointed out as the most difficult.

In other words, the self-managed team would constitute a response to cope with the environmental pressure faster and more effectively, providing, via the middle layers of the Sales and Medical departments, those pieces of information product managers needed to accomplish their tasks effectively, timely, and appropriately.

REFERENCES

Cushman, D., and King, S. (1995). *Communication and High-Speed Management*. Albany: SUNY Press.

Dower, M. (1992). "Annus Horribilis." *Script Review:* 2–17.

Jaeger, H., and Gielsdorf, W. (1992). "Europe in '92: A Changing Market and Consequencies for Drug Development." *Drugs Made in Germany* 34: 3–9.

King, S. S., and Cushman, D. (1994). *High Speed Management and Organizational Communication in the 1990s: A Reader*. Albany: SUNY Press.

Mintzberg, H. (1983). *Structure in Fives*. Englewood Cliffs, N.J.: Prentice-Hall.

Pacanowsky, M. E., and O'Donnell, Trujillo N. (1983). "Organizational Communication as Cultural Performance." *Communication Monographs* 50: 126–147.

Pelc, A. (1992). "La Structure de L'Industrie Pharmaceutique en Europe." *Les Enjeux de L'Europe* 3: 36–47.

Scott, R. (1990). *Organizations. Rational, Natural, and Open Systems*. Englewood Cliffs, N.J.: Prentice-Hall.

CHAPTER 8

Communicating the Need for Shared Responsibility in Nongovernment Joint Venture Projects: Lessons from Years of Experience

Gordon Knowles

INTRODUCTION

On an inspection tour during the construction of St Paul's, Christopher Wren is said to have asked a stonecutter "What are you doing?"
    "Cutting stone," he replied.
    Further along, he asked another stonecutter what he was doing.
    "Building a cathedral," the man said.

(Porter 1991)

The two messages given to Christopher Wren are illuminating in that they reveal something of the breadth of vision and foresight of the second stonecutter, which contrasts sharply with the narrow focus of his workmate. It also could tell us something of the management system of the project managers. The same contrast could be found in many organizations, and I would submit that in my own organization such a diversity of vision could also be found.

In this chapter I want to attempt to pull together some thoughts on the experiences of the nongovernment organization (NGO) community in developing countries. These observations and experiences are based in particular on the operations of the Salvation Army Australia.

A significant number of NGOs originate from developed countries. When they commence operations in developing countries with different languages (or a variety of languages) and differing cultural, educational, political, and economic systems, executives are presented with immense challenges in communication.

FOUNDATION STONES FOR DEVELOPMENT

Despite the confidence surrounding monetarist-inspired counter-revolution in development thinking in the early 1980s (Porter 1991, 55), burgeoning developing country debt and worsening circumstances in much of the world forced us to concede that, left to their devices, neither the market nor the state will enable the poor to lift their productivity to the level where their efforts are rewarded with longer term benefits.

Rapid democratic and economic change worldwide is positive, but profoundly unsettling and has created an era of uncertainty. Our organization has not been protected from this environment. Fundamental to that uncertainty are very real doubts about the human capacity to manipulate the present, thereby bringing about beneficial improvements to the quality of human life.

Uncertainty can be diminished by improvement in communication and building partnerships through a better understanding and an acceptance of shared responsibilities (Fowler 1992).

The involvement of NGOs with aid and development in less industrialized countries is not new. Aid and development NGOs, like the larger domestic voluntary sector concerned with welfare and social justice were largely ignored by people who wrote about organizations, politics, and social policy (Porter 1991, 55). After a long courtship of NGOs during the 1980s, the World Bank reports that NGO funding jumped by more than 300 percent in 1989 and follows this with country reviews clearly extolling the virtues of continued expansion (World Bank 1989).

What Has Caused This Escalation of Regard for NGOs?

Public disillusionment with official assistance, internationally declining official aid budgets, and tight ceilings on administrative expenditure have given NGOs enhanced credibility. NGOs benefited from international trends during the 1980s that produced an odd coincidence between two otherwise contending forces. The political Left and Right agreed on the ineffectiveness of the state and the need to foster local initiative. Market economists favored assistance to the private sector; however, the weakness of this sector in many countries has led donors to explore the alternative of working through voluntary, nonprofit agencies (Fowler 1992, 17).

NGOs from developed countries have fostered strong relationships with the donor governments and sovereign states that host their activities. NGOs have to deal with the inherent tension between the interests of voluntarism and civil society and the administrative rationalism of public bureaucracies. NGOs experience difficulties inherent in statutory and voluntary organizations such as mutual misconceptions in the absence of accepted clearly defined understandings of each other's roles, and the lack of formal agreements for cooperation in policy development, planning, funding, and reviewing.

Governments and NGOs are different species of organizations. Some governments have a preoccupation with efficiency, information gathering, corporate programming, and budgeting. This shifts attention away from efforts to localized and decentralized control, considered vital for NGO effectiveness.

Development remains a problem in the 1990s, due to the combination of three major factors:

1. The lack of consensus about the ultimate objective of development or the means to reach this elusive target;
2. The inability of poor countries to command sufficient human and capital resources to raise living standards;
3. The propensity for interest groups in poor countries to work to further their own interests so that attempts to achieve broader development objectives and reallocate resources remain suboptimal and perennially frustrated (Riddell 1992, 8).

Despite the skepticism about the impact of official government aid resources, churches and volunteer aid organizations reinforce the belief that some form of aid contributes to poverty alleviation. Continued support for aid derives from the perception not only that it ought to work, but that it has worked. Successes cited include the Marshall Plan for the regeneration of Europe and the examples of South Korea and Taiwan, which were substantially supported by aid funds in their initial growing years. Other aid successes include the development and spread of high-yielding seed varieties and a myriad of community development projects designed and managed by aid agencies, which are advertised to show that their actions make a difference to the quality of life of individuals at the village level in developing countries.

There is clear evidence, however, that some aid is wasted, that in some countries aid appears to make little difference to poverty problems, that some projects are disastrous, and that some larger aid projects seem to have paid scant attention to the environment, the rights of indigenous peoples, and sometimes the cultural taboos of the relevant people, including gender issues (Porter 1991, 62–63). The second half of the 1980s has witnessed an expansion of funding to NGOs. This is because of the significant increase in projects they were executing and the greater belief among official donors that they had an important role to play in the development process, especially in alleviation of poverty. The closeness of the NGOs to the communities in which they were working and the development by NGOs of a sense of community is regarded as an important factor for the greater use of NGOs for channelling official funds.

It is perceived that NGOs could do what governments could not, and the grassroots level of needs assessment, project development, and implementation by NGOs has seen community development and poverty alleviation successes.

How Do NGOs Achieve These Successes?

Many NGOs should be regarded as international NGOs (INGOs) because of their vast network of support agencies and their area of operations. The Salvation Army, for instance, operates in over 100 countries throughout the world. Few commercial corporations could claim that spread of operation, except perhaps the Coca-Cola Bottling Company or the McDonald's empire.

NGOs play a significant role in building esteem; creating income-generating activities or viable economic options; providing training in employable skills; providing basic health, sanitation, and educational services; and a myriad of other "community development" initiatives. As a result of these activities, it is reasonable to suggest that incomes of a significant number of people in developing countries have grown.

The World Bank in 1993 stated that nearly one fifth of the world's population lives on less than $1 per day and that in parts of Africa this average is going down. It also claimed that one fifth of the world's population had an annual income of between $2,000 and $5,000 and, over the past twenty years, watched their annual income double, triple, and quadruple in some cases (World Bank 1993). Not all of this increase can be attributable to the work of NGOs naturally.

This rapid improvement in income levels for a significant number of the world's population has enabled governments to gain access to significant investment capital for necessary infrastructure development, thus attracting the multinational corporations to various countries. Some of these countries include Mexico, Argentina, Malaysia, Indonesia, Thailand, Hong Kong, Singapore, Taiwan, and China, with resultant rapid economic growth parallelled by an appreciable increase in the quality of life for the citizens of these countries.

Each of these countries, we must acknowledge, has a vastly different cultural climate for which multinationals and NGOs must prepare, accommodate, and work within, to successfully embrace the available market and improve the quality of life for various community groups. Not only does the NGO have to adapt to this culture, but it must develop its own culture within its own operations.

DEVELOPMENT COMMUNICATION

The objective of development communication is to communicate what are supposed to be development messages. The development messages that were supposed to be communicated to audiences in the south or developing countries have, in the past, been messages of imminent failure. Despite many years of development efforts, many countries in the south are now even worse off. The concept of being developed meant that countries had to adopt Western standards of living and social organization.

Development communication has been described as "the art and science of human communication applied to the speedy transformation of a country through the utilization of appropriate expertise in a development process that will assist in increasing participation of intended beneficiaries at the grass roots level" (Moemeka 1989).

One problem faced by NGOs is that, by their nature as voluntary organizations, they need to be able to explain their plans and activities in terms that attract the participation and support of people who are naturally preoccupied with their own lives and worries. People are often quick in responding to knowledge that individuals, far from their own country, are in trouble, but they regard, as beyond their influence or responsibility, the complex economic and technological issues that underline most of the problems they wish to help with. It is much easier to raise interest and money for famine relief—vital work as this may be—than for work designed over years to assist and avoid in future famines.

In overcoming this very genuine difficulty, NGOs of the north, and of the south also, can often be assisted by cooperation on terms of equality or partnership with NGOs of the south and by sharing experiences. There is a need to understand each other from each other's vantage point.

Take for example the enormous problems faced by women in most developing countries. They work incredibly hard for intolerable hours. In the rural areas where most of them live, they have to collect wood for cooking, carry water for long distances, cultivate food for the family with a hand hoe, as well as bear and look after children, cook for the family, and seek to earn a little money on the side to provide for education, clothing, and other essential necessities of life (Streeten 1991, 39). For such women, real liberation often means having clean water brought to the village or easier access to cooking fuel or some new opportunity to improve for practical education for her or that of her children. Legal rights are almost meaningless in the face of their present economic oppression. The right to vote or participate in the democratic processes of the country are also meaningless in comparison with their pressing circumstances.

Among women, a mutual exchange of ideas, experiences, and knowledge can be of benefit to peoples in the north and south. NGOs are best placed to arrange such contacts and mutual help. The direct grassroots assistance given to people in villages or urban areas is one of the most important aspects of the work of NGOs and one of the most helpful to individuals for people-centered development in the south.

In my experience, however, NGOs involved at the grassroots level of providing services and empowering people need to be backed up by giving their attention to and lobbying about macro-economic issues. NGOs often find, for example, when they have provided or helped a village to build its school by paying for the roofing materials, a cut in the education budget means that textbooks for the children cannot be provided. When this education budget is researched, it is found to be a direct result of "conditionality" attached to external aid that includes, among other things, giving top priority to debt servicing or the direct consequences of a slump in the price of commodity exports. Many NGOs do not pay attention to the macro-economic issues that impinge on their very good work.

The application of the processes of communication to the development process has caused many NGOs to focus upon culture and sense of community. At the same time, direct people-to-people dialogue can play a vital role in helping the people of the south to develop themselves and their country. It can help them become self-reliant and therefore better partners of NGOs in the north. Our experience suggests that our partner NGOs of the south learn significantly from our management and organizing experience, and despite their organizational inexperience and frequent technical insufficiencies, developing country organizations have cultural and other knowledge we outsiders inevitably lack. We have proven that, if the work in a host country is to be sustained over the long term, the local NGO will have to carry it on, ultimately within its own resource capacities.

The objective of NGOs in the north should be to work *with* local people, not for them. This certainly is the case for the organization for which I work. NGOs of the north should enable people to fulfill their own improvement objectives, rather than to present external ideas for them to adopt.

Participants in a development program, that is, NGOs such as ours trying to improve economic, social, and cultural conditions and quality of life, work as agents and potential beneficiaries of development and change. Communication is the most important part of their work and requires different kinds of technical and cultural considerations at different stages of development, in different societies.

It is said that African tribes do not have the equivalent of the modern political party, although many nongovernment organizations are emerging. No one can claim that these tribes were democratic in any modern sense. It might be claimed that African tribes had developed their own ways of democratic governance. Small basic communities do tend to be reasonably democratic.

> The elders sit under a tree
> and talk until they agree.

This simple art of talking until agreement is reached, and partnerships established, has proved to be most effective time and time again by NGOs.

COMMUNICATION IN DEVELOPMENT—FORMAL AND INFORMAL

Any sizeable development program involves the collecting together many people and organizations of different professions, social classes, and interests, at various levels ranging from developed, First World, government officials, professionals, unskilled workers, and people at the village level. They are engaged in a variety of activities associated with policy making, planning, operations, and training. The coordination of these activities is by a network of communication and control through a variety of channels.

Development communication has its unique structure and consists of meanings, motivations, values, beliefs, customs, norms, and rules of development and communication shared or contested by individuals and organizations. The interaction of this formal and informal structure compliment each other, with the human factor being at the center of all activity. In the final analysis the human factor working through, and with each other, and utilizing the accumulated wisdom, knowledge, and information, causes development to take place.

Communicative action requires the participants to seek a mutual understanding on a number of things—the objectives, roles, and functions of participants, and the coordination of their individual activity in realizing those objectives for the betterment of the community in which they function.

Women—Sometimes Silent Participants

The frustrating thing for many NGOs from the north is that often the real doers and information providers are kept at arm's length from the NGO because of an intermediary level of decision and discussion-making people; namely, the men of the village.

Women, as I have previously stated, form the bedrock of the economies of developing countries. They provide 50 percent of agricultural labor and more than 70 percent of the work force, mostly in low technology, poorly paid industries such as clothing. They also represent by far the majority of street vendors, artisans, and domestic servants, without whose efforts millions of dependents would daily walk the fine line between subsistence and starvation.

Despite this critical social and economic role, women have few rights in relation to decision making, information providing, land tenure, marital status, income, or social security, and their place in the village is dominated by a male tier of talkers and decision makers, without whose support the NGO is unable to provide any assistance if it required.

The male contribution to the household food production begins and ends with clearing and ploughing the land. Sometimes they may grow cash crops for sale, rather than food crops. Women on the other hand do the weeding, seeding, and harvesting and often work sixteen hours a day, compared to the six or eight for men.

Because men have more time to sit and discuss and have the responsibility for making decisions, NGOs tend to assume that the men of the village and the community know what the community needs are. Numerous mistakes have been made in relation to interpreting the information provided by men through the failure to seek more appropriate guidance from women in the field: women who have practical knowledge of the implications of the particular problem and the solution about to be implemented.

The true art of development communication focuses on the utilization of appropriate expertise in the development process and the full participation of intended beneficiaries. The failure to incorporate opinions from women in the development of project proposals and project implementation has caused NGOs to significantly modify projects that were not seen to be worthwhile after they had been commenced.

NGOs are service oriented, and in much the same way that multinational corporations are conscious of their service orientation and customer service, NGOs need to focus on the opinions of the client population. Because women have such a major input to the continued sustainability of the family and because their time is almost fully utilized at present, there is a tendency to overlook the valuable knowledge and resource they possess. This is more the case in the area of leadership. NGOs should appreciate the experience of women managing the family, solving everyday problems, and using limited resources to the maximum. Women represent a vast reservoir of wisdom, a great willingness to learn, and an extensive management experience developed because of the basic need to survive.

The objective of most NGOs from the north is to work in a cooperative manner with the host government authorities and NGOs of the host developing country. We realize that education of all kinds, technical, managerial, agricultural, dealing with health, production, techniques, planning, and simple accounting, will usually be an important element of direct grassroots activity. Traditional knowledge in the south can often form the foundation for technical modernization. The essence, however, of effective north-south cooperation between NGOs can be found in people-to-people contact and mutual learning on the basis of that contact, but it can take place only on terms of mutual respect and a recognition that all involved can learn and benefit from the relationship.

To empower the people of a developing country in any field of action, NGOs, whether entirely indigenous or externally linked, must base their work on the culture and the changing circumstances, conditions, and needs of life in that particular community. NGOs should also realize that a great deal of knowledge is integrated into the particular country's culture, which needs to be drawn upon and used. The value, for instance, of African traditional medicine is now beginning to be recognized and developed by many of our modern establishments, but much other knowledge is rarely acknowledged, to the cost of Africa.

The use of traditional Chinese medicine in conjunction with modern rehabilitation techniques has been recognized by the Salvation Army and is the focus of two particularly interesting projects in Nanjing. Empowering the people is made much easier if there is a significant reliance on traditional medicine and traditional methods. It also is less costly in economic terms because of the reduced need for training and the reduced need for purchase of modern technology.

Julius K. Nyerere, the former president of Tanzania and former chairman of the South Commission, at a Conference on Empowering People, in Arusha in August 1991, claimed that there are three basic precepts for NGOs seeking to empower the people (Nyerere 1991). First, he claimed that the NGO must be very clear in what it is trying to do, why, and how it proposes to do it: it can do this only if there has been an earlier "listening to the people talking about their own problems" in the new circumstances. Second, he suggests that the design of any program of action needs to be based upon the maximum self-reliance of the group involved and its support base. Third, he suggests that built into the structure of the NGO must be a system of continuously listening, involving the concerned and supporting people in the NGO's activities. In essence, this is what development communication is all about.

In one sense, the three precepts are merely different facets of an essential approach to overcoming all the problems of Africa, he suggests that of self-reliance, using their own resources to the maximum. Nyerere also suggested that Africa's problems are directly and primarily Africa's responsibilities and that solutions need to be based on the maximum self-reliance within individual countries and within Africa as a continent.

Building self-reliance does not mean ruling out cooperation with others or help from others in the form of money, equipment, and experienced personnel. Empowering the people, creating opportunities, broadening the vision, or enhancing the quality of life will not occur unless programs, proposed by NGOs, are rooted in the local culture. Unless this occurs, they will not survive.

If they are to be effective in empowering people, NGOs from the north, and the south, need to plant their roots deeply into what we loosely call African culture. This will mean somewhat different things in different areas. An organization's failure to start from where the people start means that, whatever else it does, it cannot succeed in empowering people at all.

I am not suggesting that this means slavishly accepting all the cruelties and injustices which were part of the traditional practices in many African tribes and states. Take for example the subordinate position of women that existed and still exists. Its origins can be found in the insecurities and technologies of the past. Organizations that are concerned to overcome this subordination have to demonstrate that the technologies of today demand a very different position for women and that it is necessary both for society as a whole, for the men as well as the women of the twentieth century.

The ability of NGOs to bridge this cultural gulf places a great demand on their communications ability.

The advanced industrial nation's ability to communicate globally and process very large volumes of information at very high speed has increased dramatically over the past few decades. At the local level, however, in most developing countries, the basic telecommunications and computer networks have not yet been established. Television does not exist yet in Tanzania, for instance. Even in the developed countries, many poor and remote areas have no adequate access to the national communications networks. In many African countries where the Salvation Army operates quite large rural hospitals, it is not yet possible to telephone because of the lack of communications facilities in those countries.

CULTURE AND THE COMMUNICATION PROCESS

I recall seeing a development worker use culture and power in a very unique and what I thought was fitting manner when visiting a project site in Bangladesh. A New Zealand nurse was calling for women in the village to participate in nutrition training and demonstration sessions for their children, as well as in the immunization of all women of child-bearing age.

This nurse exerted her motivational power on these people, primarily through two personal qualities:

1. The ability to communicate—cheerfully, clearly, in a participatory way—good information about nutrition for both children and mothers;
2. The ability to identify with the people in their social and cultural surroundings, and relate to their experience of poverty and village life.

Numerous NGOs are able to cite similar examples. Organizations and individuals who are venturing forth into a developing country with a view to a commercial or development partnership would agree with the five guiding principles adopted by our organization.

1. Maintain full respect for people with regard to their sum of knowledge, life and work experience, and skills.

2. Be a learner from people and a sharer with them both of your knowledge and *their* knowledge.

3. Be a practical demonstrator of what people are taught and trained to do.

4. Avoid "the boss" attitude, and participate in the community's development.

5. Encourage sustainability, always focusing on the community as the project initiator, the goal owner, and the project beneficiary, especially in the decision-making area of project management.

Cultural differences can be likened to a person wearing a number of sets of glasses at different times, each with different specifications and purposes. The visitor who enters another culture with a filter created by his or her own cultural background may, or may not, distort all that is seen in his new environment. In a new culture where people have other ways of viewing the world, disorientation, misunderstanding, embarrassment, and possibly even offense may result from the reliance on a past cultural experience. Moreover, the ability of the visitor in this new environment to negotiate his or her way through the different processes of encoding and decoding available information and customs creates opportunities for one to gain acceptance in one's new community and become a test of one's communication skills.

We recognize that hidden barriers exist in these circumstances. Unconscious forces prevent the maximum benefit being obtained out of the communication taking place. When expanding services into new communities or areas of a country, NGOs commonly face these issues. If they want to be successful and implement or facilitate aid and development projects needed and wanted by the community, they need to be more inquiring and adapt to the local situation, not merely suffer from the "do good" syndrome.

Staff selection and staff placement by NGOs in developing countries is also a matter that should be accorded prudent consideration. Imagine the message being communicated to project staff and beneficiaries in an area in the north of Bangladesh when an NGO sent a 280 pound, overweight aid worker to that area.

Not only was it culturally unacceptable to send such a person; he was not well received by the local population who were suffering malnutrition and food deprivation. The message received by the project staff and the local community was that this particular NGO did not have respect and understanding for their particular circumstances and environment. Hence, the NGOs reputation suffered badly, and future work in that area will require significant input to redeem that lost face. Although the aid worker was recalled after only six weeks at that project site, irreparable damage had already been done. In this instance, a unique form of communication had taken place within a very special cultural and need setting.

CULTURAL PATTERNS

Culture in the context in which it is being used here includes many more things than art, literature, and music. It includes the very pattern of life people in a particular region enjoy. It includes accepted modes of behavior, beliefs about patterns of interaction between men, women, and children within the family; the types of food they eat; the way they raise their children; and it also includes the ideas, principles, and rules within a group of people in a certain geographical area. Some of these components of the particular culture may have evolved over a long period of time—others may have been imported and adapted to the particular circumstances of the people concerned.

There are variations in every culture. Social needs in a particular culture are most likely to be met by a pattern of cultural beliefs that will make social life more predictable. To make this social life more predictable, we establish some kind of order and regularity about interpersonal relationships so that the social system functions with some degree of regularity. Rules and regulations may, however, vary from group to group.

NGOs operating in the aid/development arena are especially attuned to the changes and cultural patterns within certain countries because of the significant impact on the success or otherwise of projects implemented in a diverse range of cultures.

NGOs AND DEVELOPMENT WORKERS
IN NEW CULTURAL SURROUNDINGS

Let me use, as an example, a friend of mine who has been in an African country for three years. This man, call him Chuck since he comes from the United States, holds a significant position as the public relations secretary for a prominent NGO. When Chuck arrived in this particular country, he was astounded to learn the following by experience.

- If you had made an appointment to see someone, this did not necessarily mean that the person would attend.
- If the person failed to appear for the appointment, this did not necessarily mean that an apology would result.
- Inordinate delays in queues caused a gross inefficiency in, and for, his particular organization.
- His phone was continually in disrepair, an issue he could not get used to.
- The water supply is intermittent. The people in the city where he lives accept this as normal.
- The electricity supply is also intermittent. He could not accept the inefficiency that resulted.
- Chuck could not get used to the lack of an apology for the failure to honor one's word for an undertaking previously given.
- He had to contend with a language difficulty, since in the country there were seventy-two dialects other than the official English in which he is proficient.
- Chuck found it very difficult to adapt to new customs and new food, especially after observing how it was prepared, cooked, and eaten.
- Chuck had not previously experienced a great number of divergent views about world powers and occurrences in the international arena, and he found it extremely difficult to absorb strong criticism, especially of his own country.
- The perceived laziness of the national workers, combined with their perceived lack of initiative and innovation, was a continual drain on his good nature.

In the country in which Chuck is located, it is acceptable for men to be seen in public holding hands. It is also acceptable for women to hold hands, but it is rare to see men holding hands in public with women. In many countries like Australia, the United

States, and the United Kingdom, we would tend to make assumptions about men displaying this type of behavior. In Chuck's new homeland, the holding of hands by men is seen as a gesture of friendship and a display of brotherhood. This different standard of behavior is acceptable.

NGOs, ours included, send hundreds of development workers to different countries of the world every year. Some are sent for short periods to provide specific technical assistance, whereas others are engaged for longer terms of up to four or five years. Many of these workers find themselves in similar positions to our fictitious Chuck.

The effectiveness of our public relations secretary Chuck has been greatly impeded by the problems he has encountered in his new cultural environment. His efficiency has been reduced by the "cultural glasses" he has been used to wearing in his own country. Hence the ability, both within and without the organization, to have an effective communication network has been limited by the "cultural learning curve" of the Chucks in the developing world.

Social critic Alvin Toffler, in an interview, maintains that traditional corporate bureaucracies, relics from the smokestack era of manufacturing, are poorly designed to respond to challenges and opportunities in the twenty-first century marketplace. He believes, however, that corporations must emphasize diversity and flexibility to compete in a world in which knowledge—information, communication, and technology—has become the key to economic power (Toffler 1991, 8).

Toffler's observations lead me to suggest that many CEOs encourage staff members to experiment with nonbureaucratic models. The pressures of competition, rapid change, and continually shifting market niches force companies to adopt changing organizational models and inherently undermine both the hierarchy and the departmental divisions of information. This being the case, it appears that the basic pressures do not come from the ideology of managers—growth and change find their way into the organization from the bottom, rather than the top.

It is interesting to note also that various experiments with "checkerboard organizations" have met with varying degrees of success. The example is cited of a Japanese Bank in California providing a contemporary adaptation of the Austrian postwar political experiment by alternating Japanese and Americans at every level of the organization hierarchy. This has ensured a steady stream of information from different levels and different perspectives. It has also encouraged a cultural blend within the organization (Toffler 1991). Our organization has many successful examples of expatriate-national checkerboard management teams all over the world.

We have found that a very flat administrative structure, incorporating national staff members at needs analysis, implementation, and evaluation levels, has given much flexibility and is ideal for staff development. Additionally, the use of project teams that decide on the best cultural and most economic way of doing the task has proved an effective method of gathering ideas and providing cultural input from local staff members, including women, in addition to enhancing the team morale.

The provision of an Australian input, including ideas and concepts from other cultures and projects provides, in many cases, the basis for alternative techniques or an avenue for the introduction of new and more advanced technology. Our use of a flat, three to four level at most, administration has enabled a speedier assessment of project proposals, a faster approval and funding mechanism, and a faster problem identification system through the monitoring and evaluation involvement of the Australian NGO.

Our particular version of high-speed management has improved our service delivery and overall project management. The aim of empowering people is to enable more people to have the vision to become stonecutters and build "cathedrals," rather than merely cut stones.

CONCLUSION

There are many impediments and hidden barriers to effective communication in developing countries. Let me attempt to summarize our experiences:

1. Development communication in the past has delivered defeatist messages to people in developing countries, rather than encouragement and a sense of achievement.

2. The service orientation of development NGOs should make their organizational structure more aware of the needs, opinions, and culture of the client population.

3. Organizational communication within an NGO can be enhanced by continually reappraising its achievements and paying close attention to culture, listening to indigenous people and involving them in the operations of the organization.

4. The expertise and experience of women and their leadership skills are underutilized in developing countries by NGOs and the communities from which they come.

5. Development NGOs can easily become as "bloated" as any public bureaucracy unless a continuous system of organizational appraisal and mission evaluation is implemented throughout the organization.

6. Communication in a development context is more effective in a flat administrative structure that facilitates more efficient information and technology transfer.

REFERENCES

Fowler, Alan. (1992). "Building Partnerships Between Northern and Southern Development NGOs: Issues for the Nineties." *Development, Journal of SID,* 1.

Moemeka, A. (1989). "Perspectives on Development Communication." *Africa Media Review* 13, no 3.

Nyerere, Mwalimu Julius K. (1991). Address given at Conference on Empowering People, Arusha, August 12.

Porter, D. (1991). "Cutting Stones for Development: Issues for Australian Agencies." In *Doing Good: The Australian NGO Community,* ed. Laurie Zivetz and others, 1991, Allen & Unwin Pty Ltd.

Riddell, Roger C. (1992). "The Contribution of Foreign Aid to Development and the Role of the Private Sector." *Development, Journal of SID* 1.

Streeten, Paul. (1992). "Social Development in Africa: A Focus on People." *Development, Journal of SID* 2.

Toffler, Alvin. (1991). "The Changing Business Structure." recorded in *Dialogue* 93, no. 3.

World Bank. (1989). Office Memorandum, Washington, D.C.: World Bank, September 7.

———. (1993). *World Development Report.* Washington, D.C.: World Bank.

PART 2

Public Sector Organizations

CHAPTER 9

Public Sector Performance and Private Sector Management

Ron Cullen

INTRODUCTION

In a number of countries, public sector organizations and programs have changed to make them more responsive to the demands of governments, to reduce costs, and to introduce private sector management practices. Although many of the changes aimed to improve services to the public, the gap between performance and public expectations of the public sector remains.

This chapter argues that a prerequisite for the translation of many private sector management approaches to public administration is a focus on performance that is specific and looks beyond statements of broad intent to the cost-effective delivery of services to the public at the grassroots level. The chapter draws on selected Australian changes to explore how such a focus can be developed and to identify the changes in management values required to deliver improved performance of public sector programs.

OVERVIEW

Underperformance is a major issue for public administration in the 1990s. A major cause of this gap is a lack of fit between the management and support strategies of public sector organizations and the delivery strategies they seek to implement.

This lack of fit can be related to the management values that managers and governments apply to public sector operations.

147

- Management values that see public sector performance in terms of increased freedom to manage have encouraged the dismantling of traditional bureaucratic controls over finance and personnel without developing increased accountability for delivery of services to the public.

- Management values that see structure as independent of strategy have encouraged attempts to transplant partial private sector management approaches into the public sector without developing the sort of focus on performance which guides these approaches in many private sector management situations.

- Management values that see performance as inevitable, providing malfunctions do not occur, have encouraged public sector managers to ignore the need to define performance and manage the delivery of services to the public; instead, they manage surrogates for performance. Although surrogates work well enough in a stable regulated environment, they seem increasingly ineffective in a more dynamic and deregulated environment.

This diagnosis has major consequences for the future performance of public administration. Lack of accountability combined with the deregulation that has occurred may well have exposed many public sector organizations and programs to increased risks of major failure without improving their capacity to meet public expectations for improved services.

A reversion to previous systems is not a real option. These systems also failed to deliver value to the public. Many of the old regulatory systems, and most of the middle level managers who administered them, have been abolished as part of the deregulation and cost reduction programs of recent years.

Where it is achievable, a better solution is to make the recent changes effective by introducing new approaches to defining and evaluating performance. The changes examined suggest that this can be done in selected public sector situations.

Where a performance focus is not an option, it is important to review recent changes and consider the introduction of alternative controls and regulation. Interesting applications of technology combined with audit and review procedures are being explored and seem to offer potential both to avoid major failures and ensure that clients are seen to be treated equitably.

We begin by examining shifts in the management approaches and values in the private and public sector and placing in perspective the management solutions now emerging in the public sector. Then, we outline an approach to performance management and review that has been applied in a number of public sector situations to provide a focus for the management of performance. Finally, we discuss some general results identified from a review of selected public sector changes.

CHANGING MANAGEMENT APPROACHES AND VALUES

Approaches to management are changing in both the private and public sectors. These changes can be related to changes in strategies, technology, and markets. Over the last half century, both private and public sector organizations have moved through a series of changes that can be considered in four stages; bureaucratization, market driven expansion, rationalization, and further growth and development.

Changes in Private Sector Management

- *Bureaucratization:* The early concentration was to exploit specialization and economies of scale. This led to large bureaucracies and the exploitation of emerging production technologies.
- *Market-Driven Expansion:* The focus shifted to markets and products and the devolution of management control to business units. This overcame much of the inertia created by large bureaucratic structures and enabled organizations to grow larger by diversifying production and expanding markets. The process of decentralization led to the growth of business conglomerates. In the 1970s, this led to the development of large strategic headquarters groups to add value to diverse business units by providing ideas and direction and by financing expansion.
- *Rationalization:* Many of these large conglomerates failed. Their value was often little more and sometimes less than the value of the operating business standing alone. The 1970s saw

the same advisors who had promoted large head offices advise their demolition. Divestitures assisted companies to reduce debts created by expansion and focus on core businesses.

- *Further Growth and Development:* Growth in the 1980s has centered on core businesses and exploiting products and technologies across international rather than national or regional markets. Today's conglomerates have a focus and a strategy for adding value to markets and technologies, and they use technology to control diverse business units strategically. Management practices in the private sector have used technology and the diversification of markets created by internationalization to develop devolved structures and important new forms of accountability. Performance, both financial and otherwise, is monitored against competitors and comparisons are made between markets. These controls provide a focus for devolution and adding value which was missing from some earlier experiments to manage conglomerates.

Globalization of trans National traid

Public Sector Management Changes

- *Bureaucratization:* The public sector also developed bureaucratic structures, not to focus production processes but to coordinate the huge paper factories required to administer government policies equitably.

- *Market-Driven Expansion:* The size and role of the public sector increased massively in most countries, and governments have accepted responsibility for providing many additional services. In many cases, the decision to provide services was driven by sources of funding or history rather than a detailed analysis of core priorities for the public sector. The decentralization which occurred in the private sector was paralleled by the development of a plethora of public sector agencies, each managing different groups of programs. Increasingly, governments built large central agency structures to advise on priorities between agencies and on coordination and control.

- *Rationalization:* The rationalization which occurred in the private sector occurred somewhat later in the public sector. The 1980s saw governments in many countries seek to reduce public sector costs while continuing to expand priority programs. Large bureaucracies have been dismantled; personnel systems have altered to make public sector employment more accountable; and middle layers of organizations have been eliminated to parallel private sector developments. Although technology has removed the need for many of these levels in private companies, it has offered few solutions for the public sector, where reduced coordination has led to perceptions of inequity and inefficiency. On occasion, governments have sought to revert to core businesses and recognized the value of privatizing elements that can be distanced from the government or used to reduce public sector debt.

- *Further Growth and Development:* There has been major growth in areas such as education and health and contraction in other areas. Much of the growth has occurred in partnership with the private sector. Important new priorities for many public sector programs are to leverage public funds with other funds and evaluate overall performance rather than simply the direct contribution made by public sector agencies. New forms of accountability provided in the private sector by international markets and international benchmarks for performance have been slow to emerge in the public sector. Public administration tends to be regional or national. Benchmarks and product comparison between markets are now being used, but they seldom drive public sector evaluation of performance.

Future Public Sector Management Priorities

Public sector organizations lack the simple performance focus of many business organizations; they are characterized by complex performance criteria that are often multifaceted. At a general level, broad objectives are often defined. These tend to be difficult to evaluate and only loosely linked to the delivery of services to the public.

Unless deregulation of the public sector is accompanied by new forms of accountability, underperformance will become a long-term feature of public administration. The options for transition are summarized in Figure 9.1.

Before the public sector can begin to benefit from more flexible types of management that work so well when organizations have

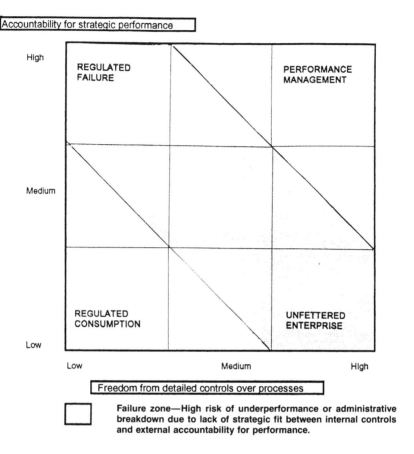

Accountability for strategic performance

High

REGULATED
FAILURE

PERFORMANCE
MANAGEMENT

Medium

Low

REGULATED
CONSUMPTION

UNFETTERED
ENTERPRISE

Low   Medium   High

Freedom from detailed controls over processes

Failure zone—High risk of underperformance or administrative
breakdown due to lack of strategic fit between internal controls
and external accountability for performance.

FIGURE 9.1.
The Performance Management Grid

direction and focus, they need to develop a similar focus. That
focus needs to extend from the broad aims of programs to the
detailed delivery of services. The next section outlines one approach to developing such a focus that has been used in several
public sector organizations.

Figure 9.1 illustrates some of the difficulties which can occur.
Although horizontal transitions might be seen as successful in
terms of shifting the organization on the grid, they do nothing to
improve core performance.

The shifts in management values required to enable public sector organizations to make the transition to performance management are considerable.

- Many public sector attitudes have their origin in the bureaucratic or machine models of organization. These organizations were based on specialized units coordinated by standards and hierarchical structures. Managers were essentially cogs in a bureaucratic machine. Performance was assumed, and management focused on correcting exceptions and failures. Failure was seen as dysfunctional. The performance of the organization was simply the sum of the performance of its parts. Performance improvement, when it became necessary, was addressed by improving the performance of individual parts.

- As discussed previously, the bureaucratic models of organization proved unable to respond to the needs of large organizations and dynamic environments. In the private sector, the movement was to decentralize business units. In the public sector the movement was often to buffer bureaucracies from external pressures and to undertake change projects.

- The various contingency theories of management focused private sector managers on external environments. For many managers, performance was seen to be a function of knowing where the organization was going in that environment. Management by objectives and a concentration on the bottom-line results enabled private sector organizations to avoid overspecialization and respond to changing external needs. These approaches failed where neat segmentation into natural business units proved difficult, where technology and production processes rather than markets proved to be the keys to business success, or where the rate of change increased substantially.

- The public sector was unable to use these techniques to provide a simple focus for many of its more complex activities. It used project structures to manage changes. Many restructures were used to change the product focus of the public sector without finding the sort of simple targets and success criteria developed by the private sector.

- Alternative approaches to management now being developed in the public sector are more strategic, change-oriented, and evaluative than their predecessors. They focus on key strategies and results and allow for failure in other areas. Such action strategies can encompass the inputs, processes, and outputs of an organization. The emerging role of management is to manage performance directly by planning impacts and evaluating progress; the emerging role of structures is to provide a focus for that performance.

- Although this approach can drive rapid change, it can also avoid the organizationwide destabilization which change often creates in bureaucratic structures. Strategic management enables those parts of organizations which do not need to change to consolidate and develop a relatively stable environment. This differs from the impact of change in bureaucratic structures, where specialization and complex interrelationships cause organizationwide destabilization.

PERFORMANCE PLANNING EVALUATION AND REVIEW

A performance planning framework which has been applied to a number of public sector organizations is summarized in Figure 9.2. It can be used to compare change strategies in selected public sector agencies.

The framework develops a plan which is strategic, change oriented, and evaluative. Many plans used in the public sector fail to meet these criteria.

- The plan must be strategic, focusing on the core elements of both short- and long-term performance and on the key performance issues facing an organization or program. Some activities are inherently more important to an organization or program than others. A strategic plan must differentiate between core program functions, support functions, and management functions. Within each of these functions, plans must concentrate on critical results rather than all the activities of the organization.

- The plan must be change oriented, focusing on critical changes required to exploit opportunities, overcome problems, and po-

FIGURE 9.2.
Performance Planning Evaluation and Review Framework

Program Functions and Strategic Fit Analysis

Program Delivery. The core outputs required of the organization or program. The results that, if delivered, would lead key external groups to regard it as successful.

Program Support. Critical management initiatives required over the planning period to support the delivery of key program results. Failure to deliver these initiatives will have a direct impact on program delivery. These initiatives will vary from time to time.

General Management. Support activities of an ongoing nature required to assist the organization to deliver programs.

    External Relations. Management of relationships with key external publics.

    Corporate Management. The development of corporate perspectives and the capacity to place individual or group objectives into that context.

    Personnel Management. Human resource management targeted to the program delivery needs of the organization.

    Planning and Resource Management. Management of the human, physical, and financial resources available to the organization to target the needs of high-priority programs, to balance resource allocations against targets, to reduce resources allocated to low priority targets, and to evaluate results against budgets.

Strategic fit analysis examines the fit between management and support action strategies and program delivery objectives, both short and long term. This involves a review of structures, values, systems, resource management, and information systems to optimize their contribution to program performance.

Action Planning and Evaluation

Key Objective	Action Strategy	Verifiable Outcome or Impact
The key contribution required from a unit, functional area, or program. Typical time span 2–5 years.	The specific action strategies developed to deliver key objective(s) over the next 12–18 months.	The specific outcomes and external impacts that can be scheduled and monitored to verify that action strategies are being implemented.

Planning involves taking existing change priorities and extending them from key objectives to impacts. Evaluation involves assessing impacts and using these assessments to evaluate performance against strategies and core objectives.

sition the organization to address its future. This requires links between current action strategies and long-term objectives.

- The plan must be evaluative, providing a basis for ongoing assessment of performance by defining the short-term impacts expected and linking them to long-term objectives. If the impact of achieving an objective cannot be noticed, it cannot become the primary focus for the management of an organization. Plans must define specific impacts as well as broad program objectives. Where there is underperformance, it is important to use evaluation constructively to improve future performance by addressing underlying causes rather than symptoms.

The framework presented in Figure 9.2 has been used to assist a variety of public sector organizations to examine their existing plans and priorities and to extend and refocus them. The framework relates change strategies to overall performance, focuses attention on key action strategies, extends the time horizon of existing plans (at least in respect of key strategies), defines specific impacts and change outcomes, and identifies areas where management and support priorities need to change.

REVIEW OF SELECTED PUBLIC SECTOR CHANGES

Selected public sector changes have been examined using the framework just discussed. A checklist of the issues explored is presented in Figure 9.3. A number of common results emerge from this analysis. They support the propositions advanced in this chapter and provide insights into the management of performance.

Change strategies are seldom related to the long-term mission of an organization. The basic reasons why an organization exists and might continue to exist are often not defined. Plans often ignore such needs in favor of solving current problems and delivering specific changes.

Change strategies seldom differentiate between core program delivery and support activities. Structures or systems often become ends in themselves, and when this occurs, the delivery of services to clients and the public can become just another performance criterion, if delivery is addressed at all.

Key Objectives or Mission. Are the long-term objectives explicit? Do they define a viable mission in terms of meeting emerging needs cost effectively? Are they the best solution for future users and for the community?

Action Strategies
Are there major gaps in the current change agenda?

To what extent are existing priorities driven by clients, rather than other factors, such as government policy commitments, government agency control debates, accountability debates, budgets, or the agenda of key managers and staff?

Is the impact on service to customers identified, evaluated, and managed directly, or is it presumed to occur as a result of various management initiatives?

Do action strategies address long-term objectives of the organization and do they provide a base for future performance?

Have the action strategies been operationalized to the point where impacts over the next year or two have been identified? Are impacts related to services and customers?

Evaluation
Is there evidence of evaluation over the last three years, either external or internal, leading to management changes?

Has the major evaluation been external, either audit or parliamentary committees, or internal?

Where internal evaluation occurs, is it directed to improved performance, as distinct from justifying past performance?

Strategic fit analysis
Do the management approaches in place and developing as a result of change strategies fit the needs of the organization and its customers at this point of time and in the future? Consider the following areas:
organizational image
organizational values and culture
organization structure
organization systems, including information systems
staff skills
resource management systems
change management

Change strategies are often not operationalized to the point where impacts are identified and can be evaluated.

There is scope to improve communications which seek to describe the short- and long-term objectives of change to those within and outside the organization. Such communication needs to address both the general and specific elements of the change and to be reinforced by action plans and targeted impacts.

The fit between management and core performance strategies is often not addressed or managed. These misfits often create new management problems and divert organizational energy from pursuing core strategies.

CONCLUSIONS

There are entrenched problems of performance in public administration, and this analysis suggests that some of the changes in recent years have created new risks without providing the sort of value the public expected of them.

Many private sector management approaches have been translated to the public sector in an attempt to make it more effective. Governments have sought greater control; managers are held more accountable; restructures abound; and middle layers of bureaucracy have been abolished to reduce costs.

Underperformance is unlikely to be solved by more time or funding or by importing solutions from other applications. The solution requires a shift in management values.

Many public sector problems can be overcome, and many private sector management approaches become feasible in public sector organizations when they commit to direct evaluation of performance, provided evaluation encompasses cost-effective delivery of services to the public.

Failure to make that commitment has been encouraged by two quite dangerous beliefs: that a focus for accountability is provided by transferring power between officials and ministers without defining results, and that performance can be managed by focusing on surrogates like structures, systems, or budgets.

Problems created by surrogates for performance can be expected to increase exponentially as the rate of change increases. An organization that focuses on budgets, processes, structures, or other surrogates for performance should not be surprised if it does those things well but fails to deliver value to clients.

SELECTED REFERENCES

Cullen, R. B. (1983). "Managing in Times of Financial Constraint." In *Proceedings of the National Government Accounting Convention of the Australian Society of Accountants, 1983.* Melbourne: Australian Society of Accountants.

———. (1986). "The Victorian Senior Executive Service: A Performance-Based Approach to the Management of Senior Managers." *Australian Journal of Public Administration* 45, no. 1 (March).

———. (1987). "Business, Government and Change: Managing Transition in the Public and Private Sectors." *Australian Journal of Public Administration* 46, no. 1 (March).

———. (1989). "Changes That Have Taken Place in the Focus of Budget-Dependent Agencies to Achieve Better Overall Performance." In *Proceedings of the National Accountants in Government Convention 1989.* Melbourne: Australian Society of Accountants.

——— and Brown, N. F. (1992). *Integration and Special Education in Victorian Schools: A Program Effectiveness Review.* Melbourne: Department of School Education.

———, Cortese, D. J., and Georgiou, B. (1987). *A Taxing Solution.* Canberra: Australian Government Publishing Service. A program management performance review of the Australian Taxation Office.

Strategic Plan for Higher Education in Victoria, 2 vols. Melbourne: Office of Higher Education.

CHAPTER 10

Communicating Health Care Reform: A Change for the Better?

John Johnson

INTRODUCTION

A dramatic evolution in the health care industry is about to take place. The end of the 1990s and the beginning of the next century could be the setting for historic changes worldwide. Thanks to advances in science and technology we can expect such significant achievements as mapping of the human genetic structure, a more complete understanding of DNA, and development of appropriate strategies to help identify and reinforce the way people care for themselves. We can expect to see technologies which will allow people to predict major illnesses, including heart disease, cancer, Alzheimer's, arthritis, Parkinson's disease and many others. Diagnostic devices and enhancers could be developed to improve memory, hearing, vision, and various other body functions. We can expect these diseases to be prevented, cured, or at least mitigated. Technologies either known to us today or on the verge of development will not only affect the quality of life and the way people feel, they will dramatically affect the cost of improving the health of whole populations. They have the potential to generate huge changes in the way health care is delivered in various parts of the world, resulting in a race by various nations and companies to be among the leaders both in the discovery and the delivery of the various technologies making this revolution possible.

Discovery is one thing, but the challenge of *delivery* of new techniques and skills to various parts of the world presents an

161

awesome task. The dissemination of this information will meet many cultural barriers—barriers springing from the relative affluence of one country versus another or one society versus another. Further complications will arise from ethnic and religious beliefs which will either permit or prohibit the new technologies from being accepted and utilized within a society. In fact, ethical and moral issues related to the discoveries will become increasingly important areas of theology and philosophy. At the same time, the expectations of people, particularly in highly industrialized and civilized cultures, will continue to grow. The quest for a better quality of life and for longer life will become more intense as the affluence of these societies grow. Even if affluence does not generally increase, there will always be some who can afford to pay or, if you will, buy up these new services.

The spread of these new technologies, and the expectations that will accompany them, will be augmented by the mobility of our society as corporations become more global, moving from local and national markets to international ones. Executives and employees will transfer from one part of the world to another with alacrity. The availability of certain health services will contribute significantly to decisions about whether or not to relocate and which job to take. It is even possible that companies will be compelled to transport health services to provide to their work force in a given area of the world, further accelerating the dissemination of available technology.

Advances in communications will play a major role in the rate at which changes are dispersed. The use of satellite dishes to receive television images, cellular telephones, computer networks, and other technologies will be commonplace around the world and allow access to databases that provide information about one's health, enabling an unprecedented degree of personal control of one's own health status.

Although all this sounds important, interesting, and even exciting and may, indeed, be the next quantum leap to the improvement of the world's health and lifespan, fundamental questions remain to be answered. Who will be the leaders? Who will set the standards? What role, if any, will governments or global organizations take? Unfortunately, as is often the case, a variety of forces will affect these issues and the ability of a society to move quickly to maximize incorporation of available technology and knowledge.

These forces will slow development in one nation or accelerate it in another. Of prime importance is the affluence of the population itself and its cultural interest in health. In cultures where food and subsistence remain the most basic consideration, bionics, genetic mapping, and other technologies will have little or no priority. In societies which place a low premium on individual life, twenty-first century health technologies will most likely not be considered with the same degree of importance or reverence as in societies in the Western world where the value of an individual life is very high.

One of the most significant impediments to the spread of anticipated advances in health care technologies will be structure and the desire for the status quo. Structure represents an organized set of rules and regulations in a given culture, be it a large organization, a neighborhood, or a country. Those rules and regulations provide stability; and human nature being what it is, stability and predictability are important in maintaining a balance in one's life. The desire for predictability and stability, both on a personal and organizational level, will create major impediments to the incorporation of important change as we move into the twenty-first century.

One of the most serious concerns for the United States, as it enters this period of enormous change in the health care field is that the motivation for the change is fundamentally wrong. The fiscal health of the nation is the driving force, and therefore, the ideal and the ultimate goal to improve the health and the quality of life of the nation may be sacrificed to the objective of cost containment. In fact, the quest to save money and at the same time increase access may even cost more money and stifle the very innovation that would otherwise bring about the result being pursued in the first place.

The role of structure in holding down constructive change can be seen in the Congress of the United States. Congress represents a system designed to bring balance to deliberation and prevent one group over another from gaining control of the country. The balance, however, can result in gridlock. How does one group make constructive compromise and get on with the work of change?

We can see parallels in corporations. Consider the term *headquarters mentality*, used to describe a condition wherein those in the corporate office believe they know what is best for all segments of the company, whether located immediately adjacent to the headquarters or in other parts of the world. In fact, this mentality has not worked for many corporations, particularly on a multinational level, because cultural differences require people to work and adapt relative to local mores specific traditions.

Global trade is affected by rules and regulations which, in turn, impact the ways in which changes are allowed to take place. Governments create laws, treaties, and regulations which often interfere with the freedom of businesses to compete, collaborate, and trade across state and country boundaries. In Japan, for example, banks, manufacturers, and distributors can all work together freely to sell a particular product line. However, in the United States, existing legislation such as antitrust laws can disadvantage corporations relative to other countries, by imposing arms-length transactions between companies.

Existing laws in the United States will have a profound impact on the delivery of health care in the year 2020 as related to issues of cost, but more important as related to the overall health status of the population. As we think of change, whether to a global economy or a new health system in the United States, it is imperative that we develop new ways of dealing with the self-interest the old structures impose. This chapter will review some of the changes taking place in the United States, problems with the current U.S. health care system, and the changes being proposed by the federal government at this time. These changes can be revolutionary in the most positive sense. However, it is critical that we assess carefully what is done to ensure that our current actions advance the desired positive results in a timely fashion rather than delaying the benefits of the new technologies.

Finally, the chapter will present an approach to health systems development and aspects of a system model for health care delivery which, in the experience of the author, has the most promising potential, not only for containing costs, but also for improving the quality of life.

THE AMERICAN HEALTH CARE SYSTEM

America is blessed with some of the best health care in the world. However, the current system is poorly coordinated and limits access primarily to those who have the ability to pay. In addition, as the health care system has evolved, a number of structural problems have developed that must be addressed before any meaningful change can be accomplished. An apparent dilemma exists in present attempts to repair the system related to the popular and reasonable desire to give equal access to all Americans while at the same time attempting to reduce costs.

Health Care Providers—Facilities

In the United States, when we think of health care providers, we generally think of hospitals and physicians. On the hospital side are acute, nonacute, and specialty hospitals. These can be structured and operated in many different organizational forms. There are religious, military, state, and federal hospitals; for-profit hospitals, with some being owned by corporations that trade their stock on the stock exchange and pay handsome profits to shareholders, and not-for-profit hospitals, not owned by anyone but controlled by a group of people, in some cases religious or other charitable organizations and in other cases by a community organized board of trustees. Many of these hospitals have the dual roles of providing health care as well as teaching and training experience for the country's physicians, with the cost of that training rolled into the billing presented to patients. Additionally, hospitals are often defined by their location as rural or urban facilities.

Nonacute health care settings include nursing homes, geared to provide skilled nursing care. Nursing homes are dominated by for-profit providers, although some are sponsored by charitable or religious organizations, and hospitals. *Home care,* another form of nonacute health care, provides care in the home for patients recuperating from an illness or chronically ill. As well, nonacute settings also include a recent proliferation of specialized, *free-standing centers* which provide diagnostic services such as MRI, CT, and other x-ray treatment, radiation therapy, surgery centers, laboratories, physical therapy centers, and many other services appropriate to this setting. Most of these organizations are operated on a for-profit motive.

The Providers—Physicians

Physicians represent the other arm of the health care provider equation. In some cases, physicians are employed by hospitals or by managed care organizations. Some are traditional fee-for-service physicians. Some are in private, solo practice; some are in single specialty group practice; and some are in multispecialty group practice.

The Payers

Perhaps one of the unique parts of U.S. health care is the payment system. For years, indemnity insurance has been the principal method of payment for most people's health care. Unions have negotiated health care insurance at the bargaining table, and employee health insurance has been financed primarily by employers. In 1965, the federal government enacted the Medicare and Medicaid programs to provide care for the elderly and poor. Now, in many parts of the country, insurance companies are initiating various programs that follow some of the pioneering work done by Kaiser and others, to shift insurance to the provider and reduce cost by restricting the places where a patient can receive care. These programs are collectively referred to as *managed care.* They offer a spectrum of options that allows a person to sign up to receive service from a given set of providers. In some instances one can go to a provider of choice. However, the penalty for this choice is usually a large patient copayment. Such arrangements are called *preferred provider organizations* (PPOs) or *point of service* (POS) plans. Another type of managed care allows no option for seeking care outside of the system. These are called *health maintenance organizations* (HMOs).

The Market

A major problem in dealing with health care reform is the tendency to think of it as one market with all the providers having similar organizations and the different parts of the country having similar expectations. This is not true. It is the same fallacious thinking that faltering companies have experienced in trying to work in a global economy with a headquarters mentality—assuming that what works in one country is going to work everywhere. It does not happen that way, and it is particularly invalid in a country as large and as diverse as the United States.

Because most health reform is thought to be organized by the federal government, the tendency to get involved in the micromanagement of any regional health system will not work. Trying to manage a Japanese subsidiary from New York headquarters has not proven successful; there is a need to localize management to conform to local customs. Health care needs in the Bronx are not the same as on a Nevada Indian reservation or in a small town in the foothills of Virginia. Labor problems are different, affluence and expectations of the publics are different. For that matter, we might as well be in different countries!

Problems with the System

Several different problems confronting the health care system need attention, including escalating costs, regional differences, inadequate attention to early detection, a payment system that is costly and risk-adverse, competition, a perverse malpractice system, difficult antitrust laws, a lack of definition of what quality really is and how it is defined, unequal distribution of physicians, and a lack of equity in choice. But, of course, the primary problem driving the efforts to reform the system is, inclusively, rampant and explosive costs.

Escalating Costs

Health care costs are one of the fastest growing components of the U.S. economy. Total health spending in the United States now constitutes approximately 13 percent of the GNP compared to 6 percent three decades ago. Current projections indicate this staggering level of growth will continue for at least the next forty years with health care costs reaching 16–19 percent of GNP by the year 2000 and 26 percent of GNP by the year 2030. Such unabated costs affect taxes at home, as well as the ability to competitively price goods abroad. Currently, the cost of care provided to those who are not insured and the costs not covered by government programs are passed on to big business. Thus, the problems of corporations and individuals are intertwined. It has been estimated that business spending on health care premiums is in excess of 100 percent of after-tax profits. Health care is a high-priority economic issue.

Regional Differences

As previously mentioned, the United States is large and diverse enough to create regional differences in the way medicine is practiced as well as wide variations in the resources and wealth of one region versus another. One thing is positive; for most people in this country a hospital is reasonably accessible. This access issue was addressed in the last major piece of health care reform, when the Medicare federal insurance program for the elderly was passed in the 1960s. Concurrently, large amounts of federal money were poured into the hospital system in grants and loan guarantees to build or expand hospitals around the country.

Inadequate Attention to Early Intervention

Current payment systems often leave the cost of preventive care or early intervention to the patient, too often causing the postponement of proper care. Such postponement can lead to full blown disease, which, although it may be covered by insurance, is considerably more costly than it would have been if there had been early intervention. In cases involving the uninsured, the impact can be greater than the mere dollar cost. The price of a high infant mortality, for example, goes beyond dollars and cents.

Despite federal programs, some 35 million people still remain uninsured and many are underinsured. These 35 million people are estimated to receive approximately 60 percent of the health care of the insured population. The cost of providing that care is shifted through higher prices to the insured population. Under this system, insured individuals, for the most part, have not been concerned about the cost of health care because it was paid for by someone else—employers or the government.

Faulty Payment Incentives

The health insurance system is not universal. It has no standard set of benefits. It screens out adverse risks, fails to cover some groups in the name of profit, and often does not pay for preventive or catastrophic care. It isolates providers and practitioners, playing one against the other, all in the interest of obtaining lower unit costs. The current system of reimbursing the costs of health care, be it by government or by private insurers, has done more to fragment the system than anything else.

This fragmented system has driven up the costs to society. It has confused the public and made any effort to truly monitor its effectiveness almost impossible. For example, a patient may go to a specialist directly. That specialist may order tests that are available in his or her practice. The patient may then go to an outpatient facility or a hospital for services, and receive the same tests because the facility does not accept the procedures performed in the physician's unit. In the hospital, the patient may be billed separately by the hospital itself, and by several consulting physicians—anesthesiologists, pathologists, radiologists, internists, infectious disease specialists, surgeons, and so forth. The result is a confusing set of bills that are difficult for those involved in the business on a daily basis to unravel, let alone the patient who may leave the hospital and enter another level of the system for follow-up care, medical equipment, home health care, and eventually back to the referring physician. In most situations, coordination among all these providers is almost nonexistent. Although a broad range of providers could be linked—vertically integrated—there is little motivation to do so. The existing reimbursement system treats all levels of the system individually and often unwittingly prevents them from working together. The fee-for-service physician is paid, in many cases, for each day he or she visits a patient in the hospital; therefore, there is little incentive for early discharge, particularly if the patient wishes to stay longer. Additionally, there is little incentive for the physician to discharge the patient early, except when reimbursed by certain government programs and HMOs that pay by the discharge rather than by the day.

If all providers were linked there would be a different scenario. The current culprits are a lack of coordination among providers and the lack of incentives to focus on the cost of a spell of illness rather than the occasion of service. As long as the system is paid for resources consumed rather than for outcome, costs will continue to escalate. We must remember that failure to collect high-quality data that includes cost as a part of the equation is an additional problem.

Competition vs. Coordination

There is expensive competition among providers—hospitals, extended care facilities, home care organizations, ambulatory care organizations, physicians' offices, HMOs, independent laboratories, and independent practitioners—for the same patient. Patients' decisions are often not made based on real quality factors, but on perceived quality factors, such as the personality of the provider and his or her staff. There is not, therefore, a large incentive for physicians to manage the cost of care, most of which is being compensated by insurance. The exceptions are in cases of managed care that motivates physicians to keep costs low and, to a lesser extent, in copayment situations in which the patient shares the cost.

Insurance That Is Complex

There are over 1,500 insurance companies, each with different forms, different coverage, and different rules. Many times consumers do not even know for what they are or are not covered, and often consumers, from fear and pressure, purchase at tremendous costs multiple insurance plans that have little value because many plans will not pay if payment has been received from another plan.

Tort System

Payments received from medical malpractice claims have been so large that physicians and other providers practice defensive medicine. This has led to ordering tests and procedures that, from a clinical assessment perspective, the physician may feel are not necessary, but provide necessary protection against the possibility of someone criticizing or suing later on.

Antitrust Laws

The antitrust laws of the United States discourage most incentives to coordinate care because they may be anticompetitive. The result is duplication of equipment and services.

Choice for Some but Not for Others

If you have adequate insurance coverage or can pay on your own (which few individuals can), you have a choice of some of the best providers in the world. However, if you cannot pay on your own, you revert to the hospital emergency room or indigent care programs that, although they provide adequate care, are also tedious and impersonal, offering little or no choice in who provides the care. In addition, many people wait until they are very sick to seek care. Sadly, many do not avail themselves of preventive or, in prenatal situations, even early care. As a result, the care ultimately provided is often more costly because the disease is more advanced.

Lack of Comprehensive Quality Control

The measurement of quality needs to take on new dimensions. Traditional quality control methods have included the review of surgical specimens, transfusion reactions, infection rates, and in more recent years, detailed, case-by-case review of specific diseases and the results of hospital-based treatment. Only recently has the idea of cost effectiveness been introduced into the quality control system. Initially, this focused on length of stay in the hospital due to the emphasis government placed on this measure followed by a government review of the medical necessity for admission. In all of these government activities, the objective of reducing costs has appeared to be the driving force rather than the pursuit of high-quality medical care. Now, all but twenty states have state-mandated data commissions gathering data related to quality. One of the most active is the Maryland Quality Indicator Program, in which over 600 hospitals from forty-six states are participating.

The idea of comparing one practitioner to another or one hospital to another, as should be done, has been met with charges that such studies would lead to "cookbook medicine" and protests that "we are different." These are valid arguments if the process is taken to an extreme and the individual physician's prerogative is significantly reduced. (Previous actions of the regulatory environment suggest this might be an outcome of a government program.) But why should a patient not know how a provider rates on these comparisons? By addressing some of these areas, the issue of resource consumption will need less direct attention and will be of less concern because the cost benefit comparison will be more demonstrable.

Maldistribution of Physicians

Regional differences exist in the supply of general practice physicians, which is short in rural and inner city areas. The training of many generalists has focused on medical care rather than on health care; they are not trained in prevention and epidemiology. Pediatricians may be the most outstanding exception. In mature Canadian and English models, the ratio of generalists to specialists is 1:1

(Straub 1993). Under most HMO arrangements, especially the capitated arrangement, the generalist is also the manager of care and the gatekeeper. The problem in the United States is the relative lack of generalists (family practitioners, internists, and pediatricians) with the current ratio around 1:4.

The current health care system has provided financial incentives for physicians to become procedure oriented. This has encouraged the education of more specialists. To expand the number of generalists will require a shift in the education system away from the tertiary care model to one that focuses on primary care. It may require the retraining of physicians and the removal of some of the legislative barriers to the use of mid-level professionals. Reimbursement reform will also be necessary to narrow the gap between the generalist and the specialist.

By the year 2000 we could anticipate a need for 49,000 or more generalists and a potential excess of 90,000 specialists (Straub 1993, 7). This demand will be modified to the extent that states opt, as they are currently allowed to do, for a single payer system that freezes the existing system and stunts the growth of HMO arrangements and the need for generalists.

Variation in Spending and Practice Patterns

Currently the spending per Medicare beneficiary ranges from the highest, Louisiana at $3,898, to the lowest, Hawaii at $1,810. ("Expenditure Limits" 1993, 55). The individual components of the cost issue vary greatly. For example, in Colorado the average number of laboratory tests per enrollee is 7.7 compared to 1.4 in Wyoming. This is a 5:1 ratio.

Technology

Accompanying this chaos is a whole new generation of technology available at minimal cost that allows procedures to be done in any number of settings—physicians' offices, ambulatory centers, nonphysician practitioners' offices, free-standing diagnostic centers, HMOs—thus further fragmenting the system and making it difficult for the consumer to "shop" on an informed basis. Procedures that formerly required hospitalization, today are commonly performed in nonhospital settings. Cataract surgery is one example. Previously this procedure required several days of hospitalization, now it is done on an outpatient basis. The patient is discharged the same day and may use the eye within a day or two. Advances in technology are also dramatically changing procedures such as joint repair, gallbladder surgery, and hernia repair. The result is further confusion, complication, duplicate records, multiple bills, and added costs—certainly not the savings that could be possible. The fact that these procedures are being performed in facilities not specifically licensed for such use raises other questions. What are the quality controls? Do incentives encourage over-utilization? What are the utilization controls? Who ensures the safety of the equipment being used?

Although new technology offers great advances in treatment, the delivery of care needs to be coordinated and placed in a structure with strict accountability if quality and efficiency are to be realized. In addition, a costly technology war is raging based on the premise that whoever wins the health care game from an economic point of view does so with the best practitioners, armed with the best equipment and the best lawyers to overcome the constant threat of malpractice litigation, burdensome regulations, and other complicated legal factors. Compounding this problem is the fact that these phenomena are, to a large extent, the result of previous attempts to cure the system.

WASTE

All these problems lead us to a word most people in the industry are loath to say—*waste*. Waste is the product of all that has been outlined before, not inefficiency and not mismanagement, because an individual provider or practitioner may be well-managed, even efficient. The system as currently operating has a lot of structurally induced waste. The Section for Health Care Systems of the American Hospital Association recently described this in their report, "Renewing the U.S. Health Care System," saying:

> It is wasteful to encourage people to wait until they are really ill to come into the hospital. It is wasteful to apply massive, often unwanted, support to an elderly, dying patient. It is wasteful to use expensive diagnostic services to confirm an already confirmed diagnosis. It is wasteful to repeat tests simply because they were done elsewhere or out of fear of malpractice.

It is wasteful to collect the same demographic information on patients at each location of service. It is wasteful to add equipment and services principally in an effort to retain or attract physicians. It is wasteful from a community prospective to build unneeded capacity just to have something that is newer and more attractive, in an effort to attract market share or physicians.

The report identifies waste resulting from unused beds and the need to help facilities whose occupancy rates are consistently low. These facilities are inefficient in areas where suitable alternative care exists, and it is recommended that they close or convert to other uses. It identifies the technological race as wasteful, the high administrative costs associated with processing claims to multiple insurers and patients as wasteful, and the abuse in Medigap insurance sales by fear-mongering sellers that provide no net value to subscribers as wasteful.

A number of cost drivers in the American health care system cannot be changed. However, structural change can minimize their impact. Again, the issues are pieces of a complex puzzle and must be factored into any solutions.

Changing Demographics

Changes in the makeup of the population is one area over which there is little control. The American population is aging. People in the over-65 age group represent the fastest growing segment of the population, and the health care needs of this group are unique. First, the population over 65 consumes five times more health care than that consumed by those under 65 years of age. Second, although the needs of those under 65 are primarily acute, requiring immediate medical intervention with a short period of recovery, the needs of those over 65 are chronic, requiring ongoing care for diseases that need progressively more care. This is a growing and increasingly burdensome demand. New ways to care for the particular needs of this age group without bankrupting the business of the country must be found.

New Diseases, Poverty, and Crime

Beyond demographic changes, other unexpected demands on the system such as AIDS and problems with TB particularly in the inner city and other areas of extreme poverty create additional expensive issues. Poverty in many cases leads to poor nutrition, drug use, and other problems that are particularly damaging to unborn infants. Crime, especially that inflicted by the use of guns, is especially costly to the health care purse.

SOLUTIONS

Clinton's Call for National Health Reform

Finally, the health care issue is now on the front burner. After years of many failed efforts by presidents and legislators, President Clinton has advanced a new plan for health reform. The middle class is today driven by a gnawing fear. They are in quicksand called *uninsurance*. For the first time in years, millions of people are facing layoffs, unemployment, and what until now they had taken for granted—health care insurance. Health care insurance may no longer be available to them or, if it is, only at astronomical cost.

In addition, many feel that they are in "job lock," if they switch employers and thus health insurance companies, an existing health problem will be termed a preexisting condition and thus will not be covered. This illness may be cancer or another long-term chronic, possibly acute, disorder that could wipe out an individual's total net worth without insurance coverage.

Beyond that, 25 million people have no insurance at all. Many work for small companies that have chosen not to provide health insurance because of its cost and the multiplicity of rules and different coverages that put a large burden on everyone.

On September 22, 1993, President Clinton proposed National Health Reform in a speech before the Congress of the United States. In this speech, President Clinton listed several principles to be the "fixed stars" that health reform must follow. These were

- *Security.* He said "Security means that those who do not have health coverage will have it and it will never be taken away from them."

- *Simplicity.* He said "We have more than 1,500 insurers with hundreds of different forms." He went on to say that those forms are "exasperating for anyone who's ever tried to sit down around a table and wade through them and figure them out." Because of this mountain of confusing paperwork, "the medical care industry is drowning."

- *Savings.* He indicated that uncontrolled "rampant medical inflation" is affecting our savings, investment capital, wages, ability to compete, confidence, and our living standard. Health reform must reduce the rate of growth of cost of medical care.

- *Choice.* He indicated that Americans want to be able to choose their own doctors.

- *Quality.* He indicated that any system resulting from reform must not throw out what is good in our existing system and must provide high-quality care.

- *Responsibility.* He indicated that everyone must pay some part of the health care costs. All employers must pick up their share of health insurance. Also, insurance companies cannot be permitted to cancel a person's health insurance simply because that person has contracted an expensive illness.

The president outlined the following structure to accomplish this reform.

National Health Care Board

There would be a National Health Care Board to monitor state compliance and the functioning of health alliances, interpret the standard benefits program, make recommendations for changes in the standard benefits to reflect changes in the delivery of care, set regional spending limits, develop indicators for quality of care, and publish these results to promote informed consumer choice.

Payment Sources

- Employers would pay 80 percent of the premium.
- Employees would pay the remaining 20 percent plus any co-payments.
- Self-employed workers would pay the full costs of the premium, with 100 percent being tax deductible compared to the current practice allowing 25 percent tax deductibility.
- Government would subsidize low-wage employees, those individuals with incomes below 150 percent of the poverty level.

Medicare would be continued for the elderly and disabled. Medicaid would continue for the poor but through the regional health alliances.

Regional Health Alliances

Regional health alliances would be established as group purchasing cooperatives to serve responsible for enrolling all residents in a given geographic area. They would also provide information to emphasize the quality and costs of the various health plans in the geographic area. This information would be formatted to help consumers make an informed choice among health plans. Alliances would also be charged with handling consumer complaints. With regard to health plans they would, among other responsibilities, contract, monitor, and regulate the manner in which health plans operate to ensure that they operate within expenditure targets and meet all federal and state standards.

Corporate Health Alliances

Corporate health alliances would be an option for employers with more than 5000 employees to provide employee coverage. These corporate alliances would have responsibilities and standards established by both the state and federal governments, as well as by the regional alliances.

Accountable Health Plans (AHP)

Formed by physicians, hospitals and other healthcare professionals, AHPs could be administered by a hospital, an insurer, or a group of physicians with responsibility for negotiating contracts for the provision of services. The AHP would negotiate per-capita premiums with the alliances based on a community rating. They would not be able to exclude people because of a preexisting condition but would be able to adjust premiums based on age and sex. In addition, they would be permitted to purchase reinsurance to protect consumers against unanticipated expenses.

Government Funding

Funding for the Clinton plan is proposed by taxing cigarettes and liquor, imposing a levy on large corporations, and cutting Medicare and Medicaid benefits. Cost controls are also included and insurance companies are given tax incentives to encourage the formation of managed competition ventures.

Other Competing Plans

In addition to the president's plan, several other plans are being proposed by members of Congress. They differ as to the method of payment. Some suggest that a single payer system would be most efficient. Others protest the requirement that employers pay employee premiums. Various proposals treat the small employer differently. Financing differs from proposal to proposal; some would pay by reducing the growth of Medicare and Medicaid; others would tax employee benefits; some would reduce the Medicare benefits of the more affluent.

PROBLEMS WITH REFORM

Structure and Self-Interest in the Status Quo

Despite the obvious benefits of the plan, structure and special interest groups are now interposing themselves as the president predicted in his September 22, 1993, speech in which he said the nation would soon "be bombarded with scare tactics by those who profit enormously from the current health care system." Whether or not scare tactics are in play, the opposition is beginning to mount. Some of the concerns being expressed include the following.

Concerns About Choice   One of the issues confronting Americans is the issue of physician choice under the Clinton Plan. It is apparent that people will be forced, if only by the economics of the situation, to join an AHP offered by an employer, using only physicians and other providers that are members of the plan. Polls have suggested that the public is deeply concerned about the loss of the right to choose a physician. The development of AHP and selective contracting is suggested by some to preserve choice, but others disagree and suggest that participation in an AHP will provide a choice of only one AHP over another, limiting the provider choices available.

Other groups favor a "single payer" plan as the only way to preserve freedom of choice, because under this system all physicians and providers will participate. Perhaps an even more fundamental issue is that the public does not believe that one plan can have all the best specialists and hospitals. Others have suggested that PPOs be an option. As described earlier, this is a program whereby a patient subscribes to a plan in which it is possible to go outside the plan for a hospital or other provider with a larger copayment. The problem, obviously, is a financial one, and some PPOs, in fact, have not paid for any service outside the plan if it was available in the plan.

Community Rating Is Another Problem   Because employers and others will all be a part of a community rating system that spreads the risk over the whole population rather than being individually rated, the premium structure will be different. A sticky part of the president's plan exists whereby the young will have to pay higher premiums than before, and the older members of the population who use more health care will pay less. The president has said that he understands the problem, but all young people will eventually be old and regain the benefit they paid for when they were younger. This problem, however, carries over to companies. Those that have traditionally employed young, healthy people will see significantly higher premiums, and the converse will be true for companies that have employed older people or have simply been in business longer and have employees who have aged with them.

The problem is exacerbated when one considers urban areas. New York City, Detroit, Boston, and others cities with large, medically indigent populations previously covered by Medicaid will now be part of community rating. Cities typically have large numbers of AIDS patients whose treatment is costly and who have been covered, in large part, by Medicaid. They will now also be part of the community rating system. When the regional health alliances are established, these factors will be significant. If cities like New York, Detroit, and others are left in a district of their own, the costs will be so large that, at the very least, there will be a loud outcry and, at worst, a large exodus of businesses from those cities to even out the costs. This problem is further compounded when we realize that, often in cities, we find the largest teaching and research hospitals, which are, by their very nature, expensive. Recognizing this as a problem, some states may exercise their option to implement a statewide system or attempt to district rural areas with inner city areas. Obviously, this will upset rural areas that, under this scenario, will pay significantly larger premiums than they paid before or would pay if in their own district. At this point no solution will solve all of these problems without some winners and losers.

Concerns of Hospitals and Physicians   Because hospitals and physicians have been the dominant providers their concerns receive a lot of attention. Among their concerns are

- *Payment of uncompensated care,* especially the coinsurance provisions, because there is no mechanism for the providers to be assured of payment.

- *Medicare and Medicaid cuts* that are proposed could be catastrophic for providers that serve large, growing populations involving these payment sources.

- *A whole new bureaucracy* is anticipated, one that is not tested, has no experience, and yet is responsible for administering and developing a far-reaching new system. Although this reform package is supposed to relieve the burden of excessive paperwork, many fear that it could impose a new layer of expensive and difficult paperwork considering its data and information gathering responsibilities. The option of large corporations to opt out of the regional alliances and form corporate alliances could in itself have a drastic impact on the proposed community rating system.

- *States' rights,* although they are appreciated as a way to deal with the various regional differences, could create their own problems, especially as states compete with one another to develop and attract new business in their region.

- *Global budgets* are of great concern, as are the difficulties alliances will face in dealing with large concentrations of high-risk populations such as those with AIDS and TB that tend to concentrate in poor, urban areas.

- *The predetermined growth rate* to be allowed in premiums in future years is considered too tight by some. This rate of growth is suggested to be less than in other industrialized countries.

- *Monitoring quality* will be difficult because no established, standardized system is accepted by the industry. Some feel that this means a lack of any meaningful information on which to judge quality.

Others Concerned   As we move from the provider side, we find
that companies of all sizes are concerned about the president's
plan. The benefits manager of the New York-based Merrill Lynch
company, which employs 40,000 people, indicated that it has enacted a number of what it considers to be innovative measures to
hold down health care costs and prefers to continue in this manner.

- *Large employers* are concerned about the 1 percent surtax on
  payroll. Others are concerned about having to deal with fifty
  different state regulatory bodies and laws. Others are simply
  concerned about being told what to do (Freudenheim 1993b,
  14f.).

- *The elderly* are concerned as well. Their concerns revolve
  around the benefit structure, the reduction in Medicare com-
  pensation, and the possible effect on the care they receive (Hey
  1993, 12).

- *The American Medical Association* (AMA) has urged doctors
  to lobby patients to oppose certain parts of the Clinton Plan,
  especially the regulation of health insurance and the cuts in the
  growth of Medicare and Medicaid (Pear 1993, 1). The AMA
  also expressed concern about patients' ability to choose their
  own physicians, the build-in incentives for physicians under
  managed care to provide less care, and the plan's inability to
  limit malpractice suits (*New York Times,* September 30, 1993,
  p. 22).

- *Drug companies* have expressed concern that using regulation
  as a method for controlling prices will slow down research and
  stifle the amount of money boards of directors will be willing
  to invest in the search for cures for AIDS and other deadly
  diseases.

- *Makers of medical devices* have voiced similar concerns about
  what all this will do to their ability to innovate (Freudenheim
  1993a, 22).

- *Anheuser-Busch* is placing placards on their trucks asking beer
  drinkers to call 1-800-beer-tax. Reportedly, thousands have
  called and were mailed brochures outlining the costs to them if
  the liquor tax in the Clinton Plan is passed (Krauss 1993).

- *A medical device company* has urged its employees to write
  their legislators opposing proposals that would limit hospitals'

access to technology. *AIDS activists* are staging theater-style demonstrations on the health plan. *Doctors* are discussing the issue with their patients during office visits. *Members of Congress* have met with dance therapists, masseuses, chiropractors, and podiatrists among many other interest groups on issues related to the plan. *Share holders of drug companies* have been warned that their profits could be hurt by this plan. *Planned Parenthood organizations* have deluged Congress requesting that their services be included in the plan. The *Health Insurance Association of America* has a toll-free number in use, to inform consumers that the Clinton Plan may mean higher insurance premiums and less choice (Krauss 1993, 20).

- *Physicians* are concerned about the Clinton Plan. Those in private practice have already seen some of their patients leave in favor of health maintenance organizations (HMOs). Many doctors have resisted the HMO movement because of lower fees and concern that these organizations limit patient choice. They have questioned whether "cookbook medicine" was going to interfere with their ability to provide high-quality health care. Other physicians, especially young specialists, are just finishing ten-plus years of training that involve huge debts, and these doctors are anticipating the opportunity for large incomes. Now the rules seem to be changing on them. On the other side are physicians that like the stability of a salary and someone else to manage the administrative aspects of their practices. They have joined HMOs as employees (Rosenthal 1993, B11).

Now the Transition   So we see that various organizations and structures are attempting to maintain the status quo. Those with a vested interest are either trying to have their role enhanced under the plan or to minimize the health reform impact. Yet, as reported by Thomas Scully, a former Bush administration official, the Republicans as well as the Democrats want to see something passed (Scully 1993, A8).

In the final analysis, will the American people be any healthier? Experts suggest that there will be no significant improvement. Statistics cited from other nations with universal coverage suggest that some of the problems, especially those associated with infant mortality, are more problems of poverty than of health insurance coverage. In fact, in the United States, infant mortality is highest among poor, inner-city people who, for the most part, have Medicaid coverage but suffer from inadequate or no prenatal care, drug and alcohol abuse, smoking, and poor diet ("Will the U.S. Be Healthier? 1993, 1 and 22).

In view of the strong opposition and criticism, will the result be worth the undertaking? The question of whether or not this is the best way to make our society healthy probably will not be the focus of the debate, but rather the question—no longer really a question in most people's minds—will be one of universal access. Another question will be how to finance this program? The debate will rage as to a balance between the status quo and change, and how all of this reform will be managed.

To a large extent, this program is designed to bring security to the American people, but with the emphasis on an immediate fiscal crisis rather than on a long-term solution. We must improve technology and bring down the cost of health care through technological innovation and emphasis on the clinical restraints. Changes in the bureaucracy can be made to reduce costs. Changes in the antitrust laws can be enacted to encourage collaboration. And changes in the effective implementation of payment programs must occur to create incentives to *manage* care rather than just sell whatever people want. Basic system changes need to be made because the current system is upside down.

There are a number of parallels in this process to the changes experienced in going from a regional market to a global market, particularly when one considers the regional differences in management methods. Different cultures, different distribution systems, different methods of practice, and different expectations of the populations being served offer problems similar to those confronting major corporations as they try to manage in different parts of the world. A potentially positive step being taken is the creation of alliances on a regional basis. To the extent that values can be similar from one region to another, this part of the program probably has the best possibility of working. When a company is operating out of one area and serving one market, the values of the organization flow on an informal basis within the organization. However, when that organization becomes decentralized into many different markets, the informal communication that was shared within the walls of one building becomes more diverse and can no longer be relied upon to convey the values of that organization. With all these regional alliances, values will have to be constructed through regulation and inspection. For this reason, spontaneity may be lost and feared differentness becomes a real possibility.

First Things First

Before we move into health care reform we must make some of the structural changes necessary for it to work. Guaranteeing health care to more people before the structure was in place to handle it was one of the mistakes encountered by the Medicare and Medicaid plans, when there was a rush to build more facilities to care for all the people who were given the right to health care. Capacity is not the problem in most sectors but rather the *right amounts* of correct capacity. We have too many hospital beds and too few primary care physicians. We have too much medical litigation with a disproportionate share of the income going into the pockets of the lawyers and not those who are damaged. We have a payment system that is too complicated and risk adverse. We have an uneven distribution of physicians. We have too many specialized facilities competing for technology. We compensate providers in a way that encourages procedures instead of cognitive and practical medicine. Perhaps these and other problems should be solved first.

At the very least, Paul M. Elwood the founder of the Jackson Hole Group, suggests the following "simple" strategies:

> "Make sure that federally-guaranteed health coverage costs cannot grow faster than revenue. For example, if we are to rely on employer-financed health benefits, obligatory entitlements cannot grow faster than wages and employment. If employment shrinks, benefits must decline or taxes must go up.
>
> "Institute an apolitical process for continuously matching revenues to health needs. The legitimacy of such a system hinges on a general commitment to improving our knowledge of which health services really benefit the public through continuous monitoring of patient outcomes and public attitudes.
>
> "Enforce cost-conscious behavior by everyone. Providers, insurers, employers, and consumers need to be rewarded for containing costs and maintaining personal health. Health reform needs to put everyone on the same team by limiting tax exclusions, encouraging use of efficient health providers, emphasizing prevention, and reducing incentives for expensive, high-tech care that may not work.

"Get Medicare and Medicaid under control, using the same methods as the private sector, before imposing new financial obligations on them. Federal policy could provide new, comprehensive drug benefits only to those Medicare recipients who choose to receive benefits through the economical health plans offered to other Americans.

"Accelerate cost-cutting reforms in the private sector. Some states are already setting up cooperatives to buy health benefits for consumers and at least thirty voluntary private cooperatives are now in place.

"Make sure that the uninsured and under-insured are covered before requiring every other American to have identical health insurance coverage. We should improve the delivery system and make sure that everyone has adequate coverage in a reformed insurance environment before we consider comprehensive employer or individual mandates." ("Balance the Health Budget" 1993, A17).

Area Health Plans

Financing and bureaucracy aside, what will the area health plans look like? The model need not be invented from scratch. For many years, people have proposed reform of the health system in the United States. Other countries' solutions have been studied and proposed as alternatives, but each of these systems required some compromises that many Americans were not willing to make, usually in the form of higher taxes, less choice, or another form of rationing that controls access to the system for nonemergency problems. However, there are ways to at least integrate care and improve both the delivery and cost issues.

As far back as 1920, one of the first works in the genesis of regionalization of hospitals was contained in a book published by the Ministry of Health of Great Britain. Known as "The Lord Dawson Report" (McNerney and Riedel 1962:2), it suggested a system of hospitals centered around a tertiary hospital, surrounded by a group of secondary hospitals like the spokes on a wheel with primary care facilities even further out on the spokes.

In the future, medicine in its simplest form would be organized similarly, with primary care physicians being the first level of patient contact, and specialists brought in when necessary. Supporting this would be alternatives for long-term care, home care, hospice care, and assisted living arrangements. With these elements in place, a system of payment would be arranged.

In the United States there are some precursors to this in parts of the country where we have already seen employers channeling patients to preferred health care providers. In these cases, corporations seem willing to sacrifice some patient choice for improved price. There is a significant copayment for the patient who opts out of the system for care. Such copayment can be as much as $200 for a hospital visit (Governance Committee, 1993:3). In these regional integrated systems, as they are called, most feel there should be a continuum of care. Care is divided into two types, wellness and illness. Wellness involves screening, early detection, prevention, and health promotion. Illness includes primary, emergency, or acute care; rehabilitation; home care; and long-term care. For this continuum to work and save costs in a high-quality manner, the various organizational elements of the system will have to be coordinated either through contractual arrangements or through common ownership. In addition, they will best be served by a common payment system that places each of the providers at risk preferably by paying them as a capitation payment. Under this system, providers get paid a single premium to provide for a person's care, whether or not the person gets sick, thus creating a financial incentive to keep a patient well. Beyond that, there is a financial incentive to provide the care in the least expensive place for those who do become ill to keep down the cost.

The financial aspects of this system are tremendous. Experience has proven that in these integrated systems, the consumption of resources is less. There are fewer hospital days per thousand population served than are provided on a national basis or even using a managed care arrangement without integration or "regionalization" as it was defined earlier. In addition, we see a decline in the use of specialists. This reduction in resource consumption translates into a reduction in the cost of the insurance for individuals involved.

The first key word is *integrated*. It means a full range of providers and practitioners, all with the same economic incentives, joined together to provide for the health of the population. *Health* is the second key word as opposed to *medical care*. The measurement should be long-term for the health status of the population served.

There are many fine examples of this type of system around the country: Kaiser in California; Mayo Clinics in Minnesota; and Lahey Clinics in Massachusetts. In recent years many more such systems have formed and are forming around the country. The author is familiar with such a system. It included two hospitals in a specific geographic region of one county. One of these hospitals had 50 beds and served primary and secondary levels of care. The second had 365 beds and served as secondary and tertiary levels of care and was also a teaching hospital. These two hospitals were under a common holding company and common management. They were, in turn, tied to a tertiary hospital. This latter hospital filled all the tertiary needs not served in the area. In addition, the hospitals combined with three home health agencies and three long-term care facilities to provide care to residents of this geographic area. The hospital also provided wellness care in various locations including homes, schools, community centers, workplaces, and in the facilities themselves. All services were tied together by a managed care program and affiliated with a third hospital in the area. Under this system, physicians and hospitals were paid a fixed amount per month to serve all enrollees whether or not they became ill. When a person became ill to the point of needing institutional care, the least costly setting was used. For example, if a patient required a hip repair this would be done in the hospital, followed by a brief hospital stay. The person could next be moved to a long-term care facility where several days of rehabilitation could take place and finally home, where the home-care company could provide physical therapy. Over a period of five years, the number of days of hospitalization per 1,000 enrollees was reduced from 750 to around 300. A significant reduction in the cost of care and in the administrative overhead associated with these facilities was realized.

Integrated Quality Control

The unifying element for such an integrated system in most cases will be economics. However, such a system would have to address *quality* in a new way, learning from examples being tested around the country in various hospitals and expanded to the network. The principle advantage of a network in terms of quality is the ability to develop a data system that can track individual patients as they move across the network. This data must be available from all participating providers and practitioners.

Physicians initially may resist the development of integrated networks and network data systems, as it means a change in traditional ways of doing business and may be seen as the beginning of a salaried relationship, which has been an anathema to the fee-for-service physician. Innovative physicians can see the integrated systems as an opportunity and will begin to form medical firms adjacent to hospital facilities, sharing equipment, data, and personnel. For example, William C. Mohlenbrock, M.D., cofounder and medical director of IAMETER, has demonstrated with actual hospital data that the cost variation among physicians treating the same disease (when adjusted for comorbidity factors, age, and sex) can vary threefold. One complication can as much as triple a hospital bill. One nosocomial infection (hospital acquired infection) can increase the cost of a hospital stay up to $2,000 ("Involving Physicians in the Quality Management Process" 1992).

What universal data source ties all providers' and practitioners' information together for meaningful review, assessing outcome, medical necessity, and cost effectiveness? None, in the current system. Each provider unit collects independent data, and there is little or no sharing this information.

Organizational Structures

Integrated networks will not solve all the problems in the health care system. However, they can have spillover benefits to other areas, and do not require government involvement. Demographics are changing the emphasis from acute to chronic care, underscoring the need for innovative systems to provide care using less expensive institutional modes of treatment such as extended care, and home health care. The new generation of technology would support such changes as they allow procedures to be done in less expensive settings. Because organizations such as extended care centers and home health care agencies are usually separately owned and operated, there is often no incentive to transfer the patient to this less expensive setting as long as payment is based on an occasion-of-service rather than outcome. In a community network system, the incentives would encourage such collaboration. The same is true with advances in technology; the potential for cost reductions associated with properly integrated use of this technology have not yet been fully realized.

Government Involvement Needed

Realistically, the system cannot be completely changed without government involvement. Government plays an obvious role in negotiating for the unemployed or those without coverage. For employers who do provide insurance, an appropriate role for government would be to prescribe a minimum set of benefits. For those who do not have such insurance, government should provide the coverage and tax the employed. This has been referred to as "play or pay," meaning that employers will either provide insurance to employees or pay the government to do so. Presumably the latter would be more expensive. Other issues, such as who pays for research, and who provides some overview of quality (especially in areas that can support only one integrated system), the transportability of benefits when employees leave employment, and so on— all of these issues imply an important government involvement in the success of any new program. In addition, there may be a role for an international organization to set standards and to assist in sharing the technological revolution taking place all over the world.

Changes will take place. Too many factors are obvious to too many people. Too much has evolved to a point where the health of this country's population can no longer be sacrificed to the status quo or special interest groups. What is necessary is the most careful, concerned consideration of all aspects of the various plans and proposals, including their criticisms to start implementing effective, meaningful health care in the United States, realizing the inevitable impact of these measures abroad.

REFERENCES

"Balance the Health Budget." (1993). *New York Times* (December 6): A17.

"Expenditure Limits." (1993). *PPRC* (July): 55.

Freudenheim, M. (1993a). "Drug Companies Feeling Pressure of Clinton's Plan to Keep Their Prices Down," *New York Times* (September 30): 22.

———. (1993b). "Corporate America's Diagnosis of the Clinton Health Plan," *New York Times* (October 31): 14f.

Governance Committee (1993). *Visions of the Future*. Washington, D.C.: The Advisory Board Company.

Hey, R. P. (1993). "Clinton Unveils Health Plan." *AARP Bulletin:* 12.

"Involving Physicians in the Quality Management Process." (1992). Naples, Fla.: The Governance Institute.

Krauss, C. (1993). "Lobbyists of Every Stripe on Health Care Proposal," *New York Times* (September 24).

McNerney, W. J., and Riedel, D. C. (1962). *Regionalization and Rural Health Care,* Ann Arbor: University of Michigan Graduate School of Business Administration, Bureau of Hospital Administration.

Pear, R. (1993). "AMA Rebels over the Health Plan in Major Challenge to President," *New York Times* (September 30): 1.

"Renewing the U.S. Health Care System." (1991). Chicago: American Hospital Association.

Rosenthal, E. (1993). "Some Doctors See Peril; Others Are Unworried," *New York Times* (September 28): B11.

Scully, T. (1993). "Outline of Eventual Deal Seems Dimly Discernible," *Wall Street Journal* (September 23): A8.

Straub, W. H. (1993). "Source Requirements for Primary Care Professionals," draft discussion paper.

"Will the U.S. Be Healthier? Maybe Not, Experts Say." (1993). *New York Times* (October 17): 1 and 22.

CHAPTER 11

Communication and Role Stress in a Government Organization

John Penhallurick

This chapter reports on some empirical data regarding the relationship between role stress and communication in a large Australian public sector organization. The data were gathered via self-report questionnaires as part of a communication audit conducted in 1989. The questionnaire was based on that of the OCD audit, developed by Osmo Wiio of the Helsinki School of Economics and his colleagues (Wiio 1978), supplemented by additional items.

The basic OCD audit questionnaire includes 105 variables:

1. General communication satisfaction (one variable),
2. Frequency of use of various written channels (four variables),
3. Amount of information received now from various sources (fourteen variables),
4. Amount of information wanted from the same sources (fourteen variables),
5. Amount of information received now about various topics (twelve variables),
6. Amount of information wanted about these same topics (twelve variables),
7. Ranking of the same twelve topics in terms of their importance to the informant (twelve variables),
8. Areas where staff would like to see improved communication (seven variables),
9. Preferred information sources for various topics (twelve variables),

10. Worst defects in communication (eleven variables),

11. Positive aspects of communication (openended),

12. Satisfaction with various aspects of work (six variables).

All of the quantitative variables were scored on a five-value Likert-type scale. Responses ranged, for example, from 1, "Very Dissatisfied" to 5 "Very Satisfied"; or from 1 "Very Seldom" to 5 "Very Often."

To better meet the requirements of the consultancy specifications, several additional questions were included:

13. Modalities used in sending information,

14. Modalities used in receiving information.

Further, five additional questions taken from Dennis (1975) were added:

15. Perceptions of superior-subordinate communication (twenty-one variables),

16. Perceived quality and accuracy of downward communication (eleven variables),

17. Superior's perceptions of communication relationships with subordinates (five variables),

18. Perception of upward communication opportunity and degree of influence (four variables),

19. Reliability of information (two variables).

Two sets of questions devised by Rizzo, House, and Lirtzman (1970) on role stress were added:

20. Role clarity (six variables),

21. Role conflict (eight variables).

Finally, information was collected on thirteen background demographics: sex, age, length of employment, classification, education, number of staff supervised, number of people communicated with, union membership, location, division, status, level, and employment stream.

The sample size for the survey was 397, with the sample drawn from staff lists by systematic random sampling.

Role stress has been the subject of an numerous studies in the organizational behavior literature, usefully summarized and critiqued by Van Sell, Brief, and Schuler (1981). The seminal work in the area was, of course, the study by Kahn, Wolfe, Quinn, Snoek, and Rosenthal (1964). As Pfeffer (1985, 398) summarizes, role theory states that

> ... individuals occupy positions in organizations and associated with these positions (or jobs) are a set of activities, including required interactions, that constitute the individual's role. Because of the nature of organizations as systems of interdependent activity, the occupant of any given role is interdependent with others. . . . Interdependence means that the performance of that individual's role depends importantly on the activities that others in the role set perform, and at the same time their performance is affected by what the role incumbent does also. Because of this interdependence . . . these others come to have role expectations for appropriate behavior. These expectations are communicated and constitute role pressures.

Kahn et al. define set role conflict as "the simultaneous occurrence of two (or more) sets of pressures such that compliance with one would make difficult compliance with the other" (1964, 19). They identify five types of role conflict (1964, 19–26):

1. Intrasender Conflict: "different prescriptions and proscriptions a single member of the role set may be incompatible . . ." (1964, 19);

2. Intersender Conflict: "pressures from one role sender oppose pressures from one or more other senders" (1964, 20);

3. Interrole Conflict: "the role pressures associated with membership in one organization are in conflict with pressures stemming from membership in other groups" (1964, 20)

The first three types all represent set role conflicts; other types involve internal forces:

4. Person-Role Conflict: where, for example, conflicts exist between the needs and values of a person and the demands of their own role set.

A rather different type is

5. Role Overload: where "various role senders may hold quite legitimate expectations that a person perform a wide variety of tasks all of which are mutually compatible in the abstract. But it may be virtually impossible for the focal person to complete all of them within given time limits" (1964, 20).

Somewhat different is the concept of role ambiguity: "the individual faces stress because of uncertainty about what behaviors are, in fact, required in the role" (Pfeffer 1985, 398).

The notion of role stress has not been utilized extensively in the literature on organizational communication, as can be seen from the paucity of references in the indexes to two recent handbooks of organizational communication: Jablin, Putnam, Roberts, and Porter (1987) and Goldhaber and Barnett (1988). An important study by Fulk and Mani (1986), examined the relationship of role stress to aspects of supervisor-subordinate communication. Their study focused largely on message distortion, which was not measured in our study. Therefore, of their three predictions in relation to role stress, only the second is relevant here: that "greater frequency of communication by the supervisor would be linked to lower role stress for the subordinate" (1986, 504). They found, "The second expectation was not consistent with our data; frequency of communication was unrelated to role stress" (1964, 20).

Another important contribution comes from King (1986, reprinted in Hutchinson 1992). This study emphasizes sources of stress outside the work environment: "The life events which produce stress in the work environment more often than not originate from outside the work environment; the communication environment which influences life stress is more often than not a function of interactions which occur both within and outside the work environment; and the relationship between communication and stress both within and outside the work environment may be one of cause, of effect, or of moderator of stress" (1992, 384).

It is, of course, true that stress arising from interactions with family and others outside the work environment may carry over into that environment. It is equally (and regretfully) true that stress arising on the job is also likely to carry on to family life. Yet there is such a thing as role stress relating to organizational life, and it is this we propose to study.

Anticipating the discussion, we find gender to be an important factor in role stress. In relation to this, there is still some tendency to treat women as marginal members of organizations. For example, a study by Aneshensel and Pearlin (1987) in a recent book dealing with gender and stress focuses on the possibility of losing one's job and conflicts between family and job demands as sources of stress, rather than on organizational communication or behavior variables. We believe that to focus only on these is to ignore that women must be recognized as core members of organizations. More generally, although we concede the two-way interaction between organizational and extraorganizational life, we argue that it is valid to focus of role stress in organizational contexts.

Before we go further, we would like to comment on the two sets of questions, relating to role clarity and role conflict, from Rizzo, House, and Lirtzman (1970), which were used to measure role stress in both Fulk and Mani's (1986) study and in ours. These have been widely used in studies of role stress. As Van Sell, Brief, and Schuler (1981, 45) comment, "most of the remaining investigations [i.e., outside some laboratory-based studies] have used the general self-report questionnaire constructed by Rizzo, House and Lirtzman (1970) to determine the role incumbent's perceived role ambiguity and role conflict. A psychometric evaluation of this instrument across six samples concludes that its continued use appears to be warranted (Schuler, Aldag, and Brief, 1977)."

Factor analysis (using promax rotation) of our data supports the distinctiveness of the constructs measured by the two sets of questions. As can be seen from Table 11.1, the variables for Role Clarity loaded heavily and positively for Factor 1 and weakly and negatively for Factor 2. The variables relating to Role Conflict show a reverse pattern.

However, it should be pointed out that, in terms of face validity, the items relating to Role Conflict are not an optimal operationalization of the five types of role conflict identified by Kahn et al. (1964) and summarized previously. Items 5 and 6 relate directly and clearly to intersender conflict. Item 1 could be related to person-role conflict, but the question as stated leaves it unclear *why* things should be done differently and does not clearly relate to a conflict between internal forces and sent requirements. Similarly,

TABLE 11.1.
Factor Analysis of Rizzo, House, and Lirtzman (1970),
Role Stress Items

	Factor 1	Factor 2
Role Clarity		
1. You feel certain about how much authority you have.	0.61	−0.10
2. There are clear, planned objectives for your job.	0.70	−0.17
3. You know when you have divided your time properly on your job.	0.68	−0.10
4. You know what your job responsibilities are.	0.77	−0.06
5. You know exactly what is expected of you.	0.89	−0.08
6. You receive clear explanations of what has to be done.	0.82	−0.10
Role Conflict		
1. You have to do things that should be done differently.	−0.09	0.54
2. You receive an assignment without the personnel to complete it.	0.05	0.61
3. You have to buck a rule or policy to carry out an assignment.	−0.03	0.65
4. You work with two or more groups who operate very differently.	−0.06	0.57
5. You receive incompatible requests from two or more people.	−0.14	0.70
6. You do things that are apt to be accepted by one person and not accepted by others.	−0.14	0.64
7. You receive an assignment without adequate resources and materials to execute it.	−0.12	0.65
8. You work on unnecessary things.	−0.23	0.47

although items 2 and 7 could be related to role overload, they focus on things external to the focal person, rather than on demands on the focal person themself. Finally, no items appear to relate clearly to intrasender conflict (e.g., why not an item like "My boss can never make up his/her mind what he/she wants me to do"?) or to interrole conflict (e.g., why not an item like "Part of my job is inconsistent with other things that I have to do"?). Despite these shortcomings, we have used the standard items for the sake of comparability with earlier studies.

In these and in some other instances, we have used indexes rather than single variables. Thus we calculated an index of role clarity and an index of role conflict using the means of the scores for the individual items. Similarly, we calculated an index of trust in supervisor from the means of Dennis's (1975) twenty-one items on superior-subordinate communication; an index of quality of downward communication from Dennis's eleven variables on "perceived quality and accuracy of downward communication"; and an index of upward communication opportunity from Dennis's four items on "perception of upward communication opportunity and degree of influence." In examining the signs on correlations, it should be noted that the orientation of all the items on which these indexes are based is that 1 is most positive and 5 is most negative, with the exception of the index of role conflict, where the polarity of items is reversed.

Other variables examined, which relate to single variables in the OCD Audit questionnaire include the following:

- General satisfaction with communication (measured on a five-point scale from 1, Very Dissatisfied, to 5, Very Satisfied; that is, 1 is most negative, 5 is most positive).
- Information received now from superiors and management generally,
- Information received now from immediate supervisor,
- Information received now from middle management,
- Information received now from senior management,
- Information received now from colleagues (these five items were measured on a five-point scale from 1, Very Little, to 5, Very Much; that is, 5 is most positive).

Finally, we include five variables, relating to satisfaction with each of the following:

- Supervision of work,
- Chances for promotion and advancement,
- Wages and salaries,
- Your work in this department,

- Participation, your possibilities to influence matters concerning your work (all measured on a five-point scale from 1, Very Dissatisfied, to 5, Very Satisfied; that is, 5 is most positive).

Data on simple statistics for these variables are included in Table 11.2.

We have included a number of variables not directly related to organizational communication because of the lack of consensus in many correlations in the organizational behavior area. For example, Van Sell, Brief, and Schuler (1981, 51) conclude: "The results of the research on the role sender-focal person relationships indicate a great deal of inconsistency across studies and a great deal of

TABLE 11.2.
Simple Statistics

	N	Mean	St Devn
1. General Satisfaction with Communication	388	2.75	1.15
Information now from			
2. Superiors and Management Generally	393	2.56	1.27
3. Your Immediate Supervisor	392	3.48	1.29
4. Middle Management	383	2.62	1.21
5. Senior Management	390	1.87	1.16
6. Your Colleagues	385	3.68	1.06
Information now about			
7. Your Own Work	393	2.98	1.36
Satisfaction with			
8. Supervision of Work	388	3.74	1.19
9. Chances for Promotion	391	2.31	1.33
10. Wages and Salaries	391	2.8	1.28
11. Your Work in This Department	388	3.61	1.16
12. Participation	385	3.09	1.36
Indexes			
13. Trust in Supervisor	382	2.41	1.36
14. Quality Downward Communication	381	3.63	0.8
15. Upward Communication Opportunity	375	2.72	0.98
16. Role Clarity	383	2.5	1.01
17. Role Conflict	378	2.99	0.89

variance in the magnitudes of the relationships between role conflict and ambiguity and different employee responses."

It is clear that as with most areas of organizational communication, we are dealing with highly contingent phenomena. It is, of course, not enough to say that the relationships are contingent. Rather, this chapter should be seen as a modest attempt to contribute further to what are the important contingencies relating to role stress.

The data on general intercorrelations are set out in Table 11.3. Significant correlations in this and following tables are indicated by asterisks; that is, * indicates $P < 0.05$; ** indicates $P < 0.005$; and *** indicates $P\ 0.0005$. Before discussing Role Clarity and Role Conflict, we will comment briefly on General Satisfaction with Communication and Satisfaction with Your Work in This Department.

As these data display some very high correlations, it might be questioned whether multicollinearity is present. To check this, we use the SAS Reg procedure, with the COLLIN option. We ran the procedure with the NONE selection (to retain all variables in the model) with four models: successively, with General Satisfaction with Communication, Satisfaction with Your Work, the index of role clarity, and the index of role conflict as the dependent variable, in each case with all of the remaining variables as independent variables.

According to the SAS Stat Guide (1987, 836), "A collinearity problem occurs when a component associated with a high condition index contributes strongly to the variance of two or more variables." According to this criterion, no collinearity problem exists. To check further, we consulted the measures proposed in Wetherill (1986, 105). He states: "Examine the condition number of the explanatory variable correlation matrix. If this number is larger than 100 conclude that there are multicollinearities. Alternatively, examine the variance inflation factors and if any are larger than about 10 conclude multicollinearities exist." No VIF in our data was greater than 2.2, and the highest condition number was less than 55. Hence we conclude that multicollinearity is not a problem.

For each of the four dependent variables, we also ran the REG procedure using stepwise multiple regression. We will present the results of these after discussing the correlation data.

TABLE 11.3.
General Intercorrelations

	1	2	3	4	5	6	7	8	9
1. General Satisfaction with Communication	1								
Information now from									
2. Superiors and Management Generally	0.37***	1							
3. Your Immediate Supervisor	0.25***	0.45***	1						
4. Middle Management	0.30***	0.58***	0.45***	1					
5. Senior Management	0.29***	0.58***	0.29***	0.52***	1				
6. Your Colleagues	0.02	0.13*	0.26***	0.17**	0.02	1			
Information now about									
7. Your Own Work	0.23***	0.43***	0.42***	0.34***	0.26***	0.25***	1		
Satisfaction with									
8. Supervision of Work	0.25***	0.24***	0.56***	0.26***	0.19***	0.12*	0.29***	1	
9. Chances for Promotion	0.20***	0.30***	0.27***	0.26***	0.26***	0.09	0.27***	0.25***	1
10. Wages and Salaries	0.13*	0.06	0.04	0.11*	0.1*	0	0.12*	0.03	0.42***
11. Your Work in This Department	0.15**	0.19***	0.29***	0.14**	0.13*	0.18***	0.21***	0.38***	0.31***
12. Participation	0.27***	0.30***	0.30***	0.28***	0.30***	0.12*	0.30***	0.36***	0.33***
Indexes									
13. Trust in Supervisor	(0.24)***	(0.27)***	(0.61)***	(0.30)***	(0.18)**	−0.1	(0.27)***	(0.62)***	(0.28)***
14. Quality Downward Communication	(0.46)***	(0.42)***	(0.28)***	(0.37)***	(0.45)***	−0.09	(0.26)***	(0.30)***	(0.31)***
15. Upward Communication Opportunity	(0.17)**	(0.25)***	(0.27)***	(0.23)***	(0.14)*	(0.19)***	(0.26)***	(0.39)***	(0.24)***
16. Role Clarity	(0.25)***	(0.21)***	(0.30)***	(0.24)***	(0.16)**	(0.17)**	(0.3)***	(0.45)***	(0.19)***
17. Role Conflict	0.20***	0.03	0.11*	0.08	0.09	−0.09	0.01	0.19***	0.06

TABLE 11.3. (Continued)

	10	11	12	13	14	15	16	17
Satisfaction with								
10. Wages & Salaries	1							
11. Your Work in This Department	0.15**	1						
12. Participation	0.22***	0.44***	1					
Indexes								
13. Trust in Supervisor	−0.07	(0.42)***	(0.44)***	1				
14. Quality Downward Communication	(0.15)**	(0.25)***	(0.38)***	0.33***	1			
15. Upward Communication Opportunity	−0.1	(0.43)***	(0.52)***	0.50***	0.30***	1		
16. Role Clarity	−0.09	(0.42)***	(0.35)***	0.52***	0.37***	0.46***	1	
17. Role Conflict	0.15**	0.07	0.11*	(0.22)***	(0.21)***	−0.03	(0.25)***	1

The highest absolute correlation with General Satisfaction with Communication among sources of information now is from Supervisors and Management Generally (0.37). Perhaps surprisingly, From Your Immediate Supervisor (0.25) is the lowest of the four managerial sources. We note that this contradicts at least the distance dimension of the distance-direction model propounded by Wiio (1978, 68–71), according to which the closer the relationship, the higher should be the satisfaction. The correlation with From Your Colleagues is weak and not significant. The correlation with Information now about Your Own Work is 0.23.

Of the satisfaction variables, the highest correlation with General Satisfaction with Communication is with Participation (0.27), followed closely by Supervision of Work (0.25). Still high is Chances for Promotion and Advancement (0.20), but Satisfaction with Your Work in This Department rates only fourth, at 0.15. Of the indexes, the highest absolute correlation by far is Quality of Downward Communication, −0.46. Role Clarity, −0.25, is greater than Role Conflict, 0.19. The correlation with the index of Upward Communication Opportunity, at 0.17, is the second lowest.

Table 11.4 displays the summary data from the stepwise multiple regression procedure with General Satisfaction with Communication as the dependent variable. Generally speaking, it supports the correlations data, ranking the index of Quality of Downward Communication (0.46) first and Information Now from Supervisors and Managers Generally (0.37) second. The Index of Role Conflict (0.20) and Satisfaction with Supervision of Work (0.25) have the third and fourth highest F-scores.

As a general measure, Satisfaction with Your Work in This Department shows a pattern of correlations different from that with Satisfaction with Communication. In terms of Information now from sources, the highest absolute correlation is from Immediate Supervisor, 0.29, followed by from Supervisors and Management in General, 0.19, and from Colleagues, 0.18. Information now about Your Work, at 0.21, is similar to the correlation of that variable with General Communication Satisfaction.

Of the satisfaction variables, the highest correlation is with Supervision of Work, 0.38, followed by Chances for Promotion and Advancement, 0.31. Participation, which was highest for General Satisfaction with Communication, is relatively low at 0.14,

TABLE 11.4.
Summary Results of Stepwise Multiple Regression for General Satisfaction with Communication

Step	Variable Entered	Number Removed in	Partial Model		$C(p)$	F	$Prob > F$
			$R^{**}2$	$R^{**}2$			
1	Index of Quality of Downward Communication	1	0.1903	0.1903	26.249	92.849	0.0001
2	Information from Supervisors Generally	2	0.0437	0.234	5.6368	22.4619	0.0001
3	Index of Role Conflict	3	0.0132	0.2472	0.8131	6.8795	0.0091
4	Satisfaction with Supervision of Work	4	0.0006	0.2532	−0.3125	3.1685	0.0758

Note: No other variable met the 0.1500 significance level for entry into the model.

just behind Wages and Salaries, 0.15. Of the indexes, the highest correlation is with Upward Communication Opportunity, −0.43, closely followed by Trust in Supervisor and Role Clarity, both at −0.42. Still high is Quality of Downward Communication, −0.25, followed by Supervisor's View of Downward Communication, at −0.17. The correlation with Role Conflict is not significant.

Table 11.5 gives the summary results of stepwise multiple regression with Satisfaction with Your Own Work as the dependent variable. Satisfaction with Participation, with the highest F score (91.66), also shows the highest correlation (0.44). There is general agreement between the rank ordering of F scores and correlation scores, with the exception of the Index of Upward Communication Opportunity, whose correlation score (−0.43) is relatively higher than its F-score (7.34), and the Index of Trust in Supervisor (correlation, −0.42; F-score, 2.24).

We turn now to role clarity and role conflict. For convenience, the correlations with these two indexes in Table 11.3 are reproduced as Table 11.6. In gross terms, the two indexes differ in that Role Clarity shows fifteen of sixteen correlations to be significant, whereas Role Conflict shows only eight of sixteen correlations to be significant. We have already pointed out that Role Clarity shows significant correlations with General Satisfaction with Communication, 0.25, and Satisfaction with Your Work in This Department, −0.42, where the negative sign reflects the orientation of the scales. According to Van Sell, Brief, and Schuler (1981, 50), our finding on Satisfaction with Work agrees with most studies.

However, our results differ from those of Keller (1975), who found that role ambiguity (the opposite of role clarity) was unrelated to supervision and promotions. In contrast, we found a strong significant correlation of −0.45 between Role Clarity and Satisfaction with Supervision of Work and a significant correlation of −0.19 between Role Clarity and Satisfaction with Chances for Promotion and Advancement. Like Keller (1975), we found the relationship between Role Clarity and Satisfaction with Wages and Salaries to be not significant. But whereas Tosi and Tosi (1970) reported no relationship between role ambiguity and Participation (for managers), our data show a strong significant correlation of 0.35 between Role Clarity and Satisfaction with Participation. As noted previously, we also found a strong correlation between Role Clarity and Your Work in This Department, −0.41.

TABLE 11.5.
Summary Results of Stepwise Multiple Regression for Satisfaction with Your Work

Step	Variable Entered	Number Removed in	Partial Model		$C(p)$	F	$Prob > F$
			$R^{**}2$	$R^{**}2$			
1	Satisfaction with Participation	1	0.19	0.19	69.79	91.66	0.0001
2	Index of Role Clarity	2	0.07	0.26	31.31	37.76	0.0001
3	Satisfaction with Supervision of Work	3	0.02	0.28	19.55	13.24	0.0003
4	Satisfaction with Chances for Promotion	4	0.02	0.3	11.16	10.22	0.0015
5	Index of Upward Communication Opportunity	5	0.01	0.31	5.77	7.4	0.0068
6	Information from Colleagues	6	0.01	0.32	4.37	3.42	0.0652
7	Information from Middle Management	7	0	0.33	3.58	2.82	0.094
8	Index of Trust in Supervisors	8	0	0.33	3.38	2.24	0.14

Note: No other variable met the 0.1500 significance level for entry into the model.

TABLE 11.6.
Correlations with Role Clarity and Role Conflict

	Role Clarity	Role Conflict
1. General Satisfaction with Communications	(0.25)***	0.20***
Information now from		
2. Superiors and Management Generally	(0.21)***	0.03
3 Your Immediate Supervisor	(0.30)***	0.11*
4. Middle Management	(0.24)***	0.08
5. Senior Management	(0.16)**	0.09
6. Your Colleagues	(0.17)**	−0.09
Information now about		
7. Your Own Work	(0.30)***	0.01
Satisfaction with		
8. Supervision of Work	(0.45)***	0.19***
9. Chances for Promotion	(0.19)***	0.08
10. Wages and Salaries	0.09	0.15**
11. Your Work in This Department	(0.42)***	0.07
12. Participation	(0.35)***	0.11*
Indexes		
13. Trust in Supervisor	0.52***	(0.22)***
14. Quality Downward Communications	0.37***	(0.21)***
15. Upward Communication Opportunity	0.46***	−0.03
16. Role Clarity	1	(0.25)***
17. Role Conflict	(0.25)***	1

In our study, Role Clarity shows significant correlations with all managerial sources of Information now: highest, −0.30, from Your Immediate Supervisor, followed by Middle Management, −0.24; Superiors and Management Generally, −0.21; and Senior Management, −0.16. Colleagues are significant at −0.17. Note that these data tend to contradict Fulk and Mani's (1986) finding (mentioned earlier) that frequency of communication was not related to role stress. The correlation with the amount of information received now about Your Own Work is, somewhat surprisingly, not significant.

Among the satisfaction variables, all correlations with the exception of that with Satisfaction with Wages and Salaries are strong and significant. The highest absolute value is for Supervision of Work, -0.45; followed closely by Your Work in This Department, -0.42; Participation, -0.37; and lower (but still significant at $P <$ 0.005), Chances for Promotion and Advancement, -0.19.

Among the indexes, we find some very high correlations. The highest is with Trust in Supervisor, 0.52, followed by Upward Communication Opportunity, 0.46; Supervisor's View of Downward Communication, 0.39; Quality of Downward Communication, 0.37; Reliability of Information (from Colleagues and Subordinates), 0.29; and Role Conflict, -0.25. Of these figures, the high figures for Trust in Supervisor and Quality of Downward Communication agree with the importance of downward communication for Role Clarity shown previously; but the high figure for Upward Communication Opportunity is surprising given the weak and nonsignificant figure with Desire for Improvement in Upward Communication, of only 0.06. The high figures for the two indexes relating to managers' communication with subordinates are also interesting. They imply that communicating with subordinates is an integral part of a manager's role, whereas this is not the case for nonmanagers.

Table 11.7 gives summary results for stepwise multiple regression with Role Clarity as the dependent variable. As with the data for satisfaction with your work, there is general agreement between the ranking of items according to F-score and correlation score, except for a higher correlation ranking for Satisfaction with Supervision of Work (-0.45, ranked third) compared with its F-score (13.28, ranked sixth); and a rather higher F-score for Role Conflict (10.20, ranked fifth) than its correlation score (-0.25, ranked seventh) would lead one to expect.

In relation to role conflict, Van Sell, Brief, and Schuler (1981, 48) state, "The best documented outcomes of role conflict are job dissatisfaction and job-related tension, which have been isolated among a variety of occupational groups . . ." They continue, "Yet even here the evidence is not unequivocal. Hamner and Tosi (1974) reported among a sample of managers a positive correlation between role conflict and job threat and anxiety but no relationship between role conflict and job satisfaction." Keller (1975) also reported no relation between role conflict and satisfaction with work among research and development professionals.

TABLE 11.7.
Summary Results of Stepwise Multiple Regression for Index of Role Clarity

Step	Variable Entered	Number Removed in	Partial Model		$C(p)$	F	$Prob > F$
			$R^{**}2$	$R^{**}2$			
1	Index of Trust in Supervisors	1	0.22	0.22	90.57	114.44	0.0001
2	Satisfaction with Your Work	2	0.05	0.28	59.22	29.18	0.0001
3	Index of Quality of Downward Communication	3	0.04	0.31	38.96	20.45	0.0001
4	Index of Upward Communication Opportunity	4	0.02	0.33	28.06	12.19	0.0005
5	Index of Role Conflict	5	0.02	0.35	19.5	10.2	0.0015
6	Satisfaction with Supervision of Work	6	0.01	0.36	13.28	8.09	0.0047
7	Information About Own Work	7	0.01	0.37	9.28	5.98	0.0149
8	Information from Immediate Supervisor	8	0.01	0.38	7.18	4.12	0.04
9	Information from Colleagues	9	0	0.39	6.26	2.95	0.0867

Note: No other variable met the 0.1500 significance level for entry into the model.

Our data also show a nonsignificant correlation between role conflict and Satisfaction with Your Work in This Department 0.07 ($P = 0.18$). Keller (1975) also found that, for research and development professionals, role conflict is negatively correlated with satisfaction with pay, supervision, and promotion. Our data show a weak and nonsignificant correlation with Chances for Promotion, but quite strong and significant correlations with Satisfaction with Supervision of Work, 0.19, $P < 0.0005$, and Satisfaction with Wages and Salary, 0.15, $P < 0.005$.

To run through the data with role conflict: It is positively correlated with General Satisfaction with Communication, 0.20, $P < 0.0005$. In terms of sources of information, it is significantly correlated only with Your Immediate Superior, 0.11, $P < 0.05$. Again, this tends to be contrary to Fulk and Mani's (1986) findings about frequency of communication and role stress. Of the satisfaction variables, with Supervision of Work, 0.19, shows the highest absolute value, followed by Wages and Salaries, 0.15, and Participation, 0.11. With the indexes, it is significantly correlated only with Trust in Supervisor, -0.22; Quality of Downward Communication, -0.21; and Role Clarity, -0.25.

Table 11.8 presents stepwise multiple regression data for role conflict. Agreement between the ranking of F-scores and of correlation scores here is rather poor. Although Role Clarity shows both the highest F-score (22.56) and highest correlation score (-0.25), in relation to the other seven variables there is considerable disagreement. We note that in absolute terms, most of the F-scores here are low, and several of the correlation scores are nonsignificant.

If we think of a possible model, the information now from variables clearly represent source variables. The satisfaction variables and the indexes represent outcomes. As possible intervening and moderating variables, we need to consider variables such as level, stream, and gender; role clarity and role conflict; we also suggest that it is worth examining information now about Your Own Work as a possible intervening variable, because it derives from the source variables and influences the outcome variables, as well as, presumably, the role stress indexes.

The first step in investigating the influence of other background variables is to look at the crosstabulation of background variables. Table 11.9 shows percentages of both sexes by level. The

TABLE 11.8.
Summary Results of Stepwise Multiple Regression for Index of Role Clarity

| Step | Variable Entered | Number Removed in | Partial Model | | C(p) | F | Prob > F |
			$R^{**}2$	$R^{**}2$			
1	Index of Role Clarity	1	0.05	0.05	25.17	22.56	0.0001
2	General Satisfaction with Communication	2	0.02	0.07	19.37	7.49	0.0065
3	Information from Colleagues	3	0.01	0.09	14.85	6.35	0.0122
4	Satisfaction with Wages	4	0.01	0.1	11.33	5.42	0.0204
5	Index of Trust in Supervisor	5	0.01	0.11	9.82	3.48	0.0627
6	Index of Upward Communication Opportunity	6	0.01	0.12	6.55	5.27	0.0222
7	Information About Own Work	7	0	0.12	6.39	2.17	0.1416
8	Index of Quality of Downward Communication	8	0.01	0.13	5.98	2.43	0.12

Note: No other variable met the 0.1500 significance level for entry into the model.

TABLE 11.9.
Gender by Level

| | Level | | | | |
	ASO 1–3	ASO 4–6	ASO 7–8	SES	Total
Female	46.8%	40.4%	11.0%	1.8%	109
Male	31.8%	40.9%	25.4%	1.9%	264

Cramer's V = 0.181
Significance = .006
Missing Observations 24

TABLE 11.10.
Gender by Employment Stream

| | Employment Stream | | | | | |
	SES	Admin	Professl	Technical	Trade/Mtc	Totals
Female	0.9%	90.8%	5.5%	0.9%	1.8%	109
Male	0.8%	54.2%	14.5%	21.8%	8.8%	262

Cramer's V = 0.360
Significance = .000
Missing Observations 26

TABLE 11.11.
GLM: Role Clarity by Gender, Level, and Stream

Source	DF	Type I SS	Mean Square	F Value	Pr > F
Gender	1	1.13	1.13	1.24	0.2663
Level	3	18.91	6.30	6.90	0.0002
Stream	4	2.88	0.72	0.79	0.5336

Source	DF	Type III SS	Mean Square	F Value	Pr > F
Gender	1	0.49	0.49	0.54	0.4633
Level	3	15.42	5.14	5.62	0.0009
Stream	4	2.88	0.72	0.79	0.5336

differences are significant, with proportionately more women at the lowest level and proportionately more men at level ASO 7–8.

Table 11.10 displays gender by employment stream. Again, the gender differences are highly significant, with women overwhelmingly concentrated in the administrative stream.

We first used general linear modeling to estimate the impact of the three possible moderating variables of Level, Stream, and Gender on Role Clarity and Role Conflict. With Role Clarity as the dependent variable, the results shown in Table 11.11 were obtained. Clearly, in relation to Role Clarity, Level displays the highest, and only significant, F score in relation to both Type I and Type III Sum of Squares and is thus a better predictor of Role Clarity than the two other variables.

Table 11.12 shows GLM results with Role Conflict as the dependent variable. Here F values and significance figures show Gender to be the best predictor of Role Conflict. These data tend to agree with the findings of Szilyagi and Sims (1975) that role ambiguity, but not role conflict, varied by organizational level for a large sample of paramedical workers. The finding that gender was more important in relation to role conflict might be linked with the findings of Penhallurick (forthcoming), that gender was a better predictor of Satisfaction with Communication than level or employment stream, but that with Satisfaction with Your Own Work, employment stream and level were better predictors than gender.

Some individual items from the audit cast light on the link

TABLE 11.12.
GLM: Role Conflict by Gender, Level, and Stream

Source	DF	Type I SS	Mean Square	F Value	Pr > F
Gender	1	5.34	5.34	7.59	0.0062
Level	3	2.39	0.79	1.13	0.3356
Stream	4	5.74	1.44	2.04	0.0883

Source	DF	Type III SS	Mean Square	F Value	Pr > F
Gender	1	7.04	7.04	10.01	0.0017
Level	3	1.92	0.64	0.91	0.4361
Stream	4	5.74	1.44	2.04	0.0883

between level and role clarity. On scales where 1 = Strongly Agree and 5 = Strongly Disagree, our results included the following:

- *You know what your job responsibilities are.*
  Cramer's $V = 0.19$, $P = 0.0007$
  Means:

Whole sample	2.06
ASO 1–3	1.75
ASO 4–6	2.15
ASO 7–8	2.37
SES	1.17

- *You receive clear explanations of what has to be done.*
  Cramer's $V = 0.18$ $P = 0.0015$
  Means:

Whole sample	2.63
ASO 1–3	2.20
ASO 4–6	2.80
ASO 7–8	2.97
SES	1.50

In both these variables, the highest degree of role ambiguity is found at ASO 7–8 level. These data are consistent with the findings of Kahn et al. (1964, 149): "Whether one orders people in terms of rank in the organization . . . or in terms of the status of their occupations, it is clear that high job status brings with it a level of tension. . . . This relationship, however, is not completely linear, such conflict being more prevalent at the middle than at the top level of management."

The influence of these potentially moderating variables was further investigated using partial correlations. A partial correlation of two variables X and Y controlling for a third, Z, is the correlation of the residuals of the regressions of X on Z and of Y on Z (Elifson, Runyon, and Haber 1982). If a strong correlation between two variables significantly weakens while controlling for a third variable, this suggests that the third variable is an intervening variable causally linking the first two variables. In the following tables displaying partial correlations, we have included only variables where the initial general correlation was statistically significant.

Table 11.13 summarizes partial correlations with General Sat-

TABLE 11.13.
Partial Correlations with General Satisfaction with Communication

	General Satisfaction Communication	Controlling for			Information About Own Work	Role Clarity	Role Conflict
		Level	Stream	Gender			
Information now from							
2. Superiors and Management Generally	0.37***	0.38***	0.37***	0.37***	0.31***	0.34***	0.37***
3. Your Immediate Supervisor	0.25***	0.25***	0.25***	0.26***	0.18***	0.19***	0.23***
4. Middle Management	0.30***	0.31***	0.30***	0.31***	0.24***	0.26***	0.29***
5. Senior Management	0.29***	0.30***	0.28***	0.28***	0.24***	0.25***	0.27***
Information now about							
8. Your Own Work	0.23***	0.20***	0.19***	0.21***	XXXXXX	0.16**	0.22***
Satisfaction with							
9. Supervision of Work	0.25***	0.22***	0.22***	0.24***	0.19***	0.16**	0.21***

10. Chances for Promotion	0.20***	0.19***	0.18***	0.18***	0.14*	0.15**	0.18***
11. Wages and Salaries	0.13*	0.11*	0.11*	0.11*	0.1*	0.11*	0.1*
12. Your Work in This Department	0.15**	0.15**	0.16**	0.16**	0.11*	0.06	0.14*
13. Participation	0.27***	0.25***	0.25***	0.27***	0.22***	0.20***	0.25***
Indexes							
14. Trust in Supervisor	(0.24)***	(0.24)***	(0.25)***	(0.23)***	(0.18)***	(0.13)*	(0.20)***
15. Quality Downward Communication	(0.46)***	(0.45)***	(0.45)***	(0.43)***	(0.40)***	(0.39)***	(0.42)***
17. Upward Communication Opportunity	(0.17)***	(0.15)**	(0.15)**	(0.16)**	(0.1)*	−0.06	(0.15)**
19. Role Clarity	(0.25)***	(0.24)***	(0.25)***	(0.23)***	(0.19)***	XXXXXX	(0.20)***
20. Role Conflict	0.20***	0.20***	0.21***	0.17***	0.19***	0.14*	XXXXX

TABLE 11.14.
Partial Correlations with Satisfaction with Your Work

	Satisfaction with Your Work	Controlling for			Information About Own Work	Role Clarity	Role Conflict
		Level	Stream	Gender			
1. General Satisfaction with Communication	0.15**	0.15**	0.16**	0.16**	0.11*	0.06	0.14*
Information now from							
2. Superiors and Management Generally	0.19***	0.19***	0.21***	0.18***	0.11*	0.12*	0.18***
3. Your Immediate Supervisor	0.29***	0.28***	0.28***	0.28***	0.23***	0.20***	0.28***
4. Middle Management	0.14*	0.14*	0.15**	0.13*	0.08	0.06	0.14*

5. Senior Management	0.13*	0.13*	0.15**	0.12*	0.08	0.07	0.12*
6. Your Colleagues	0.18***	0.19***	0.19***	0.18***	0.14*	0.13*	0.19***
Information now about							
8. Your Own Work	0.21***	0.23***	0.26***	0.21***	XXXXXX	0.1*	0.20***
Satisfaction with							
9. Supervision of Work	0.38***	0.38***	0.39***	0.38***	0.34***	0.25***	0.37***
10. Chances for Promotion	0.31***	0.34***	0.34***	0.31***	0.27***	0.26***	0.30***
11. Wages and Salaries	0.15**	0.15**	0.15**	0.17***	0.13*	0.13*	0.15**
13. Participation	0.44***	0.45***	0.46***	0.44***	0.40***	0.35***	0.43***
Indexes							
14. Trust in Supervisor	(0.42)***	(0.41)***	(0.40)***	(0.39)***	(0.36)***	(0.25)***	(0.38)***
15. Quality of Downward Communication	(0.25)***	(0.22)***	(0.23)***	(0.24)***	(0.20)***	(0.11)*	(0.23)***
17. Upward Communication Opportunity	(0.43)***	(0.43)***	(0.41)***	(0.39)***	(0.37)***	(0.28)***	(0.40)***
19. Role Clarity	(0.42)***	(0.42)***	(0.42)***	(0.40)***	(0.36)***	XXXXXX	(0.39)***

TABLE 11.15.
Partial Correlations with Satisfaction with Your Work

	Role Clarity	Controlling for			Information About Own Work	Role Conflict
		Level	Stream	Gender		
1. General Satisfaction with Communication	(0.25)***	(0.24)***	(0.25)***	(0.23)***	(0.19)***	(0.20)***
Information now from						
2. Superiors and Management Generally	(0.21)***	(0.24)***	(0.22)***	(0.20)***	−0.09	(0.20)***
3. Your Immediate Supervisor	(0.30)***	(0.29)***	(0.29)***	(0.29)***	(0.19)***	(0.27)***
4. Middle Management	(0.24)***	(0.25)***	(0.23)***	(0.23)***	(0.14)**	(0.21)***
5. Senior Management	(0.16)**	(0.21)***	(0.18)**	(0.15)**	−0.09	(0.14)*
6. Your Colleagues	(0.17)**	(0.16)**	(0.16)**	(0.16)**	−0.1	(0.19)***

Information now about						
7. Your Own Work	(0.30)***	(0.30)***	(0.30)***	(0.29)***	XXXXXXX	(0.30)***
Satisfaction with						
8. Supervision of Work	(0.45)***	(0.44)***	(0.45)***	(0.43)***	(0.38)***	(0.41)***
9. Chances for Promotion	(0.19)***	(0.25)***	(0.22)***	(0.18)***	(0.12)*	(0.18)***
11. Your Work in This Department	(0.42)***	(0.42)***	(0.42)***	(0.40)***	(0.36)***	(0.39)***
12. Participation	(0.35)***	(0.36)***	(0.34)***	(0.34)***	(0.27)***	(0.32)***
Indexes						
13. Trust in Supervisor	0.52***	0.46***	0.46***	0.47***	0.43***	0.45***
14. Quality of Downward Communication	0.37***	0.38***	0.37***	0.35***	0.30***	0.32***
15. Upward Communication Opportunity	0.46***	0.45***	0.40***	0.41***	0.36***	0.41***
17. Role Conflict	(0.25)***	(.22)***	(0.24)***	(0.23)***	(0.24)***	XXXXXX

isfaction with Communication, controlling for Level, Stream, Gender, Amount of Information about Your Own Work, Role Clarity and Role Conflict.

The partial correlations in the columns Level, Stream, Gender, Information About Own Work, and Role Conflict suggest that none of these significantly moderate links between General Satisfaction with Communication and the other variables. Role Clarity appears to have some moderating role in relation to Satisfaction with Your Work in This Department and Upward Communication Opportunity.

Table 11.14 displays partial correlations with Satisfaction with Your Work. As with General Satisfaction with Communication, it appears that Level, Stream, Gender, and Role Conflict play little mediating role. Information About Your Own Work appears to play some mediating role with information from all management sources. Role Clarity appears to mediate between General Satisfaction with Communication and Satisfaction with Your Own Work and also between Information from Middle Management and Information from Senior Management and Satisfaction with Your Work. It also seems to play some role between Information about Your Own Work and Satisfaction with Your Work.

Table 11.15 displays partial correlations with Role Clarity. There is little evidence of moderating influence by controlling variables here, with the exception of Information About Your Own Work. This moderates the relationship between Role Clarity and information now from Superiors and Management Generally and plays some role with the other managerial sources of information and also Your Colleagues.

Finally, Table 11.16 shows partial correlations with Role Conflict. The sole controlling variable that appears to exercise some significant mediating influence is Role Clarity, which plays a clear role with information now from Immediate Supervisor, satisfaction with Supervision of Work and satisfaction with Participation. It seems to play some role in relations between Role Conflict and Trust in Supervisor and Quality of Downward Communication.

We were, quite frankly, somewhat surprised at the lack of influence of potential moderating variables in the tables just examined. In conclusion, in keeping with the contingency view espoused in this chapter, we do not suggest that we have produced definitive findings, but hope that this chapter represents a contribution to the

TABLE 11.16.
Partial Correlations with Role Conflict

	Role Clarity	Controlling for			Information About Own Work	Role Conflict
		Level	Stream	Gender		
1. General Satisfaction with Communication	0.20***	0.20***	0.21***	0.17***	0.19***	0.14*
Information now from						
3. Your Immediate Supervisor	0.11*	0.11*	0.11*	0.11*	0.11*	0.04
Satisfaction with						
8. Supervision of Work	0.19***	0.17**	0.18***	0.17**	0.18***	0.08
10. Wages and Salaries	0.15**	0.17**	0.16**	0.13*	0.15**	0.13*
12. Participation	0.11*	0.14*	0.13*	0.11*	0.11*	0.03
Indexes						
13. Trust in Supervisor	(0.22)***	(0.22)***	(0.23)***	(0.20)***	(0.21)***	(0.11)*
14. Quality of Downward Communication	(0.21)***	(0.19)***	(0.19)***	(0.19)***	(0.20)***	(0.12)*
16. Role Clarity	(0.25)***	(0.22)***	(0.24)***	(0.23)***	(0.24)***	XXXXXX

literature of organizational communication, particularly that relating to role stress. It provides further evidence of the importance of role stress, and particularly of role clarity/ambiguity, in organizational communication. Role clarity showed significant correlations with fifteen of sixteen key variables. In an age of rapid change and high-speed management, role stress will become even more significant. Our findings often contradict those of earlier studies, indicating that the call from Van Sell et al. (1981) for further empirical study is still valid. Our chapter also highlights the importance of gender in organizational communication, with particular reference to role clarity.

REFERENCES

Aneshensel, C. S., and Pearlin, L. I. (1987). "Structural Contexts of Sex Differences in Stress." In R. C. Barnett, L. Biener, and G. K. Baruch, (eds.), *Gender and Stress,* pp. 75–95. New York: Free Press.

Dennis, H. S. (1975). "The Construction of a Managerial Communication Climate Inventory for Complex Organizations." Paper presented at the annual convention of the ICA, Chicago.

Elifson, K. W., Runyon, R. P., and Haber, A. (1982). *Fundamentals of Social Statistics.* Reading, Mass.: Addison-Wesley.

Fulk, J., and Mani, S. (1986). "Distortion of Communication in Hierarchical Relationships." In M. McLaughlin (ed.), *Communication Yearbook 9,* pp. 483–510. Beverly Hills, Calif.: Sage Publications.

Goldhaber, G. M., and Barnett, G. A. (eds.). (1988). *Handbook of Organizational Communication.* Norwood, N.J.: Ablex.

Hamner, W. C., and Tosi, H. W. (1974). "Relationships of Role Conflict and Role Ambiguity to Job Involvement Measures." *Journal of Applied Psychology* 59: 497–499.

Jablin, F. M., Putnam, L. L., Roberts, K. H., and Porter, L. W. (eds.). (1987). *Handbook of Organizational Communication: An Interdisciplinary Perspective.* Newbury Park, Calif.: Sage Publications.

Kahn, R. L., Wolfe D. M., Quinn, R. P., Snoek, J. D., and Rosenthal, R. A. (1964). *Organizational Stress: Studies in Role Conflict and Ambiguity.* New York: Wiley and Sons.

Keller, R. T. (1975). "Role Conflict and Ambiguity: Correlates with Job Satisfaction and Values." *Personnel Psychology* 28: 57–64.

King, S. S. (1986). "The Relationship Between Stress and Communication in the Organizational Context." *Central States Speech Journal* 37, 1: 36–44. Reprinted in K. L. Hutchinson (ed.), (1992). *Readings in Organizational Communication,* pp. 383–392. Dubuque: William C. Brown.

Penhallurick, J. M. (Forthcoming). "Gender and Communication in a Government Department." In *Proceedings of the 1993 Australian Communication Association Conference.*

Pfeffer, J. (1985). "Organizations and Organization Theory. In G. Lindzey and A. Aronson (eds.), *The Handbook of Social Psychology*, vol. 1, pp. 379–440.

Rizzo, J. R., House, R. J., and Lirtzmann, S. E. (1970). "Role Conflict and Ambiguity in Complex Organizations." *Administrative Science Quarterly* 15: 150–163.

SAS Institute. (1987). *SAS/STAT Guide for Personal Computers, Version 6 Edition.* Cary, N.C.: SAS Institute.

Schuler, R. S., Aldag, R. J., and Brief, A. P. (1977). "Role Conflict and Ambiguity: A Scale Analysis." *Organizational Behavior and Human Performance* 20: 119–128.

Szilyagi, A. D., and Sims, H. P. (1975). "Locus of Control, Role Dynamics and Job Behavior in a Health Care Organization." In J. G. Hunt (ed.), *Proceedings of the Midwest Division of the Academy of Management.*

Tosi, H., and Tosi, D. (1970). "Some Correlates of Role Conflict and Ambiguity Among Public School Teachers" *Journal of Human Relations* 18: 1068–1075.

Van Sell, M., Brief, A. P., and Schuler, R. S. (1981). "Role Conflict and Role Ambiguity: Integration of the Literature and Directions for Future Research." *Human relations* 34: 43–71.

Wetherill, G. B. (1986). *Regression Analysis with Applications.* London: Chapman and Hall.

Wiio, O. (1978). *Contingencies of Organizational Communication.* Helsinki: Helsinki School of Economics.

PART 3

Organizations in Regional Cultures.

CHAPTER 12

Communicating Change in China

Yanan Ju

Identify CCF
+ Identify CCF's
in the USA

COMMON CULTURAL FRAMEWORK: KEY TO UNDERSTANDING DOING BUSINESS IN CHINA

It is only a half-truth to say that overseas Chinese flock to Mainland China to invest or conduct other kinds of business because that is where the fastest growing economy is. It is equally insufficient to reason that rich Chinese from Hong Kong go to Guangdong Province to invest and Taiwanese Chinese arrive in Fujian Province to launch joint ventures because that is where their ancestors came from. I believe the main rationale behind the integration of the Chinese economies is that they share a common cultural framework (CCF), which makes doing business easier and more culturally and psychologically gratifying. Uniquely Chinese, this framework is unwritten and unspoken but tacitly understood and shared among those who conduct business together. It is cultural in nature and can be defined by what I call *pragmatic-humanistic rationalism,* which has a deep root in Confucianism. Before I describe the key components of this framework, I will first explain what I mean by *pragmatic-humanistic rationalism.*

PRAGMATIC-HUMANISTIC RATIONALISM

Because of the omnipresence of Confucianism in traditional Chinese culture, which moralized and politicized every aspect of Chinese way of life, Chinese society has for the past 2,000 years been very mundane, very political, and very pragmatic. Chinese philosophy, for example, never quite gained its ontological status that went beyond moral and political confines. In other words, Chinese philosophy is more of a philosophy of moralities than a philosophy in its pure sense; it is always related to "this life of this world." Religion, as a belief system or as a way of life, was never quite able to define the "Chineseness" of the Chinese people. Confucianism does that job. It is not difficult to understand why a nonreligious people tend to be more pragmatic than idealistic. Chinese science is another good example with which to explain why traditional Chinese mode of thinking was pragmatic-rationalistic in nature. In traditional China, science was never developed for the sake of developing science; science, like philosophy, was very much politicized. And more often than not people equated science with technology, which, of course, could be used to solve practical problems of "this life of this world." Deng Xiaoping's "cat theory"[1] is a modern version of pragmatic rationalism. He says: "It doesn't matter whether it is a black cat or white cat; it is a good cat as long as it catches mice." Indeed this "cat theory" has been attractive not only to Mainland Chinese, who for three decades were subjected to a Maoist utopian mode of thinking that threw the whole nation into confusion. The Chinese can never quite live comfortably without practicing pragmatic rationalism (I guess that is another reason why Maoism was destined to end like an ideological nightmare). Deng's "cat theory" was also widely acclaimed by overseas Chinese in Taiwan, Hong Kong, or elsewhere in the world as that which would save China, not without good reason. Pragmatic rationalism has served as the basis on which Chinese—mainlanders and overseas Chinese—started to build mutual trust and confidence again.

Pragmatic rationalism is only one side of the coin. The other side is Chinese humanism, or humanistic rationalism. Chinese humanism is not to be confused with Western humanism. Western humanism sees the human being as a social animal, an independent entity with reason, emotion, volition, love, friendship, equality, dignity, and human rights, who is responsible for his or her own destiny. Western humanism, a revolt against the Middle Ages churches, gave full play to human individuality. In contrast, Chinese humanism went the other way round. It is aimed at perfection of moral self (*xiushen*) to its most practical objectives: regulation of family relationships (*qijia*), good government of state (*zhiguo*), and peace under the heaven (*pingtianxia*). Without these objectives, a person is morally and ethnically deficient and inhumane. (A person who knows how to suppress individuality in order to *xiushen qijia zhiguo pingtianxia* is a moral person, an ethical person and a noble person] How could one learn to suppress one's individuality? Through *kejifuli* (control self and restore rites), according to Confucius. The key word is *li*, which can be said to represent the very core of Confucianism. Let me use a little bit more space to explain this concept because this could be key to understanding not only Chinese humanism, but the common cultural framework that is key, as is suggested at the beginning of this chapter, to understanding doing business in China.

The *li* that Confucius (551 B.C.–479 B.C.) wanted to restore during his Spring and Autumn (*chungqiu*) historical period originated from the rites of *xia* Dynasty (about 2200 B.C.–about 1700 B.C.), *shang* Dynasty (about 1700 B.C.–about 1100 B.C.), and *zhou* Dynasty (about 1100–256 B.C.), the so-called Three Dynasties in recorded Chinese history. Confucius did not create any rites by himself; all he did was try to revive the ethics and rites of the Three Dynasties. *Li* as a set of rites and properties governing social norms and institutions underwent all kinds of changes throughout Chinese history, but its essence continued to lie in the strict distinction of social ranks and strata under the so-called Three Cardinal Principles, or *sangang*.[2] The "Three Cardinal Principles" guided the practice of Chinese humanism over the past 2,000 years. A subject was a good and humane person if he did what the emperor told him to do. A son was a good and humane son if he did what his father told him to do. And a wife was a good and humane wife if she did what her husband told her to do. Things have changed greatly in the past few decades: no more emperor, no more absolutely unchallengeable parental authority, and more and more women who have become less submissive and more assertive. Despite these changes, however, a good person is still very much defined by whether one knows one's place and works hard to help maintain the existing social order, a new kind of humanistic rationalism, if you will.

Chinese humanistic rationalism, in modern business activities and practices, regulates human relationships and injects order into a seemingly chaotic objective business world. Chinese humanistic rationalism has serious implications on such important issues as organizational leadership succession, decision making, management-labor relationship, superior-subordinate relationship, promotion, corporate culture, teamwork, and others. In other words, Chinese humanistic rationalism determines how precious business resources are regulated. Although pragmatic rationalism has always been followed among overseas Chinese businesses and started its comeback in mainland China as of 1978 when Deng Xiaoping launched his economic reforms, humanistic rationalism is fast becoming a common frame of reference for both overseas Chinese and mainlanders who have very much shaken off the yoke of Maoist idealism and class struggle legacies.

Pragmatic-humanistic rationalism, as the philosophical underpinnings of the common cultural framework, is expressed in various forms through a set of culturally and socially meaningful practices, some of which are the content of the CCF. I will now discuss the key components of the framework.

KEY COMPONENTS OF CCF

The notion of a common cultural framework as a set of unwritten or unspoken norms and proprieties that help to conduct business in a socially meaningful and mutually understandable way is widely accepted and indeed well followed in business activities, whether such activities are regional, national, international, or transcultural. But how to define it and talk about it and at what level could potentially be controversial because so many dimensions could be involved. Here we are not talking about common cultural frameworks in a general sense; we are examining the common cultural framework of the Chinese. Based on pragmatic-humanistic rationalism as the cultural underpinnings of this framework and looking at it from a social-business resources perspective, I see this Chinese CCF as composed of two main aspects, what composes social-business resources and how they are regulated, both of which are uniquely Chinese. Pragmatic rationalism seems to determine what composes social-business resources and humanistic rationalism tends to affect how such social-business resources are regulated. Among what composes social-business resources are *guanxi* or connections (external resource) and entrepreneurial spirit (internal resource). How such resources are regulated pertain to social hierarchy and role communication. Let me explain each in turn.

Guanxi and Entrepreneurial Spirit as Social-Business Resources

I have to make this clear once again. I will not talk about what composes social-business resources in a general way; I will discuss only those that are uniquely Chinese. The two I have just mentioned are just part of a much longer list of such resources, as can easily be imagined. Let me begin with *guanxi* or connections.

Guanxi   No one can claim one understands China who does not even know the two-character term *guanxi*. China is a land of *guanxi*. Chinese are a people living in *guanxi*. Nothing can be done without *guanxi*. *Guanxi* is a web of an individual person's blood and social connections which define who one is and what one is capable of accomplishing without probably much to do with what other resources one has available for use. I have no doubt that *guanxi,* thus defined, is the most important social-business resource of an individual Chinese. To say Mr. so and so has a lot of *guanxi* is to say he is a man of great social-business resource, a man one is not supposed to neglect. A person who has no *guanxi* is one who is socially isolated and probably cannot go too far in his or her social space. It is not just that *guanxi* makes things easier; it is that *guanxi* makes things happen. Even though the practice of *guanxi* among the Chinese, not just mainland Chinese (though mainland Chinese are undisputedly a leader in the practice of *guanxi* in contemporary China), but Chinese in Hong Kong or Taiwan or elsewhere in the world, may go beyond the limit that is allowed by social ethics or even laws, it is nevertheless not necessarily unethical or illegal. When everybody, elite as well as commoners, and all organizations, practice it in a society, it becomes a social institution,[3] whether you like it or not. And social cybernetics will make sure that its practice, once out of balance, return to its normalcy.

Although *guanxi* is practiced in all cultures and societies, it's a way of life in China and among Chinese communities. A number of popular theories have been developed to explain why *guanxi* has become part of the Chineseness in contemporary China. One theory attributes it to the human rule being larger than rule by law, which makes perfect sense considering the fact that in China's long

history and particularly during the four decades after the founding
of the People's Republic, emperors were law, Mao was law, and
then on the island of Taiwan for not too short a period of time
Chiang Kai-shek and his Kuomintang were law. When you had a
case to present, for example, you did not go to a court, you went to
a government official, who you knew was the law or larger than the
law if there had ever been such a law. Another theory says that the
practice of *guanxi* has been caused by scarcity of resources: when
you cannot get what you want through normal channels because
too many people are waiting in the line for too small a cake, you
try to get your *guanxi* to help. Still another theory postulates that
practicing *guanxi* is simply practicing pragmatic rationalism; you
do not go against what defines Chineseness to be a Chinese. There
is also a theory that hinges on Confucianism. A related concept is
renqing, or "personal obligations and affections." The feeling of
renqing bound together many of the basically reciprocal social
relations in traditional China. A practical manifestation of *renqing*
is the asking and giving of a favor. In many instances, practicing
guanxi is practicing *renqing,* and this happens among all Chinese.

What seems to be more important to me is not so much why
guanxi is practiced as what it is and how it is practiced. First, all
Chinese know *guanxi* as a social-business resource is important
and thus must be practiced in due course, even though one need
not publicly acknowledge it. The understanding is tacitly shared.
Many Westerners are fast learning it. It is amazing that *guanxi*
seems to be becoming the most correctly pronounced Chinese
characters by some Westerners and the sound has become so communicative between Chinese and their Western counterparts that a
mere utterance of the sound *guanxi* is taken as the clearest indication that the nature of a particular business deal has been understood. The importance of *guanxi,* as many Westerners and their
Chinese counterparts understand it, often lies not as much in how
much honor one can get as in how practically useful the perceived
guanxi could be or as in how routinely it is practiced as a cultural
ritual.

Second, an effective way to understand Chinese *guanxi* is to
understand it as a system, which requires one to develop a taxology. This introduces the concept of *guanxiwang,* or network of
guanxi, which usually consists of two broad categories, blood *guanxi* and social *guanxi*. To understand one's *guanxi* is to understand

one's *guanxiwang*—the network of one's blood *guanxi* and social *guanxi*, which could be so complicated that an outsider may never quite understand how it works. Blood *guanxi* could include one's family members, relatives, and members from the same clan. Social *guanxi* are all those connections that do not belong to one's blood *guanxi*, such as friends, colleagues, and ex-classmates. For an individual Chinese, it is extremely important to have some blood *guanxi* available for use in various situations. No matter how important one's social *guanxi are*, it can seldom reach the level of unquestionable trust that one's blood *guanxi* can enjoy. Godwin Chu, a senior researcher at the East-West Center of Hawaii, and I studied the recent cultural changes in China.[4] We found that people's relations with relatives were closer than with friends and other social relations. Family members, as our study has found, are those one depends on and trusts the most. Blood *guanxi* may not necessarily be as significant as social *guanxi* in terms of their pragmatic "usefulness," but the former are what you can trust most.

When you are new in a particular field and uncertain about what is going to happen once you are in, you will definitely begin with your blood *guanxi* if you have any. For example, if I want to start a business in China and I have my brother and other important relatives living there, I would probably want to start it by talking it over with them more than with any social *guanxi*, no matter how socially important members of the latter group are. And I would willingly put my money in the hands of my brother or another trusted relative. I feel safe this way.

What about a Western business person who has neither blood *guanxi* nor social *guanxi* in China? How can one get into the business game in China? Many different ways. Go in directly. Or find a middleman in Hong Kong. Or call the official who once visited with you and left a business card. Or, assuming your best friend is a Chinese immigrant living here in the United States who has relatives living and working in China, you've got good indirect blood *guanxi!* Maybe you could talk it over with your best friend and let him talk it over with his relatives back in China. This may be a better way to start a business in China.

I am discussing the difference of blood *guanxi* vs. social *guanxi* at the level of who to trust more in a general sense. I do not imply, however, that one cannot trust one's social *guanxi* and should not start things from there. One's social *guanxi,* or rather, social *guan-*

xiwang (network of social *guanxi*) is no less important than one's blood *guanxi*. As a matter of fact, one's social *guanxiwang* tends to be larger and cover a larger social space than one's blood *guanxiwang*. Indeed an individual's social *guanxiwang*, if used skillfully, can be used with a freer hand because blood *guanxi* is easier to fall into the trap of practicing favoritism or creating problems of that nature. In real practice, one tends to pay more attention to and spend more energy on developing one's social *guanxiwang;* one need not worry too much about one's blood *guanxi*—they are always there and "evergreen" and can be mobilized anytime one wants. One's social *guanxiwang* tends to follow a separate taxology such as primary vs. secondary, long term vs. short term, and close vs. casual. It is important to remember that one's social *guanxiwang* tends to be multitiered, following a hierarchy of systems and subsystems. For example, your ex-classmate, who has his or her own social *guanxiwang*, may be willing to share a portion of it with you, and as time goes on, those newly "enlisted," or rather, "given," members may gradually become your permanent resources.

Third, the Chinese *guanxi* system is reciprocal in nature. Nothing is worse than practicing *guanxi* like following a one-way traffic, which is "unethical" in the eyes of many Chinese. A person who only gets from and never gives back to *guanxi* is unethical, someone one should avoid or stop doing business with. Each time you get something from *guanxi*, you know you are in debt in terms of *renqing*. And when you have performed a positive role in another's practice of *guanxi*, you would wait and see how the person would treat you next time when you need his or her help. In other words, you would be sensitive to the reciprocity of *guanxi*. When, for any reason, you repeatedly failed to get what you had asked for from the person who had enlisted you as part of his or her *guanxiwang*, you might decide that it was a loss of face on your part and you wanted to stop doing business with him any more, using, more often than not, implicit communication. Many Westerners never quite learned the reciprocal nature of *guanxi* even when they considered themselves an ace player in the Chinese game of *guanxi*. It is never enough to say "thank you, my friend, that's very kind of you to have done all this for me," you must consciously realize you are in debt, not in money terms, but in terms of *renqing*, and remember you may have to pay it back one way or another or you risk losing this *guanxi* of yours, who could be very important in your future business. It is not necessarily one-for-one in a mechanical way—it is seldom that way as a matter of fact, but it should be reciprocal as a whole. People tend to resent the tendency in which one quickly pays off the debt, so to speak, and terminates *guanxi* when the deal is done. A one shot kind of practice of *guanxi* suggests low taste and opportunism to many Chinese.

Fourth, *guanxi* as an individual's social-business resource should be viewed more as a way of life and practiced as such. Western misunderstanding, and in some cases, resentment of, Chinese practice of *guanxi* is well understood, but is also culturally biased. It is important for Westerners as well as many of their Chinese counterparts to correct their perception of *guanxi* and accept the practice of it as a routine cultural ritual in Chinese society. In many situations, people practice *guanxi* not because they want to get something done, but because they simply want to demonstrate their allegiance to and appreciation of their *guanxi* or because they simply want to assert their Chineseness in that practicing *guanxi* makes them an active part of the social fabric, or because it is simply a matter of ritual. In other words, practicing *guanxi* is giving structure and order to social-business life even though *guanxi* itself has no formal structure. Few Westerners, and indeed not many Chinese, think that way. Too often people associate the practice of *guanxi* with Asian types of corruption. To me, with or without the practice of *guanxi*, Chinese are neither more nor less corrupt. This being said, I am not suggesting that *guanxi* or the practice of it is always good and clean. *Guanxi*, unethically practiced—which could well be the case with anybody anywhere—lowers its level to favoritism and backdoor behavior, which is common not only in Mainland China, but among Chinese communities elsewhere in the world. But it need not be that way. *Guanxi* can be clean and can be practiced in a clean way.[5]

If I have to use one Chinese term to describe what I call the common cultural framework of the Chinese, I would not hesitate a second to say *guanxi*. To me, it is not only the greatest social-business resource an individual Chinese can hope to have, but the most important defining characteristic of the Chinese CCF. Other components tend to be at the mercy of *guanxi*, including even entrepreneurial spirit under certain situations.

Entrepreneurial Spirit   If *guanxi* is defined as a person's external social-business resource, entrepreneurial spirit is one's internal source of power. An entrepreneur, as is understood in the West, is someone who runs a business at one's own financial risk. But Chinese basically are not adventurers; they are culturally too sophisticated to be adventurers. Entrepreneurial spirit, in the Chinese interpretation, is a person's great urge to succeed at whatever cost. This may not be adventuristic. Rather, the entrepreneur has the will to do what is necessary to be ready for the challenge. Look at those overseas Chinese. They started from practically nothing. They worked hard, twenty hours a day if necessary. They saved every penny they earned. They then put their life's savings into their children's education. Then they had their business, maybe a small family business. They succeeded. Were they not entrepreneurs? When they started, they had nothing to risk because they had practically nothing. After they were in, no matter how hard it was, they would hang on there until they succeeded. They knew they were not working for their personal success. They were building their small empire, brick by brick, for their family, their ancestors. If you go to Hong Kong, Indonesia, Malaysia, Thailand, anywhere in the world where there are successful ethnic Chinese, you would hear the same story over and over again. Ask Chinese billionaire Li Ka-shing how he succeeded in building his multi-billion dollar empire in Hong Kong, which has been expanded to include ventures in Mainland China, Canada, the United States, and other parts of the world. Ask millions of Chinese small family businesses. And ask some of today's superrich in Mainland China. Are they not entrepreneurs? We are indeed talking about a special kind of entrepreneurial spirit. It is one with a Confucian imprint. It is one that, like *guanxi*, defines, at least partly, the Chineseness of the Chinese. It has been there all along; you need not cultivate it; just sprinkle some water on it, it will bloom.

It is magic that when you have such entrepreneurial spirit, you are gifted to sniff out opportunities. And the moment you decide it will take you to success, you jump onto it. The past thirty years since early 1960s have been witness to such experience. Chinese seemed to be destined to suffer during certain historical periods. For example, in the late 1950s and early 1960s, China's Great Leap Forward movement launched by Mao and the three-year human-created natural disasters that followed the movement sent millions of Chinese to die of starvation. China was plunged into an utter chaos of lawlessness and orderlessness, where millions upon millions of Chinese intellectuals and other "undesirable elements" were singled out for physical and spiritual abuse in ways unheard of in history. Nobody knows how many people died in humiliation. Nobody can possibly measure the loss China as a nation suffered in the 1966–1976 Cultural Revolution. I am sure of one thing, however. That is, the entrepreneurial spirit of the Chinese remained strong, even though very much twisted, thanks to the long years of the socialist practice of the "iron rice bowl" guaranteed from cradle to grave.

As soon as Deng Xiaoping launched the economic reforms in late 1978 and later put forward his "cat theory," the long suppressed entrepreneurial spirit among Mainland Chinese began to gradually bloom again. Just read the economic figures that keep coming from that part of the world and you know what that means. Mainland China just represents a belated magic. This entrepreneurial spirit created magic that occurred earlier in Hong Kong and Taiwan, and with other Chinese businesses in other parts of East Asia as part of the overall East Asia boom that began in the early 1960s. The magic has been a typical Chinese refusal to remain in poverty and insignificance while seeing others do well. Taiwan's GDP per head around 1960 was only $160. Mainland China GDP per head in 1962 toward the end of the three-year human-created natural disasters was a miserable $60, the world's eleventh lowest. With almost a ten-year delay after Japan, Taiwan, Hong Kong, Singapore, and South Korea—half and three-quarters being Chinese—impressed the world with their rise from poverty with real GDPs doubling every eight years during 1960–1985 (around eightfold in all).[6] This mammoth growth was achieved mainly through their export-led industrial development. The Chinese economies, except Mainland China, which was waiting for its turn, sniffed out over thirty years ago that their chance of growth lay in trade. They all jumped onto it, and they succeeded.

The Chinese entrepreneurial spirit, unlike the entrepreneurial spirit in the West, which is defined largely by a person's willingness to take risks, is characterized by three elements: one's willingness to work hard, sometimes under extremely harsh conditions; one's willingness to save as much as possibly; and one's willingness to do whatever it takes to invest in education. Let me explain each in turn.

First, the Chinese are among the world's hardest workers when they know their efforts will be rewarded. I need not go far to look for evidence to prove this. The study Godwin Chu and I did, mentioned earlier in this chapter, revealed some interesting data in this regard. We asked an open question among our subjects: "What do you think is the most important element for career success?" Respondents were allowed to answer the question whichever way they liked. Based on 1,424 respondents who gave an answer, nearly half of them mentioned "diligence," a strong indication that the traditional Chinese value of diligence (and frugality) as a way of life was still there despite the disastrous ten-year Cultural Revolution. We asked another question related to a person's work ethic: "Which is more important to you, treasure your time and work as hard as possible, or life is short and enjoy it while you can?" Nearly nine out of ten respondents (89.7 percent) said "treasure your time and work as hard as possible." We also asked some other questions related to the theme. One was "What kind of person do you prefer as your workmate, someone with a high ability even though not a close friend, or a close friend who does not have a high ability?" Not to our surprise, an overwhelming 92 percent of our respondents would like his or her workmate to be one with outstanding work ability even though not a close friend. We also asked: "If you want to pick a coworker, which one would you prefer, someone who works very hard, but has no sense of humor, or someone who does a minimum of work, but is a lot of fun?" About four out of five of the Chinese sample would like to have one who works hard; having fun does not matter.

Second, entrepreneurial spirit is mere talk if one does not have a means of coming up with needed capital with which to invest. The Chinese, and their other East Asian counterparts as well, are very good at accumulating capital by, among other means, saving. The Chinese are among the world's greatest savers, which has been another important success factor for their economies in the past thirty years. According to an *Economist* report, by the 1990s East Asia excluding Japan, but with the Chinese economies and businesses as its backbone, was saving more that 36 percent of the GDP, unmatched in any of the rest of the world's economies, developed or developing. And they have been investing almost as much as they save. Mainland China's saving rate has been between 33 and 35 percent. I heard a story that tells how a Chinese farmer saves: When the farmer has accumulated 51 cents, he would borrow 49 cents from whomever he can borrow to make it one dollar, and deposit it in his bank account. He then forces himself to work hard to earn 49 cents to pay back the debt because he can not stand the idea of being in debt. His urge to save is so strong that he borrows to save! Saving has become the farmer's way of life and he enjoys it more than anything else.

Third, when you have money plus a pair of diligent hands, you are not yet entrepreneurial in its unique Chinese sense. You are not yet entrepreneurial because you cannot go very far. To succeed big, you need a smarter head. You need ideas. You need knowledge. You need to understand modern technology. Confucius says: "One who works with his mind (knowledge) rules; one who works with his hands is ruled." Whether you like it or not, this is still very much the reality of the world we are living in. A traditional Chinese saying goes: "In books there are houses piled with gold." The Chinese—here I am referring to individual Chinese, not the government—understand that education holds the key to a person's career success. You yourself might not be lucky enough to have parents who could afford to send you to school, but you do not want to see the same thing happen to your children. Most Chinese pin their hopes on their children, who are expected to become as glorious as "dragons," as a popular Chinese saying goes. In traditional China, the only venue for upward mobility was education. If one passed the state examinations, one could enter the world of imperial service. The value of education, except during certain historical periods like the Cultural Revolution in the Mainland, has all along been highly upheld. Most Chinese parents are willing to save every penny to ensure that their children have a good education. In our previously mentioned China study, we asked our subjects a key question: "What do you want most in life?" We gave fourteen possible goals for them to choose from. Quite to our expectation, "successful children" received the second highest endorsement (66.2%) after "warm and close family," which was the number one choice (79.8%). We also asked two similar questions: "if you have a son, how far will you support him in school? If you have a daughter, how far will you support her in school?" The results for sons and daughters were nearly identical. More than 80 percent of the Chinese are willing to support their sons and daughters through either college or graduate school.

Keep in mind that, in China, only a very small percentage of high school graduates can have the privilege to attend college due to the enormous size of the population and limited availability of educational resources.

The notion of Chinese entrepreneurial spirit, which consists of a person's willingness to work hard, willingness to save to accumulate capital, and willingness to invest in education, as an internal social-business resource is widely shared between Mainland Chinese and overseas Chinese even though they have been living in quite different social and political systems. Most Chinese believe, I venture to guess, that when one has what I wish to call the *Four Treasures;* a pair of diligent hands, capital, a good education, and *guanxi,* one can be said to have arrived at the starting line of his or her success. To make it to the finish line, however, one needs to do more. This leads me to the other side of the coin: the means of regulating social-business resources, the second half of the Chinese CCF.

Social Hierarchy and Role Communication as Regulating of Social-Business Resources

Concrete means of regulating social-business resources are too many to list. But I would only discuss two broad categories, social hierarchy and role communication, which I believe, together with *guanxi* and entrepreneurial spirit based on pragmatic rationalism, define the nature of the Chinese CCF. Social hierarchy and role communication, both of which are humanistic-rationalistic in nature, are as uniquely Chinese as *guanxi* and entrepreneurial spirit.

Social Hierarchy   Respect for social hierarchy has been in Chinese society as long as Confucianism has defined, or participated in defining, the Chinese way of life. Even under Communism, which vowed to fight for social equality, social hierarchy was never quite removed from the Chinese soil; it only existed in different forms. Social hierarchy, instead of being treated as an end of Chinese society, is, in this context, viewed as a Chinese means of regulating social-business resources. This is very different from Western democracy, which is also more a means than an end. In a democracy, a decision is made based on many votes one has collected. In a society where social hierarchy is respected, one person's voice could be more decisive than a thousand votes. Which is a more effective means? The answer is, it depends. One thing I can say for sure is that Western type of democracy can hardly have a chance to land in China. It would be like pouring oil into water; they cannot become one.

I am neither for nor against democracy, which is neither good nor bad; it is a means. At this stage, China, as a society with a clearly definable social hierarchy that has been in force for thousands of years albeit in different forms, would, in my estimation, reject democracy for another fifty years. But Chinese people definitely need more liberty and freedoms, which is different from the notion of democracy. And having more liberty and freedoms does not necessarily mean less respect for social hierarchy. People do not understand that it is not just one hardliner or two who do not want democracy; it is the people, the Chinese people, who are not yet ready. If you disagree, ask the close to 1 billion Chinese peasants who until recently never quite left their land to steal a glimpse of the outside world. The peasants would say, if "democracy" is eatable like rice, give me one bag. Ask Chinese entrepreneurs who are now busy making money. If "democracy" is $100 a piece, a capital-hungry manager would not mind having some. And ask people from other sectors of social life who are struggling to get ahead economically. I guess they would tell you they do not want democracy, they want to be rich. Rich first, then democracy, they would say. When the Chinese are thirsty, they still look to Beijing for water. People still feel more comfortable calling their boss "Manager Li" or "Director Zhang" or "Secretary Wang" or simply "Head!" This is still a Chinese society, a very hierarchical one. Let me discuss, very briefly, three issues related to Chinese social hierarchy as a means of regulating social-business resources: the role of government, decision making, and social positioning.

The role of government should never be underestimated in regulating social-business resources in Chinese society. The role of government, when perceived in the context of social hierarchy, becomes the highest level of a certain social system, whether you are talking about the central government or a local one. In terms of regulating resources, Beijing has much more power to enjoy and much larger freedom to exercise it than Washington and probably any other industrialized nation on earth. Arguing which government is better, an authoritarian one or a democratically elected one, misses the point. The point is that if you have any serious business to do in China, you must have the support of the Chinese government at whichever level. If endorsement from the highest level of the social hierarchy, which is government, is lacking, you are dead even though you are still moving around. All Chinese know that and will work as hard as possible to get it, willingly or unwillingly.

Many Chinese willingly seek instructions from their government like children seeking advice from their parents. Government officials, in traditional China, were called *fumugan,* or "Father-Mother Officials," who were expected to take care of all aspects of a subject's life. What if your "Father-Mother Official" were corrupt? You would wait for a cleaner one to arrive to replace him. In present Chinese society, even though governments at various levels have been suffering from loss of credibility, they are still powerful. People no longer view them as "Father-Mother Officials" from whom to seek advice, but the former would still expect the latter to take care of all aspects of social or even business life. And this has some serious implications on how businesses are conducted in China. For example, if anything has gone wrong in your business, your immediate reaction is not to go to a professional for advice, but to seek government help. The government consciously knows it, and that is why it keeps growing in its bureaucratic apparatus at all levels. I am not just referring to mainland China; the governments in Hong Kong and Taiwan are also implied.

Decision making in a hierarchically structured system, where authority is respected, could neglect participation by ordinary system members, but can also be fast and efficient. Deals that involve billions of dollars can be decided upon within a matter of days, with or without participation of only a handful of people at the very top. This could be intuitively risky, but can also pay off big in an environment where change is the only constant and fast decision making can be crucial. High-speed decision making is one of the most important ingredients in high-speed management, a fast growing area of intensive academic inquiry in the United States. It may be interesting to note, ironically, that the best high-speed managers may not be found in the United States. They can well be some Chinese tycoons who know little about the theory of high-speed management but who can say "go" to a billion dollar deal like throwing a little stone into a pond, with style. Bureaucratic hierarchy slows action and creates tons of red tape, but not necessarily the hierarchy in the owner's hand. There is an essential difference between a typical Western management system and a typical entrepreneurial Chinese management system. In the former the decision-making power is in the hands of the CEO chosen by the Board of Directors and a multiplicity of management layers that report to the CEO or an appropriate level. In the latter it is solely the design of the owner who, for example, may put his son in the top management position to get him firsthand experience, and the son goes the direction where his father points. There could also be bureaucratic management layers in the latter, but they can be slashed or neglected any time the father or his son deems necessary. Loyalty and obedience from the lower management and employees is expected, and everybody knows that the owner is the decision maker. As I said previously, this could intuitively be risky, and the level of risk increases along with the increasing size and complexity of the business and organization. Things are changing though. Western-trained young professionals who are sons and daughters of business owners in Taiwan and Hong Kong are blowing some fresh air into this very much closed decision-making system. For example, Li Ka-shing's two sons are both American trained, and it is unlikely that Li's empire will not be influenced by what they learned in the United States. But Chinese respect for social hierarchy, along with other traditional Confucian values, is so deeply rooted in people's psychology that it will not be swept away by Western management wind. I think it will continue to exert its influence on decision-making processes in Chinese businesses and organizations, not just in Hong Kong and Taiwan but also in mainland China where state-owned enterprises are being transferred into private or collective ownership.

Social positioning refers to how a social member is positioned and positions himself or herself in the social hierarchy that he or she consciously knows should be respected. It is like taking one's designated seat in a theater or a stadium. That is how order is maintained, assuming this is the order all social members agree to uphold. A culturally respected member in the social hierarchy respects the existing social structure, where everyone has a place to stay and is supposed to remain there. It is easy to be told where you stand. It takes an awful lot of social skill and sophistication to find your place and stay there. The Chinese Communist revolution attempted to destroy the existing social order—quite successfully.

But the old social hierarchy was replaced by a new one. The position of emperor was replaced by the chairmanship of the party. The traditional "Father-Mother Officials" were now party officials. And so on down the line. The new social order is now fast returning to the old again, with modifications and confusion. Whichever order you are in, you are in a hierarchy and must find your position, probably more so in Mao's period than either earlier or later on. Social hierarchy, tacitly understood among social members, may follow a more complex taxonomy than many of us think it does. It not only defines how power is shared, but categorizes and then regulates such social-business resources as wealth, age, education, seniority, and experience.

As I said before, it would be easier to be told where to position than to position oneself. The real challenge lies in how one learns to take one's position in the social hierarchy in a given system, whether in an organization or in a particular social context. Positioning occurs at different levels: division of labor, task assignment, value congruence, need compatibility, and observance of social rituals. One who lacks the seniority or experience or talent or *guanxi* would not ask for promotion to a senior managerial position, but would stay at a lower level and be happy. "Let me vacuum the floor. It's my job!" you may say to your colleague in the office who you know is older than you are. Zhou Enlai would always walk a step behind Mao to show his humbleness each time they had a public appearance either in the Great Hall of the People or at the rostrum of Tiananmen. Premier Zhou was never confused about his position in relation to Chairman Mao. Had he been half a step confused, he should have been eliminated like Liu Shaoqi[7] during the Cultural Revolution, I guess. And all Chinese understood 100 percent the way their premier behaved. Therefore even the observance or violation of social rituals could have serious consequences on whether or not one is determined to be socially mature. I used to teach at a Chinese university in Shanghai. I knew who I was and my students knew who they were, and we were never confused about our positions. If we, for example, walked into a meeting room where there was only one soft armchair and all other seats were wooden. Almost always as expected, the students would put me in the armchair before they took their seats. This has never happened in my experience in the United States since I came to teach here quite a while ago; students were never culturally programmed to behave that way. Indeed I would intentionally take a wooden seat to assert equality between professor and students. China and the United States are very different in social hierarchical structure and the handling of it.

Social positioning is closely related to role communication, which is a means with which to reinforce the existing social hierarchy. I will end this chapter with a brief discussion of role communication that I believe characterizes, in addition to *guanxi*, entrepreneurial spirit, and social hierarchy, the common cultural framework of the Chinese. Like social hierarchy, role communication is used to regulate social-business resources in a uniquely Chinese way.

Role Communication   Role communication is a process where interactants use communication to emphasize each other's role identity. "I" identity tends to be suppressed in the interaction. According to not a few communication scholars in the United States, only interpersonal communication is high-quality communication—one where interactants reveal who they are and assert their "I" identity. Role communication, with interactants' individuality suppressed, is superficial. This is a half-truth. To me, role communication is as high in quality in China as interpersonal communication is in the United States. Indeed, in China as well as in the United States, or in any other culture, interpersonal communication can never occur without interactants playing a certain role, the role of a parent, a daughter, a son, a friend, a lover, a talker, or a listener. In the United States, it is possible that one, when talking with one's parents, is more a unique "Michael" or "Jennifer" than a son or daughter. In a typical Chinese family, one talks more like a son or daughter—one's role—than as a unique self. Which is higher in quality? To the Chinese, talking like a son or daughter when one is talking with one's parents is more acceptable, hence higher quality, culturally speaking. Confucius says: Behave like a father when you are a father; behave like a son when you are a son. This is the essence of role communication, which, as a ritual, is performed to maintain the existing social hierarchy and further regulates social-business resources.

To make a clearer case, let me take the issue to the extreme. Suppose you are greeting a person who happens to occupy a higher social or organizational position. If this were your section chief, you lean your body a little bit forward to show your humbleness. If this were your division head, you bow 30 degrees. If he were the CEO of your company, you bow 45 degrees. If, all of a sudden, this person changed to the governor of your province, you bow further down to 90 degrees. Then, my goodness, the "last emperor" is standing right in front of you. Instead of bowing, you kneel down and kowtow to the ground. This looks like something that happened a long, long time ago. People no longer bow that much and seldom kowtow unless in a ceremony worshipping one's ancestors. However, in present day mainland China, as well as in Hong Kong and Taiwan I guess, an average Chinese would still work hard weighing between 30 and 45 and 90 degrees not necessarily in bowing behavior but in other role communication situations.

Language is a primary tool with which to conduct role communication. My son has been fast adjusting to American way of life including the use of what I call nondiscriminatory language in role situations. In a Chinese context, children learned to be careful in the use of *you* or *she* or *he* or *they* when talking or referring to their parents. Instead of saying "What do you think?" one should say "What does Dad think?" with the father being right there. And my son does not quite buy that. When he comes home, for example, he could ask Grandma: "Where are they?" He means father and mother. I would insist, teaching him how to communicate in a Chinese way, that he ask "Where are Dad and Mom?" If he is talking to his uncle, he would have to learn to make role statements like "Would uncle have time to have dinner with Dad and Mom?" and "Uncle should take care of yourself."

In formal business situations, I would call, for example, the manager of a factory "Manager Wang" or "Manager Li" instead of using his or her given name. In a face-to-face discussion, I would say "Would Manager Wang like me to present a written proposal?" or "May I have the pleasure of inviting Manager Li to come to visit with our facility at any time Manager Li thinks convenient?" In other words, I would try hard to avoid the use of *you*. In China, this is called *giving face* or *gaimianzi*.

Face, *mianzi* or *lian,* is an extremely important variable in role communication, in the process of which you are concerned not only about your face, but about another's face. If you fail to give face to another this time, you risk "losing face," called *diulian,* next time, depending on how serious the situation is. Lin Yutang[8] writes:

> Face is psychological and not physiological. Interesting as the Chinese physiological face is, the psychological face makes a still more fascinating study. It is not a face that can be washed or shaved, but a face that can be "granted" and "lost" and "fought for" and "presented as a gift." . . . Abstract and intangible, it is yet the most delicate standard by which Chinese social intercourse is regulated. . . . Face cannot be translated or defined. It is like honor and is not honor. It is hollow and is what men fight for and what many women die for. It is invisible and yet by definition exists by being shown to the public. It exists in the ether and yet cannot be heard, and sounds eminently respectable and solid. It is amenable, not to reason but to social convention.

To me, face is more an interpersonal construct than part of a person's psychological entity. Face is a person's public image one claims for a set of roles one plays. A manager may enjoy being perceived as a generous person while in fact he is a miser, which he himself may know very well. But this public perception is part of his face, and he will fight to preserve it if he decides this is an important social resource. One of the most important functions of role communication is to assert one's face or give face to another, which is more a performance of a ritual than seeking instrumental goals. A master communicator is one who accomplishes what one intends to accomplish and gives another enough face so that he or she will be equally happy. This is particularly useful in negotiations and handling of conflicts.

In business negotiations with Chinese, a higher ranking Western negotiator could get more than a lower ranking, one not necessarily because the former has better negotiation skills but because the Chinese may give him or her (or, rather, his or her rank) more face. Confrontational and aggressive negotiation styles could particularly be agitating and annoying to the Chinese because such styles are generally deemed to be unsophisticated and subject one to the risk of losing face. The best way to negotiate with Chinese is to never forget to give face. It almost always pays to send someone whose Chinese counterpart at the negotiation table is a former friend; no matter how tough this Chinese negotiator is, he or she would be willing to give some face to the friend. It is a dangerous situation when the face of a Chinese negotiator is completely lost. It is dangerous because he or she may turn around to do whatever is possible to tear your face apart, called *sipolianpi*—and this could indeed be a last resort to restore face. If the American government wants a deal with its Chinese counterpart and the deal a tough one, send Nixon or Kissinger or Bush over. They would each get more than a nonfriend. That is what *guanxi* is, is it not? Things like what happened in the Yinghe incident on the Indian Ocean in 1993 could be very dangerous. It was very unusual that the Chinese did not blow up even under the pressure of a whole group of generals. That is not a good way to solve conflicts with the Chinese. Nothing could be more ineffective than imposing sanctions on the Chinese to solve a conflict or make them change behavior. China is big and has a big space to move around. Economic sanctions will have little chance to work no matter how hurting they could be. The Chinese would be more concerned about how much face they will lose than about how much business they will lose. And they would retaliate one way or another to tear your face apart in order to reclaim their lost face. This part of Chineseness is never quite understood by the West. On the one hand, the Chinese can be extremely pragmatic, so pragmatic that they can become opportunistic; on the other hand, the same Chinese can be extremely sensitive, defensive, and idealistic when it comes to a big face thing, in which case they may want to practice a different kind of rationalism, tear your face apart. It is called "attack poison with poison." Chinese are all that way, not just Mainland Chinese or Taiwanese Chinese.

NOTES

1. This so-called cat theory was one of the weapons that the Chinese reformists used to counterattack, in the early years of the economic reforms, hardliners who claimed that reformists were betraying the ideal of socialism.

2. *Sangang,* i.e., the Three Cardinal Principles, refers to *jun wei chen gang,* or ruler guides subject; *fu wei zi gang,* or father guides son; and *fu wei qi gang,* or husband guides wife.

3. It is always risky to criticize another culture's social institution as being immoral or unethical using one's own cultural criteria because morality and ethics are in themselves cultural formulations.

4. The findings of that study were reported in Chu and Ju's *The Great Walls in Ruins: Communication and Cultural Change in China* (Albany: SUNY Press, 1993).

5. In this sense, it is absolutely necessary that a Westerner who is going to China to represent a Western company receive a special training in the "Chinese Practice of *guanxi*."

6. For details, refer to *The Economist* (October 1993).

7. Liu, the late chairman of the People's Republic of China, was stripped of power by Mao for his allegedly anti-Mao policies. Liu died as a result of cruel physical and spiritual abuse at the hands of Mao's Red Guards during the Cultural Revolution.

8. Lin was a prominent contemporary Chinese scholar. The quote was from his *My Country and My People* (New York: John Day Company, 1939), pp. 199–200.

CHAPTER 13

Communicating Change in Australia

Robyn Johnston

INTRODUCTION

[handwritten margin note: Students learn How the Aus's Train their work force]

The last decade has been an era of turbulence for Australian organizations. The floating of the Australian dollar, deregulation of banking, mergers and takeovers in the private sector, downsizing in both the public and private sector, the emergence of the environmental movement as a real political force along with the growth of the economies of Asia, and the lifting of a protectionist trade policy are among the factors that have both created and resulted from such turbulence. As a consequence both employers and employees have recognized well that they must learn to survive in what is commonly referred to as an age of *discontinuity* and in Morgan's (1988) words, to ride the white water.

Learning to operate in this environment has led to considerable change in many Australian organizations. New approaches have been initiated by organizational leaders both in response to government policy and as they search for more efficient and effective strategies to attain organizational competitiveness. With the introduction of new systems, processes, and approaches, the role of communication in organizational functioning has received increased attention and the need for organizational communication competence has been recognized.

INDUSTRIAL RELATIONS REFORM

Significant change has occurred in the industrial relations domain. Until recently Australia has had one of the highest rates of unioniz-

[handwritten margin note: What parts of This could be used for org to change itself]

ation in the world, with an arbitration system that has encouraged the formation and growth of unions. During the 1980s and 1990s there has been a steady decline in trade union membership in Australia, particularly with the fall of employment within the manufacturing sector and a growth of jobs in the service sector, where unionism has traditionally been weakest. By the end of the decade approximately 300 unions represented 45 percent of the working population. The decline has been most severe in the private sector where only about 33 percent of the work force was unionized by 1990.

Our response to the decline in membership has been the movement to reduce the large number of small unions through amalgamations into larger unions based on industry groupings. Commentators argue that this move will lead to improved labor-management relations (Lansbury and Spillane 1991). At the same time the union movement generally has supported the reconstruction of many of the industrial awards to which union members have worked. Archaic restrictive work practices are being eliminated from awards and new job classification structures created. These revisions have encouraged the broadening of jobs and the deepening of skills at the enterprise level as unions accept the need for a multiskilled work force.

Such revisions have taken place in a climate that has allowed for increased employer-employee communication with a trend toward greater participation by employees in aspects of decision making at industry and enterprise levels. Changes in approach by the key industrial relations body, the Australian Industrial Relations Commission, and recent pronouncements of the High Court have clearly played an important part in the reshaping of Australian industrial relations and creating a more consensual climate. Lansbury and Spillane (1991, 264) claim: "The changes in approach of both these bodies in terms of the encouragement of a more informing and participative style of management is significant."

An example of the heightened focus on communication can be seen in the decision resulting from the social welfare union case of 1983. This decision established the requirement for employers to notify the union (in this case the Federated Clerks Union) and employees of any decision to begin feasibility studies concerning technological change, to consult and to advise these groups as soon as any decision was made. Further, the employer was also obliged to consult with the union and employees on the issue of alternative proposals. One judge, in summing up, commented that the workers' claim "is a demand to be treated as more than wage hands, to be treated as men and women who should be informed about decisions that might materially affect their future and to be consulted on them. It is a demand . . . to be treated with respect and dignity." In industrial relations terms this case challenged the existing definition of managerial rights previously accepted by industrial courts.

In a similar vein the following year saw the termination, change and redundancy decision, with the Australian Industrial Relations Commission giving workers rights to information and consultation with employers over plans for technological change and organizational restructuring to be set down in awards.

Interest in employee participation is not new as unions have sought industrial democracy since the 1970s. Perceptions of progress toward this goal, however, can been linked to the establishment of the Accord of 1983 between the union movement and the Hawke opposition and then government. Australian Council of Trade Unions (ACTU) officials have argued that the accord represented a blueprint for industrial democracy. It was seen as encouraging greater employee participation at the national industry enterprise and workplace levels.

The union movement has not been alone in its endorsement of increased participative practice in the workplace. The support of employer groups was shown in the joint ACTU/CAI Statement on Participative Practices in 1988, which asserted "communication, information sharing and consultation are the keys to developing co-operation and a spirit of trust between management and the worker" (ACTU/CAI 1988, 7). Similarly, the Business Council of Australia (BCA), formed in 1983 to represent the views of large private sector employers, summed up its position stating: "Employee participation with its primary focus on the individual employee would contribute significantly to personal development, attitudinal change, healthy relationships at work, increased productivity and economic revitalization." With recent trends toward enterprise agreements, the focus on increased communication and joint consultation between employers and employees has continued. A review of the first 100 agreements by the Department of Industrial Relations (1992) showed that many agreements contained provisions for consultative mechanisms to facilitate the development and implementation of changes to workplace.

Much of this increased workplace consultation has taken place through joint consultative committees (JCC), which have been established in both unionized and nonunionized workplaces. The extent, nature and effectiveness of such committees was recently measured through the Australian Workplace Industrial Relations Survey. This survey was conducted into 2358 workplaces with five or more employees. Marchington (1992), in analyzing responses to this survey, reports that two thirds of the respondents to the survey indicated that the main objectives they sought through the formation of joint consultative committees was improved communication between employers and employees. The AWIRS data also indicated that most participants were highly satisfied with the operations of the consultative committees. Ninety percent of managers surveyed claimed that the JCC had improved their relations with employees.

In summary, then, from a macro perspective of industrial relations, a trend to greater employee participation in determining work practice can be observed in Australia. Put another way, work environments are more communicative because of changing approaches to industrial relations. This process, however, is not being achieved without difficulty. Tensions exist between unions and employers about primary communication channels. Many employers do not accept that the unions and their representatives should be the single conduit of communication with employees.

A second issue concerns the lack of power preparation for participation. To illustrate, the Administrative and Clerical Officers Association (ACOA) claimed that so many initiatives for union and management consideration have flourished that unions have not been able to offer adequate responses because they have not had the resources to train staff for joint consultation (Lansbury and Spillane 1991, 205).

ORGANIZATIONAL RESTRUCTURING

Another expression of the more communicative organizational environment has arisen through organizational restructuring. Outcomes from such restructuring, facilitated by the advent and adoption of new technologies and the broadening of industrial awards, have included the establishment of self-managing multiskilled work teams working on specific assignments in some organizations (e.g., steel refining, Shell Refining, ICI plants, Tubemakers Pty Ltd, Boyer Mills in Tasmania). In other organizations there has been a heightened focus on team work. Accompanying the move to a more team-oriented approach has been a recognition that the communication skills required to work in such teams are as essential as the broader range of technical skills. For example, Bishop and Graham (1992), in a case study describing the implementation of self-managing teams in the Boyer Mill in Tasmania, cite examples of training module development that has taken place to support the introduction of self-directed work teams. Modules such as interpersonal communication, working together, and team decision making are among the portfolio of materials being developed to ensure effective implementation.

QUALITY APPROACHES

An interest in quality and the adoption and adaptation in many large organizations of customer-focused systems of total quality management has resulted in a heightened awareness of the importance of workplace communication. The concept of quality initially appeared with the quality circle movement in the late 1970s. These circles met with only isolated success. The 1980s has seen the evolution of the TQM approach in more all-embracing programs of change that attempt to alter the entire operational stance of many organizations. There is evidence of increasing interest in this approach to workplace functioning in both the public and private sector (Osborne 1991) to the extent that the former premier of NSW Nick Greiner (1992) asserted that the philosophies and practices of TQM were to be adopted by the NSW Public Services. There has been to date no indication from the current Premier that his policy direction should change. Evidence of the acceleration of interest in quality issues can also be seen in the proliferation of organizations servicing the quality movement and the number of corporate members of the largest of these organizations, the Australian Quality Council. This organization, which supports research, education, and implementation of quality programs and conferences in both large and small organizations, has 900 corporate members.

The relationship between quality approaches and enhanced workplace communication was recently emphasized at the First International Quality Management Institute Conference (1993), Quality and Organisational Culture Change, held in Australia. At this conference a number of speakers signaled the importance of training staff in dimensions of communication and team work and in communicating progress of programs for the successful implementation of successful quality programs. Similarly Anna Booth, joint national secretary of the Textile and Clothing Union of Australia, in reviewing the effect of a best practice program initiated to develop models of quality change programs, cited the following as desired outcomes for workplace change programs directed to achievement of quality:

> Whilst it would be wrong to be put forward one formula for a workplace achieving Best Practice there are certain features we should aspire to:
> The process of management
>
> - flatter management structure replacing old hierarchical ones
> - communication and consultation replacing the dictates from on high and the outmoded notion of managerial prerogative
> - cellular workteams, self directed workgroups regulating their own affairs.

She also called for "an emphasis for raising the levels of English language literacy and numeracy as a base to build further skills and for improving communications between management and workforce and between employees" (1993, 85).

These themes pertaining to the importance of communication in quality programs have also been reflected in writing and case study reports from this area. For example, Gray (1993, 7) argued, "Communication handled well can provide strong support to the quality process providing it transfers meaning." He accentuated the importance of knowing what to communicate, the importance of face-to-face supervisor-employee communication, and emphasized that communication is more than words, stating "actions, and workplace experiences and examples are often more powerfully communicative than organisational communication by the traditional communicative media."

Additional evidence of the emphasis being given to communication in quality change programs can be seen in a case study describing the internal communication strategy implemented by the South Queensland Electricity Board (Flynn 1993). The internal communications strategy adopted by this organization included the incorporation of internal communication activities with corporate planning. Each SQEB division and region was asked to include activities relating to improving communication with staff members in their divisional strategic plan. There was an encouragement of management by walking around, with supervisors being urged to regularly leave their office to talk informally with staff. The program was supported by staff consultative committees—a mechanism designed in response to a staff survey that indicated a need for staff members to be given opportunity to present ideas and suggestions. Team briefing sessions were initiated to provide accurate up-to-date information on policy issues and to allow time for the identification of difficulties resulting from these policies. A rumor hotline was established with clarification of rumors being provided weekly by computer network or staff notice boards. An in-house magazine was also maintained. In an evaluation of this five-pronged approach to communication staff members indicated increased communication satisfaction (Flynn 1993).

Another facet of the search for quality in Australian organizations has been adoption of quality assurance practices. Many Australian organizations are currently documenting work practices and procedures to attain quality endorsement for their products and services. Both in establishing quality systems and the associated documentation process many organizations have had to confront and address problems resulting from literacy and linguistic deficiencies of members of their work force. A number of workplaces have embarked on literacy in the workplace programs to remedy these deficiencies. These programs although focusing on the reading ability of participants are also addressing the more general area of communication competence.

Thus the need for and processes associated with "reconstruction" have led to a heightened focus on communication in the workplace. Both the changing industrial relations environment along with new organizational structures and approaches are resulting in increasing opportunities for employee participation in decision making and hence a more communicative organizational climate.

THE NEW MANAGER

Paralleling the search for organizational quality has been an emphasis on developing the skills of Australian managers and in this endeavor an increased focus on communication can also be observed. In a benchmark study of management development in Australian private enterprises, commissioned by the National Board of Employment, Education and Training (1990), a survey of Australian CEOs highlighted the importance of "the ability to communicate and the ability to motivate" as the most important factors for progression to senior levels of management in Australian organizations (1990, 7). This report argued that, although the practice of management development is well established in Australian organizations, the absolute amount remains low at approximately four days attendance at development programs per manager per year. The report also established that the priorities for management development are mainly in the "softer areas of leadership, vision and entrepreneurship rather than in functional expertise." With one exception the functional competence of Australian managers was highly rated. Critical areas for improvement that were identified included communicating plans and instructions, building interpersonal relationships, leadership, and team building.

This survey revealed that respondents nominated short courses as the most effective method for achieving development goals. There is extensive provision of short course training programs for managers provided by tertiary institutions, in-house training, and external providers, particularly since the passing of the training guarantee legislation. Many of these programs have a considerable focus on transformational approaches to management and leadership and include sessions directed at the skills of vision creation and capacity to communicate that vision. The importance of communication for effective management is also reflected through professional development journals for practitioners. Advice to managers to address their communication practice "that the performance of most organisations and the quality of working life of their employees depend upon the quality of management communication" (Hockley 1991) are relatively commonplace.

TRAINING REFORM AGENDA

The reconstruction process has revealed that insufficient attention to work-force development in past years has led to an underskilled work force in Australia. The Australian federal government has responded to this situation with its national training reform agenda, which has elevated the status of workplace learning. Vocational training has become a significant part of the business development strategy and is being seen as an element in increasing organizational effectiveness. This has meant that, particularly for enterprises that have been among the "early changers" to modern systems of skill formation, there has been a shift from traditional training values, beliefs, strategies, and practices and the emergence of a new culture associated with training and the need for organizational learning (Whitely 1993).

The training reform agenda has proposed change on a broad front. It has involved ongoing efforts by federal and state governments, the industrial relations system, the ACTU, and employer groups to influence the emergence of large-scale and systematic employment-based training in the private sector (Carter and Gribble 1992). The implementation of the often-criticized training guarantee legislation, to increase industry and enterprise commitment and contribution to training, is one aspect of such reform initiatives. The training reform agenda has also promoted increased collaboration between higher education, vocational education, and industry, a move to nationally consistent training and accreditation and the implementation of a competency-based training system that allows for the recognition of prior learning and current competencies.

Development of National Industry Competency Standards

Central to a number of the training reform agenda initiatives has been the development of sets of national industry competency standards. These competency standards are the productes of industry Competency Standards Boards (CSBs). Currently there are CSBs for thirty-nine industry groups covering 80 percent of all workers. Each board has the prime responsibility for overseeing the development of a set of competency standards for the industry and those occupations within the industry it represents. These standards, once endorsed by the National Training Board, establish the specifications for the kinds and levels of knowledge and skill to the standard required for employment in that industry. Competency standards are based upon the structure of work within a particular industry and expressed in terms of workplace outcomes (National Training Board 1992).

While varying methodologies are being used by CSBs to establish occupational standards, such as DACUM techniques, functional analysis, delphi techniques, focus groups and interview, all standards are being written to a standardized format made up of units, elements and performance criteria that describe the performance of elements within the unit. A second important common feature of all sets of industry competency standards is that they have been developed in consultation with those working in the particular industry. The standards, therefore, reflect what currently happens in industry and the essential skills and attributes needed by employees to carry out their workplace activities. The industry parties and the National Training Board are confident of having 50 percent of the work force covered by industry competency standards by the end of 1993 and are aiming for 90 percent of the work force covered by the end of 1995 (NTB Network 1993).

Sets of endorsed competency standards, which are subject to regular review to ensure they represent the competencies required by workers within a level and an industry, will form the basis of training and vocational education for initial training and up-skilling, reskilling, and multiskilling. Delivery, assessment, and certification of training is to be related to the identification and demonstrated attainment of the knowledge, skills, and effective performance as detailed in the national competency standards.

Industry competency standards therefore form the basis for building employee career paths within an industry and across industries where there is evidence of common competencies by comparing sets of competency standards from various industries and occupations it is possible to see similarities and differences in the competencies required in different occupations and between different levels within occupations or industries. This information can be used to establish training programs that will help eliminate skill deficits thereby increasing employers' opportunities to move either horizontally to another occupation or vertically to a position of increasing complexity. Competency standards form the benchmarks for vocational education and training. They can be used to ensure that occupational training programs are relevant to industry needs and provide the basis for greater consistency for Australian work-force development. Although there is concern that such standards do not always encapsulate some of the more nebulous or difficult to define elements necessary for excellence in the workplace such as vision, creativity, or imagination (Ramsey 1993), they provide, at least in x-ray form, a picture of what the employee who is to take the Australian economy to the year 2000 within an industry should "look like."

② *Australian Standards Framework*

A second major component of the training reform agenda has been the establishment of the Australian Standards Framework (ASF) by the National Training Board. This framework provides a ladderlike structure with each of the eight steps of this ladder generally defining a level of work practice for Australian industry. The characteristics of each level are described in a general way rather than reflecting the performance requirements of a particular industry or enterprise. Positions requiring the possession of basic or minimal competencies to perform routine proceduralized tasks with extensive supervision would be attributed to ASF level 1–2 status. Positions requiring more refined or higher level differing competencies would be aligned to higher level status. Levels 6–8 are generally attributed to positions dependent on high-level theoretical and applied knowledge that have required expensive training or experience and in which the participant will operate with autonomy and may be accountable for the output of others. Industry competency standards are aligned to ASF levels with the standards documents showing the clusters of units of competence within an industry that are necessary for each ASF level of performance. The framework allows for a recognition that not all industries have employees working at each of the eight ASF levels.

The framework is designed to provide a bridge between the competency requirements of the workplace and the vocational and educational training system. It facilitates articulation between different levels or fields of study and the movement between various types of education (on-the-job, TAFE, university) and education and employment. The framework also assists with allowing for

comparability and achieving consistency of levels within and between industries (NTB networks 1993, 8).

Competency Recognition and Assessment

A third dimension of the training reform agenda concerns the
assessment and recognition of skills and attributes of members of
the work force. The reform agenda, which has encouraged extensive industry participation in shaping the training and vocational
education system, has stimulated the increased use of workplace-
based competency approaches to training. This in turn has led to
the need for more systematic methods of workplace-based assessment of competency.

The reform agenda has also legitimized acknowledging the pri-
or learning of employees. As a result employees will have greater
opportunity to demonstrate their possession of competencies as
outlined in industry competency standards. No longer will the
possession of a degree or diploma or time-based qualification from
a formally accredited institution be the sole method for being considered skilled in an area to the required level. Currently industry
and organizations are developing mechanisms through which employees can demonstrate their competence however this competence has been gained. This process commonly referred to as recognition of prior learning (RPL) does not give credit simply for
experience. RPL programs do, however, allow people credit for the
skills they have and can demonstrate, whether those skills were
gained through formal programs of study or from incidental or
informal learning.

This increased activity in assessing workplace competence
however gained is therefore leading to the formalization of the
work role of workplace assessment. Competency standards for
workplace assessors have been established and endorsed by the
National Training Board. Workplace assessors will have as a prime
role the responsibility for assessing employees attaining levels of
competence as specified through industry and the related enterprise standards.

Communication Dimensions of the Training

These three interrelated dimensions of the training reform agenda
have therefore given impetus to exploring the question of what

employees at various levels of competence within specific industries of the 1990s should look like. In the process traditional expectations of employee competence have become outmoded in much the same way as conventions of management practice have limited relevance in our changing work environments. One particular dimension of employee competence that would seem to be the focus of increased attention is related to communication competency. The need for such competency is well illustrated in the following comments describing the essential skills of workers in the reformed Australian workplaces.

For example, Laurie Carmichael, assistant secretary of the ACTU and chairman and author of the Carmichael report argued in 1989, "Let's see what kind of skills are predicted by new forms of work organisation. If you are looking for people who will exercise responsibility, deliver quality and work co-operatively, they need interpersonal skills. They need communication skills. They need a range of skills that sit alongside of their technical and dexterous skills. That wasn't there before." In a similar vein researcher Giselle Mawer (1992) commented: "The new competencies needed in the restructured workplace include co-operation, communication, working in groups, decision making and multicultural skills. Standards for managers and team leaders need therefore to include an emphasis on these skills as well." These two excepts certainly highlight the centrality of communication competency on the part of both workers and managers for the reconstructed organizations in Australia.

Although popular management writers, communication academics, and those describing generally the requirements of the new worker may herald the importance of communication, for communication competence to be really recognized as an essential element of the workplace for employees of the future it needs to be formally included in national industry competency standards, as these documents will provide the blueprints for institutional and workplace-based training and education. The documents will also provide a consistent basis for the assessment of workplace competency and potentially organizational reward and promotion systems. A study that examined the communication dimensions of industry competency standards was conducted by Johnston in 1993.

From this study of a sample of industry competency standards documents it could be seen that communication was being identified as an essential competency required by workers at a range of ASF levels. Analysis of the sample also revealed that communication competencies were identified as discrete skills or units of competence as well as embedded in other identified skills.

This study also sought to determine which dimensions or sub-skills of communication were being nominated as necessary for workplace competence and whether particular skills were associated with various levels of workplace activity. Analysis by levels showed that at lower skill levels (ASF 1 and 2) the required listed competencies included receiver and reactive skills such as understand basic information and instructions, receive and acknowledge feedback. Such skills were not listed as frequently in higher level industry standards. Analysis by levels further revealed that required competence for lower level employees included what could be called the reproductive communication skills involving the application of industry or enterprise communication protocols like formal correspondence, telephone answering, responding to simple or routine questions, relaying messages, following instructions. In some industries there was a requirement for more proactive involvement and communication of the lowest skilled employees. For example, employees of the clerical and administrative industry (private sector) were expected to have competence in negotiating their own roles within their work unit.

This study also showed that as the employees' skill level increased there was a much greater expectation of more proactive, "productive" and adaptive (able to adapt to different others) communication. Employees across most industries were expected to contribute to the decision making within work teams and to encourage the participation of others (usually subordinates), to liaise with subordinates and superiors and to some extent external agencies or other stakeholders. For employees of ASF levels 4–6 there was consistent evidence of expectations of competency in providing effective feedback on work performance to individuals or teams, the need to be able to explain or clarify work goals, provide work directions, provide counseling to staff members, and resolve conflict. For employees at ASF level 6 additional requirements included communicating the corporate vision both internally and externally, displaying shared values, and boundary spanning in terms of using and maintaining networks are indicated.

A typology that moved from reproductive, routinized communication skills for employees working at lower ASF levels through to contributory, collaborative, and more demanding adaptive and finally proactive skills for employees at higher ASF levels could be seen to exist from the sample of selected documents.

This study showed a recognition of the importance of effective communication in at least some Australian industries. Aspects of competence in communication have been identified as fundamental components of skill for employees at all levels across a range of industries through direct inclusion in units, elements, and performance criteria in the selected competency standards. Communication skills have been identified in these documents as employee "must haves." The analysis also suggested the requirements for progressively more complex and abstract dimensions of communication competency as employees seek positions at higher levels within their industries in the same ways as they could be expected to demonstrate higher order skill and understanding to complete tasks of greater technical complexity. The complexity and abstraction at higher ASF level results from a need for employees at these higher levels to relate to wider audiences both within and outside the organization often about more diverse or abstract topics.

To summarize, a range of initiatives are currently being implemented through the national training reform agenda in a bid to enhance international competitiveness through work-force development. As part of the process there has been considerable attention to identifying the repertoire of skills required by the "new" employee, and at least at a superficial level, there is some evidence of a growing perspective of the importance of employee possession of enhanced forms of communicative competence.

ISSUES AND CHALLENGES

The first challenge involves separating rhetoric from reality. It could be argued that, as a result of the reconstruction being undertaken in Australian industries and organizations, systems and approaches are being established that acknowledge the importance of communication effectiveness for organizational functioning. A gap may, however, exist between the rhetoric about communication and the reality. Recent comments about communication deficiencies in our workplaces suggest there is still room for improvement. To illustrate findings from a survey by the BCA in 1992 suggested that managers are often deficient in leadership, human relationship, and communication competencies despite the commonplace exhortations of management writers. A comment by Peter Ritchie, chairman of McDonald's Australia, to the Australian Institute of Directors illustrates this further deficiency (West 1993). He argued that Australian business had almost universally overlooked communication and interpersonal skills, stating, "to my mind they are vital and they are the factors which make McDonald's stand out. Now the question in my mind is 'why more Australian companies don't adopt the same approach.'" This problem is not one confined to managers. Weil and Emmanuel (1992) suggested that employers often find graduates lacking in problem-solving skills and unable to communicate accurately and effectively.

not that diss. from Here.

The problem may be explained partly by the place the formal study of communication has been given within our education and training system. Despite a growth in the formal study of communication in some schools and faculties, particularly through what was the college of advanced education sector (More and Bordow 1991), such study is not included in the curricula in the more traditional universities. The situation in further education has until recently varied only slightly with communication subjects often being seen as soft options, not central to the real learning and sometimes relegated to undesirable spaces in the curriculum and times on the timetable. This situation arises not necessarily from a failure to acknowledge that communication is important in the work life of professionals and graduates, however, it is often seen as a "nice to have" competency rather than a "must have." It has therefore frequently been given a peripheral role in students' study programs. This is a challenge that communication educators and curriculum designers need to address. The task may become salient with the development of competency standards by professions and greater professional input into the design of tertiary education programs.

A second challenge requiring continuing attention arises from a multicultural work force being confronted with workplace reform. The issues of workplace literacy and language competence are becoming increasingly important as both technological advances and the move toward employee multiskilling and job broadening in workplaces are requiring higher levels of English literacy and oracy. While language and literacy initiatives are taking place in Australia, ongoing efforts will be required to remediate the deficiency among migrant and less-skilled nonmigrant members of the work force. The effort however must not be confined to literacy remediation. In the new work organization, as shown through the competency standards and as required with total quality approaches, employees are expected to participate more frequently in a workplace problem solving and decision making. This therefore requires not only literacy, oracy, and linguistic competence but a more general communication competence. It also requires a new sensitivity on the part of those working with and leading teams of newly empowered workers.

As Mawer (1992) argues from her research in the metals industry, "factors affecting worker's participation in industry decision making often had nothing to do with worker's own level of language and were outside their immediate control e.g. the role of the Chair in setting a comfortable atmosphere, encouraging participation, regulating turntaking e.g. paraphrasing, clarifying, showing respect and tolerance for workers struggling to express themselves in English."

A third challenge remains in maintaining the consultative patterns resulting from the new approach to industrial relations. Lansbury (1991) and Marchington (1993) emphasize that even though both managers and union delegates appear to be highly satisfied with the operation of joint consultative committees in their workplaces, there continues to be indifference if not opposition to providing a legislative base of the kind found in some Western European countries for joint consultation in Australia. The relatively undeveloped systems of consultation and lack of tradition for the process lead Alexander and Green (1991) to the conclusion that there may be considerable obstacles to overcome before the benefit from workplace reforms will be achieved. Heather Carmody (1993) in arguing the value of enterprise agreements as part of the process of ongoing organizational change and a new direction for industrial relations also warns of the difficulties that will arise resulting from enterprise agreements requiring people to work together in a collaborative way. She claims, "collaborative behaviour in the sophisticated senses is going to take a fair bit of undoing of stereotypes about people at work."

A study cited in James (1992) reinforces Carmody's concerns. This study revealed significant employee opposition for participative management and the devolution of responsibility. This suggests that new types of training and innovative attitude change programs are necessary to reduce such resistance. Lansbury (1991) and Marchington (1993, 81) emphasize the need for training and development for both employees and managers in the new industrial relations climate. Australian unions, they argue, will need to acquire the skills necessary for effective consultation, which differ from those required in the more traditional roles of advocacy and bargaining. Such skills will require time, commitment and resources.

Fourth, the interest in quality approaches poses continuing demands related to communication in organizations. Despite an expansion of interest in the processes associated with quality management, there is an ongoing need to maintain attention on the communicative dimension of this process. Palmer and Saunders (1992, 76) argue that TQM provides a framework for management decision making based on a theory of the behavior of staff members and customers and the use of scientific method. However, they warn, "it can become a recipe: the obvious features like statistical process control quality improvements, the 'Seven Tools of TQM' etc. have the potential to replace the substance. . . . The philosophy of TQM can only be taken seriously by companies using it, if they adopt policy deployment to unify direction of the parts of the company and ensure constancy of purpose, training of managers in the appropriate use of statistical tools and an emphasis on effective communication as the key to quality."

A fifth challenge emanates from the identification of communication skills and subskills in the development of national competency standards. The identification of such skills clearly gives prominence to the importance of communication skills. The standards provide a defined basis for development of workplace training and a more systematic basis for assessment of competence. However a danger exists that workplace-based communication competence may be seen too simplistically or as competencies isolated from contextual determinants.

It is therefore in the design of training programs that particular care must be given to ensure that atomization of communication is avoided. The process of effective communication must be addressed as a meaningful whole, and training must provide trainees with a repertoire of skills from which trainees can appropriately select according to the demands of the situation and relationship between interactants. The writings and research from communication competence scholars needs to be applied to the development of training programs to equip both managers and employees with a wide range of capacities that go beyond organizational protocols. These programs need to provide participants with both a cognitive understanding and a behavioral flexibility to adapt to different others and heed cues from the immediate environment.

The words of Bostrom in 1984 could well be considered in the design of training programs: "Communication competence requires not only the ability to perform adequately certain communication behaviors. It also requires an understanding of those behaviors and the cognitive ability to make choices about behaviors." Hockley (1991) asserts that the dubious reputation of communication training of the past is being dispelled; however, attention will need to be given to communication trainer training. As indicated earlier in this chapter, the tradition of academic and vocational preparation study in the field of communication in Australia, particularly at the graduate level is comparatively new and as a consequence increased activity in this arena will be necessary.

A sixth, related challenge pertains to the assessment of such organizational communication competence. The competence movement has intensified an interest in workplace-based assessment of employee competencies. Workplace assessors will be responsible for evaluating competencies of employees based on competency standards. Hence they will be responsible for assessing communication competence as part of overall employee competence. Competence in communication, however, is not solely in the control of the individual because of the transactional nature of communication and the relational dimension of communication competence. Robert Bostrom (1984, 265) illustrates this difficulty when he argues: "Making ideas and feelings clear to others is more than making ideas and feelings clear. Communication does not exist without a receiver, and what is clear to one receiver is not necessarily clear to another receiver. Clearly then we must measure not what the person does but what impact what the person does has on the receiver. Clarity (or any other outcome variable we might choose) is in the mind of the receiver, not in the mind of an observer or in the behaviour of the communicator."

Kaye (1992) and Irwin (1992) both have highlighted some of the difficulties of assessing communication competence. Irwin claims, "Any assessment of learning with respect to competency must be confined to global assessments inferred from successful performances and understanding of the process and must involve norm referenced rather than criterion referenced procedures" (1992, 6). A request for norm referenced procedures could be seen as a luxury or not appropriate to process of the current competency movement. However, the call for a global assessment inferred from successful performance of a number of subskills is not at odds with the approaches to assessment advanced by the current competency movement and competency standards development.

Assessors of communication competence, particularly when making an assessment by observation or based on self or other reports of competence will require a cognitive understanding of the dynamics and processes of communication. This means that they will also need an awareness of a repertoire of communication behaviors and the microskills constituting those behaviors as well as an understanding of the impact organizational culture or subculture on communication behaviors to make an assessment on the appropriateness and effectiveness of the displayed behavior in the given situation.

Assessors may often have received training and have broad understandings related to technical dimensions of tasks being observed and have had intuitive success in communicating themselves. This is not to say, however, they will have an understanding of or a sensitivity to the range of communication behaviors that may be required or possible in a given situation.

Hence training of assessors in the dynamics of communication will be a prerequisite to ensure fair assessment of communication competence in employees. The desired outcome of various interactions and communication activities may be elusive through no particular deficiency of the assessee. Conversely success in the demonstrated situation by the assessee may be fortuitous and not generalizable to a range of situations because of a lack of cognitive understanding of the dynamics that produced the outcome on the part of the assessee.

Guides to assessment with examples of evidence of competence are being provided within some sets of competency standards or in separate publications. Judgment of communication competency, however, may be difficult because of the diversity of communication solutions that may be appropriate. Assessor communication competence training may ensure more adequate decision making.

CONCLUSION

In conclusion, new ways of operating at industry and enterprise levels are determining the nature and outcomes of a reconstructed Australia. As part of the reconstruction process communication is being recognized for the vital role it plays in employee competence needed for achieving improved organizational and industry outcomes. This is not the time for complacency. Significant challenges now exist for researchers to explore strategies for increasing communication effectiveness in organizations and to determine barriers and patterns limiting competent performance and effective reconstruction. Challenges also exist for those working in the field of tertiary education, workplace training and industry education, and trainer and assessor preparation to ensure that organisations of the 1990s and their employees singularly and collectively have a communication repertoire with which to work appropriately to achieve the outcomes so necessary for the country's prosperity.

REFERENCES

Alexander, M. J., and R. Green. (1991). "Workplace Productivity and Joint Consultation." *Australian Bulletin of Labour* 18, no. 2: 95–118.

Australian Council of Trade Unions and Confederation of Australian Industry (ACTU/CAI). (1988). *Joint Statement on Participative Practices: A Co-operative Approach to Improving Efficiency and Productivity in Australian Industry.* Canberra: Australian Government Printing Service.

Australian Council of Trade Unions and Trade Development Council. (1987). *Australia Reconstructed,* Canberra. Australian Government Printing Service.

Bishop, C., and C. Graham. (1992). "Self-Directed Work Teams—The Search for a Better Way." *Training and Development in Australia* 19, no. 1.

Booth, A. (1993). "Quality—The Key to Workplace Change." In *Proceedings from Quality and Organisational Change International Conference.* Sydney.

Bostrom, R. N. (1984). "The Elusive Construct." In R. N. Bostrom, *Competence in Communication. A Multidisciplinary Approach*. Beverley Hills, Calif.: Sage Publications.

Carmichael, L. (1989). "It's Time to Bite the Bullet." *Training and Development in Australia* 6, no. 1 (March).

Carter, E. M. A., and I. A. Gribble. (1992). "Work Based Learning. A Discussion Paper." TAFE National Staff Development Committee.

Commonwealth Department of Education, Employment and Training (Mayer Report). (1992). "Employment Related Key Competencies. A Proposal for Consultation," Report of Australian Education Council.

Business Council of Australia with Towers Perrin and Cresap Australia Pty Ltd. (1992). *Workforce 2000 BCA.*

Department of Industrial Relations. (1992). *Workplace Bargaining: The First 1090 Agreements.* Canberra: Australian Government Printing Service.

Dwyer, M. (1992). "Universities Under Attack." *Australian Financial Review* (May 12).

Flynn, M. (1993). "Internal Communication and Quality." *The Quality Magazine* [Australian Quality Council] (February).

Gray, R. (1993). "Successfully Communicating Quality." *The Quality Magazine* [Australian Quality Council] (February).

Greiner, N. (1992). *New South Wales: Facing the World.* Sydney: NSW Premier's Department.

Hockley, R. (1991). "Quality Communication in Management." *Training and Development in Australia* 18, no. 3.

Irwin, H. (1992). "Enhancing Interpersonal Communication Quality. Can the Competency Movement Help?" Paper presented at National Conference of the Australian Communication Association, Bond University, Gold Coast, Queensland.

James, D. (1992). "Why Changing Our Employees' Attitudes Is No Pushover." *Business Review Weekly* 14, no. 42: 68–69.

Johnston, R. (1993). "Competence via Communication: A Communication Perspective of Training Reform in Australia." Paper presented to the International Conference Communication in the Workplace, Culture, Language and Organisational Change. Centre for Workplace Communication, Sydney.

Kaye, M. (1992). "Assessing the Interpersonal Competence of Vocational Teachers: Contemporary Issues and Dilemmas." Paper presented to the twelfth annual international seminar for Teacher Education, University of New England, Armidale.

Lansbury, R. D., and R. T. Spillane. (1991). *Organisational Behaviour. The Australian Context.* Melbourne: Longman Cheshire.

Littlejohn, S., and D. Jabusch. (1982). "Communication Competence Models and Applications." *Journal of Applied Communication Research* 10, no. 1: 29–37.

Marchington, M. (1992). "The Practice of Joint Consultation Australia: A Preliminary Analysis of the AWIRS Data." *ACIRRT Working Paper*, no. 21. Sydney: ACIRRT.

More E, and A. Bardow. (1991). *Managing Organisational Communication*. Melbourne: Longman Cheshire.

Morgan, G. (1988). *Riding the Waves of Change: Developing Managerial Competencies for a Turbulent World*. San Francisco: Jossey Bass.

National Board of Employment, Education and Training. (1990). *Interim Report on the Benchmark Study of Management Development in Australian Private Enterprises Commissioned Report No. 5*. Canberra: Australian Government Printing Service.

National Training Board. (1992). *National Competency Standards: Policy and Guidelines*. Canberra: NTB.

Osborne, P. (1991). "Total Quality Management Supplement." *Australian Financial Review* (November 8).

Palmer, G., and I. Saunders. (1992). "Total Quality Management and Human Resource Management: Comparison and Contrasts." *Asia Pacific Journal of Human Resources* 30, no. 1: 67–77.

Ramsey, G. (1993). Competence, Excellence and Curriculum." *Journal of Vocational Education and Training* 1, no. 1.

Weil, S., and D. Emmanuel. (1992). "Capability Through Humanities and Social Sciences." In J. Stephenson and S. Weil, *Quality in Learning: A Capability Approach to Higher Education*. London: Kogan Page.

Whitely, A. (1993). "Competency, Culture and Change: The Organisational Context of Competency Based Training." *Training and Development in Australia* 20, no. 1.

West, M. (1993). "McDonald's Puts a Side Order for Success on Table." *Sydney Morning Herald* (September 17): 21.

CHAPTER 14

Communication in Asian
Job Interviews

Ernst Martin

Cultural Dis.
Read Book for
Diff. In - Inter Viewers
+ Interviewes

INTRODUCTION

In an environment of change within an organization, high-speed management is characterized by a system that is innovative, a-daptive, flexible, efficient, and rapid in response (see King and Cushman, Chapter 2). When change is occurring in cross-cultural company ventures—joint ventures, outsourcing, joint product agreements, licensing, joint marketing, or equity technology exchange—communicating organizational perspectives in diverse cultures require an awareness of cultural differences (see Kozminski, Chapter 15). Interviewing, within the field of organizational communication, is vitally important for managers as they communicate change using the interviewing forms of selection, appraisal, job satisfaction, discipline, exit, research, and others.

The topic of interviewing has attracted a vast amount of attention in recent years. The issues surrounding it are highly relevant to Asia given the dynamic growth and rapid modernization. Asian organizational communication takes place in distinctive socio-cultural environments of the region (Westwood 1992). Much of the conceptualization and research on interviewing, however, is from a North American and British orientation, reflecting Anglo-American backgrounds and concerns that may or may not be relevant to Asia.

The theory of interviewing, as typically constructed in current textbooks and other literature, is not related to the cultural, social, economic and political situations of non-Anglo-Americans (Westwood 1992). Although the Western-based classic work should not be discounted, it must be critically examined to see to what extent it is applicable and relevant. Asian theory and research, to the extent it currently exists, should then form the basis of a new or modified perspective.

The theoretical framework for most of the research applicable to interviewing communication fall within twelve categories, with contrasts and differences.

1. *Integrating vs. analyzing.* Are details of phenomenon integrated and configured into whole patterns, relationships and wider contexts (integrating) or analyzed by breaking into parts such as facts, items, tasks, numbers, units, points, or specifics (analyzing) (Lewin 1951)?

2. *Particularism vs. universalism.* should an exceptional case be considered on its unique merits (particularism) or should the most relevant rule be imposed, however imperfectly (universalism) (Parsons and Shils 1951)?

3. *Polyocular viewpoint vs. objective viewpoint.* Is perception from the viewpoint of two eyes in a single head (objective viewpoint) or from the viewpoint of what four, six, eight, or a score of eyes might perceive from positions all around the phenomenon being scrutinized (polyocular viewpoint) (Maruyama 1982)?

4. *Synchronized time vs. sequential time.* Is time seen as telescoped in a circular view, with past experience working with present situation for future aims (synchronized time) or as moving forward, increment by increment, in a chronological line (sequential time) (Peters and Waterman 1982)?

5. *Inductive reasoning vs. deductive reasoning.* Does thinking move from the particulars to generalizations and synthesis (inductive), or are universal propositions tested to see if objective data (primarily numerical) supports the initial hypothesis (deductive) (Boisot 1987)?

6. *Helical vs. linear thinking.* Which is better: circular or "loop" thinking, exemplified *yin-yang* in terms of interactive cycles (helical thinking), or a course of direct movement in one dimension from the beginning to the conclusion (Senge 1990)?

7. *Collectivism vs. individualism.* Is it more important to pay attention to the advancement of the family, community or corporation, which all members serve (collectivism) or to focus on the enhancement of each individual, his or her rights, motivations, rewards, capacities and attitudes (individualism) (Tonnies 1957)?

8. *Outer directed vs. inner directed.* Which are the more important guides, the signals, demands, and trends in the outside world to which we must adjust (outer directed) or the judgments, decision, and commitments coming from inside us (inner directed) (Ozbekhan 1971)?

9. *Consensual vs adversarial decision making.* Is it better for people to discuss things until almost everyone agrees, or have viewpoints voiced and debated with the decision based on majority vote (Hampden-Turner and Trompenaars 1993)?

10. *Hierarchy vs. equality.* Is it more important for authority to flow from position (hierarchy) or for everyone to be treated as equals (equality) (Hampden-Turner and Trompenaars 1993)?

11. *Ascribed status vs. achieved status.* Should status depend on characteristics such as age, seniority, education, gender, strategic role (ascribed status) or should status depend on what has been achieved (achieved status) (Hampden-Turner and Trompenaars 1993)?

12. *Benevolence vs. autocracy.* Is the hierarchy accompanied by relations of *amae,* roughly translated from the Japanese as reliance and dependence on the indulgent love of an older person (benevolence), or is hierarchy necessarily domineering and repressive and dogmatic (autocracy) (Maruyama 1985)?

The twelve contrasts are not necessarily contradictory from the Asian perspective—as indicated by the *vs.*—but rather can be complementary. However, they do indicate differing cultural orientations and assumptions.

This is not to say that everything in Asia is different from the West; however, communication is shaped within the general societal milieu and traditions. This is also not saying that there is a homogenous "Asian" perspective. Many differences are due to culture, stage of development, political and institutional arrangements, and so forth. Yet some commonalties tend to hold through-out Asia (Westwood 1992b).

DEFINING THE INTERVIEWING PROCESS

Many situations in which two people interact can be called an *interview.* In the classic literature in the West the definitions of interviewing center on interviewing as a specialized form of human communication. Downs, Smeyak, and Martin (1980) define an *interview* as "a specialized form of oral communication between people in an interpersonal relationship that is entered into for a specific task related purpose associated with a particular subject matter." Stewart and Cash (1978) define it as "a process of dyadic communication with a predetermined and serious purpose designed to interchange behavior and involve the asking and answering of questions." Kahn and Cannell (1963) define an interview as "a specialized pattern of verbal interaction—initiated for a specific purpose, and focused on some specific content area, with consequent elimination of extraneous material."

We put interviewing into an appropriate Asian context, using this as a working definition: Interviewing, as a specialized form of human communication, is the process in which feelings and ideas, for a specific task-related purpose, are exchanged, within a context of interpersonal relationships and the situational environment, through verbal and nonverbal means, with the goal of achieving shared meaning.

1. It is a specialized form of human communication, including many of the elements of other communication (intrapersonal, interpersonal, public) (De Vito 1991), but taking forms such as selection, appraisal, counseling, disciplinary, exit, research, negotiation, journalistic, medical, and so on.

2. It is a process because it never stops and shows continuous change. As the attitudes, expectations, and feelings and emotions of individuals who are in the interview change, the nature of their communication changes as well.

3. It involves feelings and ideas, which implies that we cannot separate the ideas we are presenting from the feelings we have and the feelings that are evoked, no matter how specific a focus we try to keep on the subject area.

4. It is task oriented, meaning there is a specific purpose or end objective for each participant in the interview.

5. It involves verbal and nonverbal means of communicating messages. Communicating in the interview situation is done in many other ways than simply with words.

6. The complex interpersonal relationship of interviewer and interviewee, as well as the communication environment, directly influence the interview process.

7. The interview exchange should result in creation of "shared meaning"—a common interpretation of the message (Daniels and Spiker 1987) or a shared view of behavior, event, or idea.

MODEL OF INTERVIEWING COMMUNICATION

The basic components and the process of interviewing communication from an Asian perspective is illustrated in the model shown in Figure 13.1.

Interviewer: Communicator A

The interview process starts when the Interviewer, Communicator A, is consciously or unconsciously stimulated by some event, object, or idea in the interview situation. A need to send a message is then followed by a memory search to find the appropriate language (verbal or nonverbal) with which to encode the message. Such factors as perceptions, expectations, attitudes, and physical state effect the sending of messages. Berlo (1960) defined elements of communication skills, attitudes, knowledge, social skills, and culture affecting the communicator. These and other elements will be discussed.

Interviewee: Communicator B

The Interviewee, Communicator B, is represented with a different shape than Interviewer, Communicator A. This represents individual uniqueness, but also that the two people in the interview communication situation will never be "the same." It is most obvious in cross-cultural interview communication situations, but applies even to subcultures within cultures as well as other segmentation schemes including demographics, geographics, and psychograph-

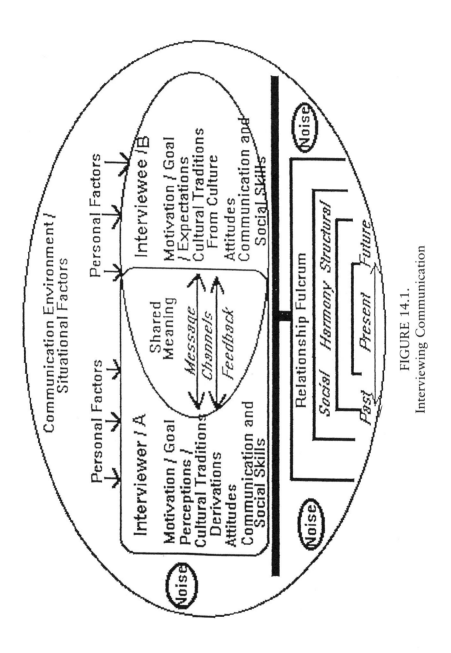

FIGURE 14.1.
Interviewing Communication

ics. The best participants can hope for is to maximize the area of shared meaning, without either "becoming the other."

The Interviewee receives the verbal and nonverbal signals through the channel and decodes them. They are processed through a memory search so that the signals are translated into the interviewee's language system. This decoded message will not be identical to the one encoded by the Interviewer, because each person's symbol system is created by a unique set of perceptions, knowledge, culture, communication skills, and social skills.

The interview communication can best be thought of as a transaction in which variables are found simultaneously within both communicators, and Interviewer and Interviewee play interchangeable roles throughout the act of communication (Stewart 1986). Communicator A encodes a message and sends it. Communicator B then encodes the feedback and sends it to A, who decodes it. These steps, however, are not necessarily mutually exclusive or sequential, because encoding and decoding may occur simultaneously.

Goals and Motivation

Central to the definition of interviewing is the function—the specific-task related purpose—that it is intended to achieve. The goals of both Interviewer and Interviewee are vitally important because the goals of both parties must be compatible for the interview to be effective. People pursue goals when motivated by needs. Lopez (1975) argues that a complex series of motives underlies every human action; a motive is a connection between a felt need and a perceived goal. Westwood (1992c) contends that motivation is affected by the culture and value system of a given country.

There are a large number of human needs. Maslow's (1954) hierarchy of human needs is one of the dominant Western analyses. At the bottom of the hierarchy—and the most important—are physiological needs. Second is safety—needs for a basic level of security and protection, freedom from fear of physical danger or harm. Needs for social relationships, belonging, and love and affection are third. The next set of needs is esteem needs, including both self-respect and the respect of others. The highest level is self-actualization—to realize one's potential and experience a sense of self-growth and development. Maslow proposes most humans have these five needs, and when not satisfied (through deficit and progression) they provide the motivating mechanism for all actions. Hofstede (1980a) argues that motivation theories, including Maslow's hierarchy of human needs, reflect United States cultural values of high individualism, weak uncertainty avoidance, and lower power distance. Further, Hofstede (1984) points out that some motivation concepts like "achievement" are not translatable in some languages. Redding (1977) questions the strong emphasis on individual-oriented needs like self-actualization. Redding and Martyn-Johns (1979), based on research in Hong Kong, Thailand, Malaysia, Indonesia, Vietnam, and the Philippines, also argue that culture affects basic thought processes and leads to different motivations. Kanungo (1983) accepts that needs motivate, but cultural values and socialization influence the structure of those needs. From research in Thailand, Runglertkrengkrai and Enkaninan (1986), using Porter's (1961) instrument of needs importance and satisfaction found self-actualization diametrically opposed in satisfaction and importance. This supported the multiple country findings of Haire, Ghiselli, and Porter (1966). A study of Malaysian bank managers found differences according to education level and age (Rashid 1989). However, the importance of needs identified by Maslow does show some consistency across cultures (in Africa), even if the needs structure is not the same (Blunt 1973, Howell, Strauss, and Sorenson 1975, Blunt 1976). Graham and Leung (1987) found financial rewards substantially stronger in motivating middle managers in Hong Kong than in the United States and Australia. Martin and Wilson (1993), in Hong Kong, found differences in motivating job expectations based on varying levels of individual modernity or traditionalism and Chinese and Western value orientation. Yang (1986), in summarizing a pooled sample of several studies of Chinese, found relatively high scores on achievement, order, affiliation, introspection, self-abasement, nurturance, change and endurance, relatively low scores on exhibition, heterosexuality and aggression, with deference, autonomy, and dominance falling in the middle. Additionally, when summarizing value research in Taiwan, Yang (1972, 1986) says the values center on one building a moderate and balanced life with action, contemplation, and enjoyment combined in proper proportions, in strict control of oneself, warm and benevolent in the treatment of others, social restraints willingly accepted, and good human achievements and traditions carefully maintained. Taken as a whole, the results of the research studies while inconclusive, throw doubt on a rigid hierarchy of needs applicable in the West and Asia. However, they do suggest certain needs are significant and there is some similarity across cultures on what people consider important (Westwood 1992c).

As an alternative view of motivation from an Asian perspective, Hsu (1971) identifies three basic needs in Chinese culture: sociability, security, and status. Importantly, these needs are satisfied through interpersonal interaction. The theory is built on the principle that basic needs and motivation are a relational, social phenomena rather than the Anglo-American conception of an individual, independent motivation (collectivism vs. individualism). Satisfaction of basic needs depends on being able to bring behavior in line with social norms and expectations. A key motivating force is avoidance of social disapproval and social shame (Yang, 1981). With a similar conception, Andres (1985) developed a Filipino management system based on *pakikisama* ("going along") as a significant motivator that aims to keep interpersonal relations smooth. Cushman and King (1985) point out that Japanese interactions must take place in *kuuki,* referring to a feeling of commonalty or group harmony in direction. Interpersonal relations as motivating factors were also found by Lynch (1970), Torres (1981), and Arce (1978). Particular human satisfactions are wrought into the whole combination (particularism vs. universalism) (Hampden-Turner and Trompenaars 1993). In summary, the social aspects of motivation are of high significance in interviewing situations in Asia, with sociability, security, and status or social needs, and then other needs including self-actualization.

Perception and Expectations

The perceptual system provides information about the physical environment and other people through the five senses. Perception involves selecting, organizing, and interpreting messages in ways that make sense to the person or suits his or her purpose (Downs, Smeyak, and Martin 1980). Using it is an unconscious activity and often dominated by learned habits. Additionally, any interview communication situation has a wide variety of cues (verbal and nonverbal messages) that are a part of the communication. Because one cannot pay attention to all of the communication cues, the person selects some and leaves others out—a process called _ab-stracting_ (Haney 1973). A person perceives a message but actually hears or sees only very few characteristics of that message. The parts represent the whole. Selective perception and selective retention operate for both parties (Downs, Smeyak, and Martin 1980). In the interview situation all are abstracting or selecting those items most vital to them or that make the most sense in their worlds. Therefore, two people hear the same message, yet their experience of abstracting leave the definition of the message not identical. Differences in perception are to be expected.

 Differences of personality effects perception. Some people would find a certain interview situation stimulating and exciting, while others perceive the same situation stressful and demanding.

In the Asian context, perception within an interview communication situation also involves trying to understand how the other party will perceive the situation. Maruyama (1982) described Japan as a polyocular culture in contrast to the American search for so-called objectivity. In North America and northwestern Europe the world is defined as existing of objects, the description of which would be agreed on by all detached observers. The Japanese, on the other hand, take the view that all phenomena can be seen from multiple points of view, with the additional angles make reality more whole and comprehensive. Prior to Western imperialism, the Japanese had no word for "objectivity." Now, _kyakkanteki_ (the guest's point of view) connotes objectivity while _shukanteki_ (the host's point of view) means subjectivity, knowing the dynamics of the whole (Maruyama 1982). Additionally, traditional Chinese landscape painting, and their assimilation into other Asian painting traditions, is easily differentiated from Western painting because of the multiple rather than single point of view within one painting (Minick and Ping 1990).

In social orientation, Chiu (1972), comparing Taiwanese and American subjects, found that the Chinese tended to have a relational-contextual style—to categorize stimuli on the basis of their functional and thematic relationships—while the Americans had an inferential-categorical style—to categorize stimuli on the basis of inference made about the stimuli that are grouped together (integrating vs. analyzing).

Hampden-Turner and Trompenaars (1993) found that the United States is the most analytic and reductive culture of twelve they studied, while Japan and Singapore in Asia are the most oriented to larger, integrated wholes.

Cultural Traditions

In its broadest meaning, *culture* refers to the way of life of a group of people that is passed on from one generation to another. Terpstra and David (1985) define culture as a learned, shared, compelling interrelated set of symbols that provide a set of orientations for a society.

History, including the collective memory of colonialism or imperialism and being the birthplace of some of the world's greatest religions, has shaped contemporary Asian attitudes. Colonialism and imperialism are blamed for having imposed Western values on Asian societies. Special, somewhat unflattering names for Westerners are throughout Asia—*gweilo* in Hong Kong and China, *geijin* in Japan, *farang* in Thailand, *mat salleh* in Malaysia, and *villaiti* in India (Bedi 1991). Additionally, romanticized but cherished ancient beliefs include China as the middle kingdom, India's Ram Rajya, Malaysia's Melaka Sultanate, Korea's Hermit Kingdom, and Thailand's Sukothai. Modern life is to some extent judged by old values.

Religions and ethical-philosophical traditions are a significant feature of most cultures. Among the most influential and widespread in Asia are Buddhism (widely spread but especially in Thailand, Tibet, Laos, Vietnam, Cambodia, Burma, Korea, and Chinese communities), Islam (Malaysia, Indonesia, and other pockets of Asia), Hinduism (Malaysia, Indonesia, and Indian ethnic groups spread throughout Asia), Christianity (widespread throughout Asia, dominant in the Philippines), Confucianism (influential in China, Hong Kong, Taiwan, and overseas Chinese communities as well as a force in Korea and Japan), Popular Daoism (influence within Chinese communities, with elements of Taoism, Confucianism, and ancestor worship), Shintoism (indigenous religion of Japan), ancestor worship (beginning with Neolithic Chinese, still influential), animism (belief that all objects have spirit, still influential with other religious views), Maoism-Marxism-Leninism (influential philosophical-political position). The religious and ethical-philosophical traditions come into play in shaping a particular culture's value system (Westwood 1992d). For example, Cushman and King (1985) point out that, philosophically, life in Japan is influenced by Japan's fusion of Confucian, Shinto, and Buddhist beliefs. Confucianism regulates human relationships, Shintoism emphasizes economy of expression, a practical view of reality, and public service. Buddhism has as its ultimate goal the selfless spiritual state through contemplation, distrust of oral language, and a fusion of thought and action.

Derivations From Culture

Esteem for Power and Status Hierarchy

Asian cultures especially revere status and power and accept the hierarchical structure of society, and in many they accept the upward mobility of people in the lower social and power hierarchy (Kao and Young 1992). A vast body of research, with classic literature typified by Earle (1969), Meade and Whittaker (1967), Singh, Huang and Thompson (1962), indicate the significant importance of acceptance of power in the Asian personality (see the discussion of the relationship fulcrum later). Chinese tend to have a higher degree of authoritarianism than Americans and British, but less than Indians. Yang (1986) contends that Chinese are conspicuously deferential toward anyone or anything considered an authority (person, situation, institution).

Japanese business people hesitate to say "no"—being deferential—because they are addressing themselves to the interpersonal relationship rather than to the concrete things being asked for (Hampden-Turner and Trompenaars 1993). When Americans hear the words "Yes, but it is difficult . . ." with meaningful pauses, they believe assent when what it means is "Yes, you have a right to ask me, but I cannot do that particular thing" (March 1988). With each other they say "no," but still politely (Pascale and Athos 1981).

Conformity Tendency   Related to the power hierarchy and status is the tendency for conforming behavior in Chinese, Japanese, and other Asian cultures, submission to authority, status, and tradition. Workers in Japanese companies, spending several hours socializing in the evening with colleagues, even at the price of physical exhaustion, conform because social sanctions and supervisor suspicion could result (Kao and Young 1992). However, Hampden-Turner and Trompenaars (1993) found conformity among Japanese is not a conformity to skills and attainments of one another, except in superficial ways, because the basis of harmony is complementary heterogeneity. Maruyama (1963) found close Japanese teenage groups spontaneously organized on the principle of heterogeneity, with particular individuals having particular expertise to bring the widest possible variety of information on diverse pastimes to the group as a whole. Furthermore, conformity to superiors in the hierarchy, however, is done subtly and with circumspection (Bond and Lee 1981) and may not be related to private belief (Tedeschi and Piess 1981; Bond and Hui 1982, Leung and Bond 1982, Bond and Hwang 1986).

Self-Disclosure and Trust   In Western interviewing communication situations trustworthiness is a critical characteristic (Corrigan 1978). In the counseling interview communication, the assumption of a trustworthy helper is the start and then it is tested over and over (Egan 1986). However, for some people, especially those in minority groups, trust must be earned, with proof provided (La Fromboise and Dixon 1981). A key behavior in the development and maintenance of trust is self-disclosure (Millar, Crute, and Hargie 1992). Di Matteo and Di Nicola (1982) provide a three-stage Western model of trust building through self-disclosure in a patient-helper interview situation. (1) Patient engages in risk-taking behavior, primarily by self-disclosing personally sensitive information. (2) The helper greets the patient's self-disclosures with acceptance and understanding. (3) The helper returns the trust with self-disclosures signifying an open relationship and climate. The distinctive features of an open climate are a great willingness to trust, an avoidance of evaluation, and an apparent willingness to accept whatever information the interviewee wants to give (Downs, Smeyak, and Martin 1980).

Openness is generally strongly advocated as desirable from an Anglo-American perspective. However, in the Asian context, a particular relationship may require flexibility in deciding whether it is appropriate to be open or not (Chua 1992). Hwang (1982) found that Chinese subjects were more willing to self-disclose highly personal matters to "expressive ties"—family members and close friends—while "mixed ties"—business associates, friends, public officials, and teachers—remained on superficial topics. In summarizing self-disclosure and trust in Asia and the West, Chua (1992) points out disclosure requires a healthy level of trust between the parties, developed through frequent interaction and shared experience. Hampden-Turner and Trompenaars (1993) suggest that while Americans and northwestern Europeans require that human relationships submit to universal truths and rules (universalism), for the Japanese the particular relationships of *honne,* a spirit of intimacy between persons, is the moral cement of society; and to the extent that relationships are trusting, harmonious, and aesthetic, rules of wider generality can be derived. Trust and openness are developed from experiences (particularism). In Asia, relationship levels (*guanxi*) and the hierarchical structure of the situation determines self-disclosure behavior, but more research is required to investigate patterns and reasons for trust and self-disclosure.

Emotions   Emotions play an important role in interviewing communication. Frijda (1986) defines three components of emotion: the direct conscious experience or feeling of emotion, physiological processes that accompany the feeling of emotion, and the actual verbal and nonverbal expression to convey emotion. Izard (1977) indicates that emotional states inevitably affect the perceptions, thoughts, and actions of a person because virtually all the neurophysical systems of the body are involved to some degree. Emotional states of both the interviewer and interviewee are of importance as they communicate with each other.

In many Asian cultures there is the apparent modernation with which emotions are expressed compared with Westerners. Bond (1991) points to implicit rules surrounding the display of emotions in Chinese and Japanese culture that are ingrained during socialization, in addition to a cultural background of respect for hierarchy and moderation. Uninhibited emotional display is a disruptive and dangerous luxury for Chinese, whereas Westerners, operating under a different social logic, are often amazed by apparent Chinese control in the face of arousing events (Bond 1991). Strong display of emotions is related to a person's inner-directedness. Hampden-Turner and Trompenaars (1993) found that Singapore Chinese and Japanese scored substantially lower than America, German, Canadian, and Australian samples on being inner directed. Asian managers tend to see themselves as driven by external forces, often out of their control—a maelstrom in the tides of events. Rather than fighting, with great inner-directed emotional effort, adjustment should be made by agility and wit to redirect the force and momentum of the opponent, as demonstrated many cartoon heroes in Japanese pop culture.

Individual Modernity and Individual Traditionalism   In the wake of modernization and Westernization throughout Asia, a number of studies have dealt with changes in the Asia character. Martin et al. (1993) and Martin and Wilson (1993) found the combined concepts of individual modernity and traditionalism and Chinese-Western orientation is desirous in segmenting Hong Kong students and the Hong Kong Chinese population with its very diverse backgrounds, status, and life experiences. Despite the modern, deceptively Western look of the society, the ethnic Hong Kong Chinese have maintained a strong cultural identity (Bond et al. 1985). In summarizing the previous findings in the field, Bond (1991) and Yang (1986) contend that individual traditional and modern attitudes do not necessarily exist in opposition to each other, especially when mediated with Chinese values. In studies in North American, Taiwan, Hong Kong, and China, a "Modern Chinese" is a person who retains the essential Chinese virtues (especially familism, achievement, and moderation) in a creative amalgam with Western technical mastery. A "Traditional Chinese" maintains valued traditional characteristics like filial piety and thrift as well as traits of noncompetitiveness, superstition, and authoritarianism (Bond 1991). A review of literature dealing with the Chinese personality based on individual modernity of Chinese students (primarily in Taiwan) indicates increased individual modernity develops a greater concern with self-expression, self-assertion, independence, personal achievement, dominance, tolerance, as well as less inhibition in associating with the opposite sex, less concern with conforming to customs, achieving organization, and orderliness, less likely to blame and belittle oneself, persevering in a task or activity until finished, seeking approval or admiration from others or society, and striving to achieve goals set by others or society (Yang 1986, Vernon 1982, Yang 1981, Hwang 1976, Abbott 1976, Fried 1976, Lee 1973, Li and Yang 1972, Hchu and Yang 1972, Abbott 1970).

Personal Factors

Personal factors are those features of the individuals (both interviewer and interviewee) that are readily visible to others. During
the interview process we make a number of judgments based on
appearance, and these judgments influence how we interpret and
respond (Millar, Crute, and Hargie 1992). From a Western perspective, Hargie and Marshall (1986) identified four main personal factors that directly bear on interviewing communication: gender, age, dress, and physical appearance.

People tend to hold different expectations of, and respond differently to, others depending on their gender (Martin and Tsui
1993, Stewart, Powell, and Chetwynd 1979). Mayo and Henley
(1981) indicate sex, as cued by appearance, is a powerful force in
human interaction. Females tend to smile more frequently, require
less interpersonal space, are touched more, use more head nods
and engage in more eye contact than males. Females have been
found to use more intensifiers ("*really* exciting"), more modal expressions ("might," "could," "possibly"), and more formal language. In interviewing situations, the gender of interviewer and
interviewee sometimes affects responses (Martin 1993) and questions asked (Breakwell 1990).

Age is an aspect that can be estimated in the interview situation, regardless of how far people go to disguise their true age.
Older interviewers are seen as more experienced, and younger interviewers are regarded as more up-to-date (Millar, Crute, and
Hargie 1992). In cross-cultural research, Hampden-Turner and
Trompenaars (1993) found that Singapore, Japanese, and Korean
samples ascribe status by age compared to American, Australian,
and Canadian samples believing in achieved status. Although status by age does not preclude status by achievement, the personal
factor of age is important in the Asian context.

Clothes and accessories convey information about a range of
factors in interviewing communication including gender, status,
individual identity, and personality (Downs, Smeyak, and Martin
1980). Kleinke (1986) found that interviewees prefer counselors
who dress formally enough to show competence yet stylish rather
than old fashioned so to not convey unapproachability.

Physical appearance refers to body size, shape and attractiveness. Millar, Chute, and Hargie (1992) contend that a thin figure

tends to be seen as clean, tidy, quiet, and conscientious, yet nervous; muscular people are strong, healthy and forceful; heavier figures as lazy, sloppy, and untidy, yet happy. Height also has an impact. Stewart, Powell, and Chetwynd (1979) found that height and higher status are perceived in direct proportion. Attractiveness is also important, with those who are rated as attractive also seen as more popular, friendly, interesting to talk with. They receive more eye contact, smiles, self-disclosures, body accessibility with openness of arms and legs, and closer bodily proximity (Kleinke 1986).

In general, personal factors are important for interviewing communication in the Asian and Western contexts. However, the ramifications need to be investigated in future research.

Message and Feedback

The interview communication process is complex because it is symbolic, using language to represent the objects and ideas about which we are communicating. Symbols can be misunderstood. Confusion and misunderstanding can result, especially in cross-cultural or second language situations and with Asian contextual languages.

For example, by Anglo-American standards, Japanese are far more deferential to superiors and authority generally, utilize a language indicative of the relative status of the communicators, and are most reluctant to openly criticize or challenge those in charge (Hampden-Turner and Trompenaars 1993). The Korean language has specific forms for address, depending upon the relative status of the speakers.

Additionally, Millar, Chute, and Hargie (1992) note that change in tone, volume, pitch of voice, as well as formality of language, varies across situations.

A range of concepts is associated with messages in the interview communication situation (Downs, Smeyak, and Martin 1980). A common error made by professionals is the mistaken assumption that clients are familiar with the concepts being used. Dickson, Hargie, and Morrow (1989) points out doctors assume patients understand concepts (blood pressure, cholesterol) when, in fact, the concepts are not fully comprehended.

The approaches to messages are based on circular thinking— "circling around" with "feedback loops." It has been tried to the mandala—a symbol in Hinduism and esoteric Buddhism meaning a circle (Tatsuno 1990), the *Tai Chi,* and *yin-yang* (Hampden-Turner and Trompenaars 1993). Rather than the Anglo-American preference for "getting to the point" with messages, circling around can determine people one can trust, to discover how sensitive, responsive, and subtle they are, before moving on to specifics (Hampden-Turner and Trompenaars 1993). De Mente (1992) found a similar pattern among Chinese business executives.

Once meaning is assigned to the received message, the Interviewee, Communicator B, is able to respond. This response is called *feedback*—a verbal or nonverbal reaction to the message. The feedback should be carefully observed because it will indicate whether the message is received and understood. The act of responding with feedback actually shifts the roles of the communicators.

Fitts and Posner (1973) give three functions of feedback: (1) provides knowledge of results, (2) serves as motivation to continue, and (3) acts as reinforcer. Careful attention must be paid to verbal and nonverbal behavior for optimum communication effectiveness (Leathers 1992, Burgoon, Buller, and Woodall 1989). In interviewing, feedback is a two-way process because the behavior of the interviewer is the source of social feedback for the interviewee. Therefore attention must be given to the feedback given as well as received (Millar, Crute, and Hargie 1992).

Because of differing backgrounds and experiences, people process information differently and solve problems with a variety of types of logic and reasoning (Hocker and Wilmot 1991). It must be recognized that people do not come to conclusions based on the same reasoning system. A major breakthrough in understanding the communication process takes place when we accept that it is possible to respect others' beliefs without actually believing as they do.

For example, the Japanese see *prajna*—an intuition of the whole—as the source of *vijnana*—reason (Tatsuno 1990). In some of the creative processes, everyone's ideas are first written down and later harmonized, utilizing inductive thinking—moving from the particulars to generalizations and synthesis. This contrasts with the Anglo-American preference for deductive thinking, with universal propositions tested (Hampden-Turner and Trompenaars 1993). Messages can be visualized as spirals, with each communicator starting on the outside and slowly circling inward. It represents the message structure or "ritual" remarks, starting from a collectivist rather than individualist perspective, which provides clues to the quality of relationship to be expected with the other person (De Mente 1992, Hampden-Turner and Trompenaars 1993).

The underlying core of what a person says and how a person acts in an interview communication situation is the ethical system. Ethics are the values that have been instilled through socialization, either knowingly or unknowingly. Research in the field of speech (Nelson 1966) has isolated some traits of what can generally be considered an ethical speaker: (1) speaks with sincerity, (2) does not knowingly expose an audience to falsehoods or half-truths that cause significant harm, (3) does not premeditatedly alter the truth, (4) presents the truth as he or she understands it, (5) raises the listeners' level of expertise by supplying the necessary facts, definitions, description, and substantiating information, (6) employs a message that is free from mental or physical coercion, by not compelling someone to take an action against his or her will, (7) does not invent or fabricate statistics or other information intended to serve as a basis for proof of a contention or belief, and (8) gives credit to the source of the information.

Some observers describe an Asian notion of situation ethics operating. It is said that, although one kind of behavior is appropriate in one setting to the Japanese, it is natural that another kind of behavior is appropriate in another setting (Holstein 1990). Hampden-Turner and Trompenaars (1993) contend the moral core of "the good" is an elegant pattern and fine arrangement at different levels of intimacy rather than a single ethical value.

Shared Meaning   Shared meaning is represented by the overlap of the two communicators in a transactional model of interviewing communication. Because the participants will never be identical (represented by different shapes) the best scenario is a large area of shared meaning. Achieving a high level of shared meaning is partially from message considerations, but also understanding and comprehending all of the other variables in the interview situation.

Part of shared meaning depends on the role of cognition in interviewing communication. Neisser (1967) identified cognition as all the processes by which sensory input is transformed, reduced, elaborated, stored, recovered, and used. Individuals use cognitive schema to process information (Hawkins and Daly 1988), and experienced counselors have a number of schema (i.e., she is becoming embarrassed) with accompanying plans of action (i.e., use reassuring self-disclosure) (Millar, Crute, and Hargie 1992). From an Asian perspective, a helical process generates shared meaning from a circular approach.

In some of the Asian research on cognition, Liu, Chuang, and Wang (1975), based on the conceptual framework that specific stimulus conditions are retained in individuals' memories as stimulus-response rules that affect later behavior, found more Chinese than English words and frequency of use related to loyalty, filial piety, officials. Chinese acquire the "respect superiors" sets of rules during childhood (Liu 1986).

Morita (1986) used an analogy of a bricklayer versus the stonemason. Americans have the framework laid out in advance and proceed to order bricks to fit the slots available. The Japanese order irregular lumps of stone that the mason then shapes so they fit together harmoniously.

Bloom (1981) found that Chinese-speaking subjects were less likely than English-speaking subjects to give counterfactual interpretations of constructed stories (i.e., ". . . would have happened"), possibly because English has a counterfactual cue ("would have") with no corresponding cue in Chinese (Au 1983). However, Liu (1986) proposes that semantic relativity—the thought conveyed by a language affects the thinking of the people who use that language—is more relevant than linguistic relativity—that language predisposes people to cognitively process in one way or another. Experimental factors are more responsible for differences in cognition than race. As a consequence of having acquired "rules" and behavioral patterns from their childhood, the verbal and ideational flow of Chinese is less smooth, but they excel in tasks requiring memorization. Liu (1986) contends that if the Chinese think differently from Westerners, the difference is superficial and can be explained by semantic relativity.

Channel(s)

Within the interview communication setting, the encoded message is carried through a channel or channels. If the communication is face to face, these channels may be some or all of the five senses.

Typically we rely on sight and sound for channels in speaking and listening, but also use touch, smell, and sometimes, in situations like banquets, the sense of taste. The Interviewer, Communicator A, and Interviewee, Communicator B, should exercise as much care in selecting the channel for communication as each does in choosing the symbols to be used. This is because different channels require different methods of developing ideas. Communication is not the same on the telephone as in the face-to-face situation.

Noise

Noise is internal or external interference in the communication process. There are several types of noise: (1) environmental noise (others talking, music playing, traffic); (2) physiological impairment (deafness, speech impediment); (3) semantic problems (using dialects, jargon, heavy regional accents); (4) ambiguity (meaningless or obscure words); (5) syntactical problems (flawed grammatical usage); (6) organizational confusion (confusing structural order of ideas that inhibit understanding); (7) social noise (preconceived, unyielding attitudes derived from a group or society); and (8) psychological noise (stress, frustration, irritation). Although noise interferes with communication, we must learn to adapt to it and compensate for it because noise is always present. For example, the Interviewer should offer opportunities for feedback to make sure the message has been received and understood.

Situational Factors and the Communication Environment

The situation in which the interview communication takes place influences the behavior of the participants. Argyle, Furnham and Graham (1981) identify features of social situations.

1. *Physical environment.* The size of the room, the color of the walls, the available lighting, crowding, temperature, decor, smells, and so forth have an impact on effective communication. People feel more relaxed in "warm" environments; that is, soft seats, subdued lighting, carpets, curtains, potted plants (Millar, Crute, and Hargie 1992).

2. *Situational goal structure.* Although the individual goals of each participant were considered previously, there is also an overall situational goal structure for the interview communication. For example, organizational goals (proposed reduction in staff) that may be external to both participants in an appraisal

interview may be operating that influence the communication situation.

3. _Roles_. In any situation, people will play, and be expected to play, certain roles. The roles carry with them expectations about behavior, attitudes and values. Problems occur if one participant holds mistaken views about the other's role. In an Asian context, roles can be viewed as inverted Chinese or Japanese puzzle boxes, related to time. As the role is higher in hierarchy, the role looks farther past and farther forward then the level beneath it, encompassing longer and longer time spans of orientation (Hampden-Turner and Trompenaars 1993).

4. _Rules._ Every situation is "rule governed," with implicit rules that have to be adhered to have effective communication. From an Asian perspective, rules, like everything else, are all encompassed within a circle that ebbs and flows like the lighter, whiter mountain mist and the darker, heavier mountain mist that alternate in the original _Tai Chi_ (Hampden-Turner 1981). Each part is a piece of the larger whole, and—_yin-yang_—can be seen as either excluding or including one another (Hampden-Turner and Trompenaars 1993). However, in the cross-cultural study of management values, Singapore Chinese were more likely to allow the particular claims of friendship to overshadow legal duty, but the Japanese were as a "rule" universal as it related to their corporations as Germans, Americans, and British.

5. _Expected sequences of behavior._ A set sequence of events is expected by the participants. Smooth interaction requires both interviewer and interviewee to be aware of the expected behavioral sequence and adhere to it as far as possible. Byrne and Long (1976) identified a six-episode behavioral sequence in doctor-patient interviews. De Mente (1992) identifies ritual behavior for Chinese business banquets.

Relationship Fulcrum

The important foundation for interviewing communication from in an Asian context is the relationship fulcrum. Inherent in the conduct of the interview, the concepts of social and structural harmony result from inner goodness and are coupled to exterior grace and social decorum (Redding 1990).

Social harmony can generally be called *virtuous behavior* (*Ren/Li*). *Ren* is, in general, human-heartedness in which the person can be considered fully human only when she or he takes proper account of others and acts toward them as she or he would want to be acted towards (Westwood 1992d). *Li* are rules (or more accurately, cultivation of an awareness) of propriety or proper behavior in any given situation. It serves to structure social relationships and maintain order in hierarchical situations (Westwood 1992d). The key elements of the *Ren/Li* social harmony is collectivism/relationship-centeredness with related concepts of (1) reciprocity, (2) *guanxi*, (3) face and shame. There are differences among Asian societies in the degree that collectivism/relationship-centeredness present. Meindl, Hunt, and Lee (1989) propose that collectivism can be present at different levels. The United States belongs to the high individualism (low collectivism) category, whereas China belongs to high collectivism (low individualism). Hong Kong, Taiwan, and Korea are in the moderate collectivism category. Cushman and King (1985) point out Japan's traditions and culture reflect homogenous collectivist values, a strong sense of hierarchy, and maintenance of public face. In Thailand, a Buddhist cultural value of harmony augments a core Thai value of *kreng chai*. This complex set of values includes self-effacement, humility, respectfulness, consideration, not intruding on others, and avoidance of embarrassment or trouble to oneself or others (Siengthai and Vadhanasindhu 1991). In Indonesia, harmony (*keselarasan*) and honor (*kehormantan*) form traditional values (Widyahartono 1991). In the Philippines, *kapwa*, expressing a fundamental unity between "self" and "others" is a "shared identity", as well as *hiya* (sense of propriety and shame), *pakikisama* (going along with others), *amor propio* (sensitivity to personal affront), and *utang na loob* (gratitude) reinforcing the relationship-centeredness (Westwood and Chan 1992). In Malaysia, a *halus* person is courteous, sensitive to others, modest, avoids anger and aggression, respectful of others, and generally shows a sense of propriety (Westwood and Chan 1992).

The sense of self is not the Anglo-American idea of a separate ego, but based on sets of relationships (Tu 1984). People are very group oriented with strong attachments formed to significant groups. The chief Chinese collective is family—the extended family and kinship groups. Family relationships are strong, persistent, and tightly structured, with roles clearly defined and implicit rules for appropriate behavior. Key is filial piety—respecting and obeying one's father. In addition to family, Bond (1991) points out that generally Chinese choose to communicate mainly with people they know and, within this circle of acquaintances, with family members in particular. Given that Chinese social needs are met by these existing associations, there is little need to interact with strangers.

Reciprocity means that a favor given by someone must be returned. Yang (1957) says a Chinese who acts normally anticipates a response or return. Westwood (1992d) calls it *social investments*. Cushman and King (1985) point out that the Japanese exchange of gifts (*oseiba*) and favors (*ochugan*) lead to feelings of trust, reciprocity, and obligation. In the Philippines, *utang no loob* is a similar concept of reciprocity (de Leon 1987).

An additional element of relationship-centeredness is *guanxi*, the status and intensity of an ongoing relationship between two parties. People seek to build the relationship, to intensify the bonds, and build on reciprocation. The quality of *guanxi* governs how one should behave within it, with implicit rules governing the behavior (Westwood 1992d).

"Face" in Asia, for the Chinese and Japanese especially, is a major mechanism governing social relationships and providing the strongest social sanctions. Gaining and giving "face" is within the context of particular relationships. Bond and Hwang (1986) identify six forms of "face" behavior: enhancing one's own face, giving face to another, losing one's own face, damaging another's face, saving one's own face, saving the face of another. Face is closely tied to status and social structures and, in Chinese cultures, is the ultimate social sanction. (Hsu 1971).

Several Asian cultures, particularly Chinese cultures, are cultures of "shame" as opposed to the Western "guilt" cultures. In a collectivist and relationship centered culture, a person who breaks the norms is judged by peers. The person will know that she or he acted improperly and will feel shame. In a guilt culture, a person will refer to an internalized set of moral standards and will feel guilty if she or he breaks them (Westwood 1992d).

In addition to the social harmony half of the relationship fulcrum in interviewing communication, the second half is structural harmony—hierarchy—with related concepts of (1) respect for authority, (2) patriarchy, (3) limited and bounded trust, (4) personalism (Westwood 1992d).

The firm hierarchical relationships, identified in Confucianism in the *Wu Lun*, are unequal relationships with reciprocal obligations and duties between prince-minister, father-son, husband-wife, older brother-younger brother, friend-friend. Clear role positions are represented, and role behavior is guided by *Li* (Westwood 1992d). Chinese children are socialized to internalize the values and behavior patterns accompanying acceptance of the role positions (Bond 1991). These hierarchical and paternalistic structures have been reported in research in Hong Kong (Redding 1990, Redding and Wong 1986), Singapore (Chong 1987), Taiwan (Silin 1976), Korea (Cho 1991), the Philippines (Andres 1985), Thailand (Thompson 1989), Indonesia (Widyahartono 1991), and Japan (Iwata 1982).

Respect for authority is an essential element of hierarchical role position. Several research studies have shown that Chinese are quite deferential toward whomever or whatever they consider an authority. Chu (1967), in studying persuasibility—change of opinion—among different population sectors in Taiwan compared with non-Chinese data, found submission to the authority of age, status, and tradition. Hiniker (1969) experimented with a forced-compliance paradigm for attitude change, with Hong Kong Chinese who were post-1959 mainland refugees, finding easy inducement to comply with authority, although compliance did not indicate private acceptance. Yang (1970) found role behavior of acquiescence, subordination, and dependency in equal-power role pairs among Taiwan university students, suggesting that for Chinese, unless one clearly knows one is the authority in a role relationship, the best policy is to behave like a subordinate and treat the other like an authority. In the Malay culture, Sendut, Madsen, and Thong (1989) found high respect for authority and deference to superiors. Thompson (1989) found that submissiveness, obedience, and loyalty were considered as important as ability among Thai supervisors and workers. Hofstede's (1980b) high power distance measure means people are willing to accept sharp power-status differences and generally Asian cultures were high on this measure.

Patriarchy, referred to by Weber (1951) in Chinese social order, means that power is held and expressed personally by the male head, regardless of the structural arrangements, as contrasted with the Anglo-American systems with emphasis on impersonal and abstract rule systems. Relationships have mutual obligations. As long as the power of the head is accepted and legitimized and everyone stays with their respective roles and abides by the implicit rules of behavior, order is assured with relations remaining personal (Westwood 1993e). Cho (1991) points to strong patriarchal order in Korea.

All aspects of hierarchy, including patriarchy, operate with the concept of personalism; that is, it is the quality of relationships between people that matters and determines what happens, not aspects of a formal and impersonal system (Westwood 1992d).

Limited and bounded trust also relates to hierarchy and personalism. If a good relationship has developed between people, then trust will be high and formal mechanisms such as contracts will not be seen as necessary. In the absence of a proper relationship, however, trust may be withheld. The extent of trust depends upon the relationship (Westwood 1992d).

Although explicit links to Confucian texts are not made, the socialization of children and the lessons in proper behavior and proper structures are still passed on to Chinese children (Westwood 1992d, Bond 1991). The impact is great in most parts of Asian society. Based on Confucian principles, Bond and Hofstede (1989) showed a partial causal relationship between the cultural values in "Confucian work dynamism" and economic growth. Hui (1992) argues that people favoring Confucian values including interpersonal harmony, hierarchy, family integrity and kinship affiliation, and individual responsibility are characterized by a strong entrepreneurial spirit, desire for success, and that a society that adopts such values has a high growth potential.

INTERVIEW COMMUNICATION PROCESS

In the complex process of interview communication it is not enough simply to be able to identify the component parts. How do they fit together? Looking at the process of interviewing communication (Figure 13.1) illustrates how the various elements relate to each other. The Asian perspective model shown is a transactional communication model. Perhaps interview communication can best be thought of as a transaction in which source and receiver play interchangeable roles throughout the act of communication (Stewart 1986). A transactional model of communication represents what we now know about human communication—variables are found simultaneously within both communicators. Both communicators in the interview can be, to some extent, understood with varying goals and motivations, perceptions and expectations, cultural traditions, and derivations from that culture. Communicator A encodes a message and sends it. Communicator B then encodes the feedback and sends it to A, who decodes it. These steps, however, are not necessarily mutually exclusive or sequential, because encoding and decoding may occur simultaneously. In the interview situation, we may send a verbal message, and at the same time, we may receive and decode a nonverbal feedback. This process of encoding and decoding can occur continuously throughout our exchange. Because we can send and receive messages at the same time, this model is multidirectional.

The channels are the pathways used for the message and feedback, both verbal and nonverbal. The degree of shared meaning is accomplished by adaptation in the process of common interpretation. Noise interferes with the communication process, potentially affecting all parts of the process. Personal factors and the communication environment and situational factors make each interviewing communication situation different.

From an Asian perspective, each of these elements is affected by some uniqueness. Importantly, the interview communication is built upon a relationship fulcrum. Functioning like a seesaw, harmony and hierarchical systems tilt the model in relative proportions, with the possibility of small shifts even during the course of the interview. The effectiveness of any particular interview communication exchange works within a context of the relationship fulcrum.

In summary, Asian theory and research applicable to interviewing communication, to the extent it currently exists, forms the basis of this model. With this theoretical framework, it is possible to begin a more complete analysis of factors within the process, determining the commonalties and differences among Asian contexts. It is also possible to begin to begin to analyze each of the interviewing forms, each with different task orientations, to determine the commonalties and differences between Asian selection appraisal, job satisfaction, discipline, exit, research, and other interview forms. There are more unanswered questions than answered questions at this point in time; the more we learn, the more we know we do not know. However, once the break is made from the conceptualization and research on interviewing primarily from a North American and British orientation, reflecting Anglo-American backgrounds and concerns that may or may not be relevant to Asia, organizational communication of change can be improved with interviewing skills relevant to the distinctive socio-cultural environments of the region.

References

Abbott, K. A. (1970). *Harmony and Individualism.* Taipei: Oriental Cultural Service.

———. (1976). "Culture, Change and the Persistence of the Chinese." In *Response to Change: Society, Culture, and Personality,* ed. G. A. De Vos. New York: Van Nostrand.

Andres, T. D. (1985). *Management by Filipino Values.* Quezon City, Philippines: New Day Publishing.

Aree, W. F. (1978). "Exploring Explanations for Job Attitudes and Behaviour in a Metro Manila Factory." *Philippine Sociological Review* 26: 3–30.

Argyle, M., A. Furnham, and J. Graham. (1981). *Social Situations.* Cambridge: Cambridge University Press.

Au, T. K. F. (1983). "Chinese and English Counterfactuals: The Sapir-Whorf Hypothesis Revisited." *Cognition* 15: 155–187.

Bedi, H. (1991). *Understanding the Asian Manager: Working with the Movers of the Pacific Century.* North Sydney: Allen and Unwin.

Berlo, D. (1960). *The Process of Communication.* New York: Holt, Rinehart, and Winston.

Bloom, A. H. (1981). *The Linguistic Shaping of Thought: A Study in the Impact of Language on Thinking in China and the West.* Hillsdale, N.J.: Lawrence Erlbaum.

Blunt, P. (1973). "Cultural and Situational Determinants of Job Satisfaction Amongst Management in Africa: A Research Note." *Journal of Management Studies* 10: 133–140.

———. (1976). "Management Motivation in Kenya: Some Initial Impressions." *Journal of East African Research and Development* 6: 11–21.

Boisot, M. (1987). *Information and Organization.* London: Fontana.

Bond, M. H. (1991). *Beyond the Chinese Face: Insights from Psychology.* Hong Kong: Oxford University Press.

———— and G. Hofstede. (1989). "The Cash Value of Confucian Values." *Human Systems Management* 8: 195–200.

———— and H. C. C. Hui. (1982). "Rater Competitiveness and the Experimenter's Influence on Ratings of a Future Opponent." *Psychologia* 25: 91–99.

———— and K. K. Hwang. (1986). "The Social Psychology of Chinese People." In M. H. Bond (ed.), *The Psychology of the Chinese People.* Hong Kong: Oxford University Press.

———— and P. W. L. Lee. (1981). "Face-Saving in Chinese Culture: A Discussion and Experimental Study of Hong Kong Students." In A. Y. C. King and R. P. L. Lee (eds.), *Social Life and Development in Hong Kong.* Hong Kong: Chinese University Press.

————, K. C. Wan, K. Leung, and R. Giacalone. (1985). "How Are Responses to Verbal Insult Related to Cultural Collectivism and Power Distance?" *Journal of Cross-Cultural Psychology* 16: 111–127.

Breakwell, G. M. (1990). *Interviewing.* London: Routledge.

Burgoon, J. K., D. B. Buller, and W. G. Woodall. (1989). *Nonverbal Communication.* New York: Harper and Row.

Byrne, P., and B. Long. (1976). *Doctors Talking to Patients.* London: HMSO.

Chiu, L. H. (1972). "A Cross-Cultural Comparison of Cognitive Styles in Chinese and American Children." *International Journal of Psychology* 7: 235–242.

Cho, D. S. (1991). "Managing by Patriarchal Authority in Korea." In *Management Asian Context,* ed. J. M. Putti. Singapore: McGraw-Hill.

Chong, L. C. (1987). "History and Managerial Culture in Singapore: 'Pragmatism,' 'Openness' and 'Paternalism.'" *Asia-Pacific Journal of Management* 4: 133–143.

Chu, G. C. (1967). "Sex Differences in Persuasibility Factors Among Chinese." *International Journal of Psychology* 2: 283–288.

Chua, B. L. (1992). "The Communication Process." In *Organizational Behaviour: Southeast Asian Perspectives,* ed. R. I. Westwood. Hong Kong: Longman.

Corrigan, J. D. (1978). "Salient Attributes to Two Types of Helpers: Friends and Mental Health Professionals." *Journal of Counseling Psychology* 25: 588–590.

Cushman, D. P., and S. S. King. (1985). "National and Organizational Cultures in Conflict Resolution: Japan, the United States and Yugoslavia." In *Communication, Culture, and Organizational Process,* ed. W. B. Gudykunst, L. P. Stewart, and S. Ting-Toomey. Beverly Hills, Calif.: Sage Publications.

Daniels, T. D., and B. K. Spiker. (1987). *Perspectives on Organizational Communication.* Dubuque, Iowa: William C. Brown.

de Leon, C. T. (1987). "Social Categorisation in Philippine Organizations: Values Toward Collective Identity and Management Through Intergroup Relations." *Asia Pacific Journal of Management* 5: 28–37.

De Mente, B. (1992). *Chinese Etiquette and Ethics in Business*. Lincolnwood, Ill.: NTC.

De Vito, J. A. (1991). *Human Communication: The Basic Course*, 5th ed. New York: Harper and Row.

Dickson, D., O. Hargie, and N. Morrow. (1989). *Communication Skills Training for Health Professionals: An Instructor's Handbook*. London: Chapman and Hall.

Di Matteo, M. R., and D. D. Di Nicola. (1982). *Achieving Patient Compliance: The Psychology of the Medical Practitioner's Role*. New York: Pergamon Press.

Downs, C., G. P. Smeyak, and E. Martin. (1980). *Professional Interviewing*. New York: Harper and Row.

Earle, M. J. (1969). "A Cross-Cultural and Cross-Language Comparison on Dogmatism Scores." *Journal of Social Psychology* 79: 19–24.

Egan, G. (1986). *The Skilled Helper*, 3d ed. Monterey, Calif.: Brooks/Cole.

Fitts, P., and M. Posner. (1973). *Human Performance*. London: Prentice-Hall.

Fried, M. H. (1976). "Chinese Culture, Society, and Personality in Transition." In *Response to Change: Society, Culture, and Personality*, ed. G. A. De Vos. New York: Van Nostrand.

Frijda, N. H. (1986). *The Emotions*. Cambridge: Cambridge University Press.

Graham, R. G., and K. Leung. (1987). "Management and Motivation in Hong Kong." *Hong Kong Manager* 23: 17–24.

Haire, M., E. E. Ghiselli, and L. W. Porter. (1966). *Managerial Thinking: An International Study*. New York: Wiley.

Hampden-Turner, C. M. (1981). *Maps of the Mind*. New York: Macmillan.

——— and A. Trompenaars. (1993). *The Seven Cultures of Capitalism: Value Systems for Creating Wealth in the United States, Japan, Germany, France, Britain, Sweden, and the Netherlands*. New York: Currency Doubleday.

Haney, W. V. (1973). *Communication and Organizational Behavior*. Homewood, Ill.: Richard D. Irwin.

Hargie, O. D. W., and P. Marshall. (1986). "Interpersonal Communications: A Theoretical Framework." In *A Handbook of Communication Skills*, ed. O. D. W. Hargie. London: Routledge.

Hawkins, R. P., and J. Daly. (1988). "Cognition and Communication." In R. P. Hawkins, J. M. Wiemann, and S. Pingree (eds.), *Advancing Com-*

munication Science: Merging Mass and Interpersonal Processes. Beverly Hills, Calif.: Sage Publications.

Hehu, H. Y., and K. S. Yang. (1972). "Individual Modernity and Psychogenic Needs." In *Symposium on the Character of the Chinese: An Interdisciplinary Approach,* ed. Y. Y. Li and K. S. Yang. Taipei: Institute of Ethnology.

Hiniker, P. J. (1969). "Chinese Reactions to Forced Compliance: Dissonance Reduction or National Character?" *Journal of Social Psychology* 77: 157–176.

Hocker, J. L., and W. W. Wilmot. (1991). *Interpersonal Conflict,* 3d ed. Dubuque, Iowa: William C. Brown.

Hofstede, G. (1980a). "Motivation, Leadership, and Organization: Do American Theories Apply Abroad?" *Organization Dynamics* 9: 42–63.

———. (1980b). *Culture's Consequences: International Differences in Work Related Values.* Beverly Hills, Calif.: Sage Publications.

———. (1984). "Motivation, Leadership, and Organization: Do American Theories Apply Abroad?" *Hong Kong Manager* 20: 7–18.

Holstein, W. J. (1990). *The Japanese Power Game: What It Means for Americans.* New York: Charles Scribner and Sons.

Howell, P., J. Strauss, and P. F. Sorenson. (1975). "Cultural and Situational Determinants of Job Satisfaction Among Management in Liberia." *Journal of Management Studies* 12: 225–227.

Hsu, F. L. K. (1971). "Psychological Homeostasis and Jen: Conceptual Tools of Advancing Psychological Anthropology." *American Anthropologist* 73: 23–44.

Hui, C. H. (1992). "Values and Attitudes." In *Organizational Behaviour: Southeast Asian Perspectives,* ed. R. I. Westwood. Hong Kong: Longman.

Hwang, C. H. (1976). "Change in Psychological Needs over Thirteen Years." *Bulletin of Educational Psychology* 9: 85–94.

Hwang, C. H. (1982). "Studies in Chinese Personality: A Critical Review." *Bulletin of Educational Psychology* 15: 227–240.

Iwata, R. (1982). *Japanese-Style Management.* Tokyo: Asian Productivity Organisations.

Izard, C. E. (1977). *Human Emotions.* New York: Plenum Press.

Kahn, R., and C. Cannell. (1963). *Dynamics of Interviewing.* New York: John Wiley and Sons.

Kanungo, R. N. (1983). "Work Alienation: A Pancultural Perspective." *International Studies in Management and Organization* 13: 119–138.

Kao, H., and L. Young. (1992). "The Individual and the Organisation." In *Organizational Behaviour: Southeast Asian Perspectives,* ed. R. I. Westwood. Hong Kong: Longman.

Kleinke, C. (1986). *Meeting and Understanding People*. New York: W. H. Freeman.

La Fromboise, T. D., and D. N. Dixon. (1981). "American Indian Perception of Trustworthiness in a Counseling Interview." *Journal of Counseling Psychology* 28: 135–139.

Leathers, D. G. (1992). *Successful Nonverbal Communication*, 2d ed. New York: Macmillan.

Lee, P. H. (1973). "Personality Correlates of Chinese Individual Modernity." *Acta Psychologica Taiwanica* 15: 46–53.

Leung, K., and M. H. Bond. (1982). "How Americans and Chinese Reward Task-Related Contributions: A Preliminary Study." *Psychologia* 25: 2–9.

Lewin, K. (1951). *Field Theory and Social Science*. New York: Harper and Row.

Li, M. C., and K. S. Yang. (1972). "A Study of Values Among Chinese College Students." In *Symposium on the Character of the Chinese: An Interdisciplinary Approach*, ed. Y. Y. Li and K. S. Yang. Taipei: Institute of Ethnology.

Liu, I. M. (1986). "Chinese Cognition." In *The Psychology of the Chinese People*, ed. M. H. Bond. Hong Kong: Oxford University Press.

———, C. Chuang, and S. Wang. (1975). *Frequency Count of 40,000 Chinese Words*. Taipei: Lucky Books.

Lopez, F. M. (1975). *Personnel Interviewing: Theory and Practice*, 2d ed. New York: McGraw-Hill.

Lynch, F. (1970). "Social Acceptance Reconsidered." In *Four Readings on Philippine Values*, ed. F. Lynch and A. de Guzman II. Quezon City, Philippines: Ateneo de Manila University Press.

March, R. M. (1988). *The Japanese Negotiator*. Tokyo: Kondanshi International.

Martin, E. F., Jr. (1993). "Survey Research Validity in the Brave New World: Interviewer Effects and Respondents Falsification." In *Proceedings of the Second International Conference on Research and Development in the Brave New World: Futuristic Perspectives*, ed. N. Charoenpit and P. Brudhiprabha. Bangkok: Srinakharinwirot University.

——— and G. B. Wilson. (1993). "Hong Kong Chinese Individual Modernity and Western Orientation Related to Job and Educational Expectations: A Preliminary Study." Paper presented at the fourth International Intercultural Conference. San Antonio.

———, Y. M. Cheng, G. B. Wilson, and Y. W. Tsui. (1993). "Advertising Images Among Hong Kong Chinese: A Preliminary Study of Individual Modernity and Western Orientation." Paper presented at Asian Mass Communication Information Centre Conference on Communication, Technology and Development: Alternatives for Asia, Kuala Lumpur.

————— and Y. W. Tsui. (1993). "Hong Kong Chinese Opinions Toward the Portrayal of Women in Advertising." Paper presented at the University Women of Asia (UWA) Triennial Conference, Hong Kong.

Maruyama. M. (1963). "The Second Cybernetics." *American Scientist* 51: 164–179, 250–256.

—————. (1982). "New Mindscapes for Future Business Policy and Management." *Technological Forecasting and Social Change* 21: 55–65.

—————. (1985). "Mindscapes: How to Understand Specific Situations in Multicultural Management." *Asia-Pacific Journal of Management* 2: 124–149.

Maslow, A. (1954). *Motivation and Personality.* New York: Harper and Row.

Mayo, C., and N. Henley. (1981). *Gender and Nonverbal Behavior.* New York: Springer-Verlag.

Meade, R. D., and J. O. Whittaker. (1967). "A Cross-Cultural Study of Authoritarianism." *Journal of Social Psychology* 72: 3–7.

Meindl, J. R., R. G. Hunt, and W. Lee. (1989). "Individualism-Collectivism and Work Values: Data from the United States, China, Taiwan, Korea, and Hong Kong." *Research in Personnel and Human Resources Management,* Supplement: 59–77.

Millar, R., V. Crute, and O. Hargie. (1992). *Professional Interviewing.* London: Routledge.

Minick, S., and J. Ping. (1990). *Chinese Graphic Design in the Twentieth Century.* London: Thames and Hudson.

Morita, A. (1986). *Made in Japan.* New York: Signet Books.

Neisser, U. (1967). *Cognitive Psychology.* New York: Appleton-Century-Crofts.

Nelson, T. (1966). *Ethics in Speech Communication.* Indianapolis: Bobbs-Merrill.

Ozbekhan, H. (1971). "Planning and Human Action." In *Systems in Theory and Practice,* ed. P. A. Weiss, pp. 123–230. New York: Haffner.

Parsons, T., and E. Shils. (1951). *Toward a General Theory of Action.* Cambridge, Mass.: Harvard University Press.

Pascale, R. T., and A. G. Athos. (1981). *The Art of Japanese Management.* New York: Simon and Schuster.

Peters, T., and R. H. Waterman. (1982). *In Search of Excellence.* New York: Harper and Row.

Porter, L. W. (1961). "A Study of Perceived Need Satisfaction in Bottom and Middle Management Jobs." *Journal of Applied Psychology* 45: 1–10.

Rashid, M. Z. A. (1989). "Job Satisfaction and Motivation Among Bank Managers in Malaysia." In *Proceedings of the International Conference on Personnel and Human Resource Management,* pp. 674–683. Hong Kong.

Redding, S. G. (1977). "some Perceptions of Psychological Needs Among Managers in Southeast Asia." In *Basic Problems in Cross-Cultural Psychology*, ed. Y. H. Poortinga. Amsterdam: Swets and Zeitlinger.

———. (1990). *The Spirit of Chinese Capitalism*. New York: Walter de Gruyter.

——— and T. A. Martyn-Johns. (1979). "Paradigm Differences and Their Relation to Management, with Reference to Southeast Asia." In *Organisational Functioning in a Cross-Cultural Perspective*, ed. G. W. England, A. R. Negandhi, and B. Wilpert. Kent, Ohio: Kent State University Press.

——— and G. Y. Y. Wong. (1986). "The Psychology of Chinese Organizational Behaviour." In *The Psychology of the Chinese People*, ed. M. H. Bond. Hong Kong: Oxford University Press.

Runglertkrengkrai, S., and S. Enkaninan. (1986). "The Motivation and Need Satisfaction of the Thai Managerial Elite." *Asia Pacific Journal of Management* 3: 194–197.

Sendut, H., J. Madsen, and G. Thong. (1989). *Managing in a Plural Society*. Singapore: Longman.

Senge, P. M. (1990). *The Fifth Discipline*. New York: Doubleday.

Siengthai, S., and P. Vadhanasindhu. (1991). "Management in a Buddhist Society—Thailand." In *Management: Asian Context*, ed. J. M. Putti. Singapore: McGraw-Hill.

Silin, R. H. (1976). *Leadership and Values: The Organisation of Large Scale Taiwanese Enterprises*. Cambridge, Mass.: Harvard University Press.

Singh, P. N., S. Huang, and G. C. Thompson. (1962). "A Comparative Study of Selected Attitudes, Values and Personality Characteristics of American, Chinese, and Indian Students." *Journal of Social Psychology* 57: 123–132.

Steward, R., G. Powell, and S. Chetwynd. (1979). *Person Perception and Stereotyping*. Farnborough: Saxon House.

Stewart, C., and W. B. Cash. (1978). *Interviewing*. Dubuque, Iowa: William C. Brown.

Stewart, J. (1986). *Bridges, Not Walls*. Reading, Mass.: Addison-Wesley.

Tatsuno, S. M. (1990). *Created in Japan*. New York: Harper and Row.

Tedeschi, J. T., and M. Piess. (1981). "Verbal Strategies in Impression Management." In *Ordinary Language Explanations of Social Behavior*, ed. C. Antaki. London: Academic Press.

Terpstra, V., and K. David. (1985). *The Cultural Environment of International Business*. Cincinnati, Ohio: South-Western Publishing.

Thompson, A. G. (1989). "Cross-Cultural Management of Labour in a Thai Environment." *Asia-Pacific Journal of Management* 6: 323–338.

Tonnies, F. (1957). *Community and Society*. New York: Harper and Row.

Torres, A. T. (1981). "The Filipino Worker in a Transforming Society: Socio-Psychological Perspectives." Ph.D. dissertation, University of the Philippines.

Tu, W. M. (1984). *Confucian Ethics Today: The Singapore Challenge.* Singapore: Federal Publishing.

Vernon, P. E. (1982). *The Abilities and Achievements of Orientals in North America.* New York: Academic Press.

Weber, M. (1951). *The Religion of China.* Glencoe, Ill.: The Free Press of Glencoe.

Westwood, R. I. (ed.). (1992a). *Organizational Behaviour: Southeast Asian Perspectives.* Hong Kong: Longman.

———. (1992b). "Convergence, Persistence, and Difference." In *Organizational Behaviour: Southeast Asian perspectives,* ed. R. I. Westwood. Hong Kong: Longman.

———. (1992c). "On Motivation and Work." In *Organizational Behaviour: Southeast Asian Perspectives,* R. I. Westwood, (ed.) Hong Kong: Longman.

———. (1992d). "Culture, Cultural Differences, and Organizational Behaviour." In *Organizational Behaviour: Southeast Asian Perspectives,* ed. R. I. Westwood. Hong Kong: Longman.

———. (1992e). "Organizational Rationale and Structure." In *Organizational Behaviour: Southeast Asian Perspectives,* ed. R. I. Westwood. Hong Kong: Longman.

——— and A. Chan. (1992). "Headship and Leadership." In *Organizational Behaviour: Southeast Asian Perspectives,* ed. R. I. Westwood. Hong Kong: Longman.

Widyahartono, B. (1991). "The Pancasila Way of Managing in Indonesia." In *Management: Asian Context,* ed. J. M. Putti. Singapore: McGraw-Hill.

Yang, K. S. (1957). "The Concept of *Pao* as a Basis for Social Relations in China." In *Chinese Thought and Institutions,* ed. J. K. Fairbank. Chicago: University of Chicago Press.

———. (1970). "Authoritarianism and Evaluation of Appropriateness of Role Behaviour." *Journal of Social Psychology* 80: 171–181.

———. (1972). "Expressed Values of Chinese College Students." In *Symposium on the Character of the Chinese: An Interdisciplinary Approach,* ed. Y. Y. Li and K. S. Yang. Taipei: Institute of Ethnology.

———. (1981). "Social Orientation and Individual Modernity Amongst Chinese Students in Taiwan." *Journal of Social Psychology* 113: 159–170.

———. (1986). "Chinese Personality and Its Change." In *The Psychology of the Chinese People,* ed. M. H. Bond. Hong Kong: Oxford University Press.

CHAPTER 15

Lessons from the Restructuring of Post-Communist Enterprises

Andrzej K. Kozminski

Complexity

REASONS FOR ENTERING POST-COMMUNIST COUNTRIES

It is generally acknowledged that the core markets of the Triad (North America–Western Europe–Developed Far East) are becoming increasingly "crowded" and, because of market saturation and high costs, cannot provide any more for sustainable healthy rates of growth. More intensive and more globalized competition follows (Thurow 1992, Carnevale 1992). Because of that global leaders such as GE are drastically refocusing and betting their future on the markets from outside of the Triad such as China, India, Mexico, and newly emerging Southeast Asian economies (*Business Week* 1993).

Global value-creating networks linking Triad and non-Triad entities are being created. "Increasingly successful companies do not just add value, they reinvent it. Their focus of strategic analysis is not the company or even the industry but the value creating system itself, within which different economic actors—suppliers, business partners, allies, customers—work together and co-produce value. Their key strategic task is reconfiguration of roles and relationships among this constellation of actors in order to mobilize the creation of value in new forms and by new players" (Norman and Ramirez 1993, 65–66).

Such networks based on the gain-sharing principle enable bypassing head-to-head competition by refusing to play the competitive game as it is currently defined and by formulating a new network as the best equipped to win (Kieman 1993). In such a way IKEA has involved furniture buyers in value creation and has built the world's largest global business system in home furnishings. IKEA has 1,800 suppliers located in more than fifty countries.

Over 500 of IKEA's suppliers are located in the post-Communist countries of Central and Eastern Europe. The first Eastern European store (out of 100 worldwide) was recently inaugurated in Poland. IKEA's examples proves very clearly that today's global networks cannot and should not ignore post-Communist countries.

Networks built and led by global leaders such as IKEA, GE, AGG, or GM are practicing a full-line strategy of market entry, servicing the needs of the total global market. Possible benefits of such resource intensive strategies include recognition as a category leader, economies of scope and scale in R&D, manufacturing, marketing, and service (Teplensky et al. 1993, 511).

When entering the post-Communist environments, global firms are looking for the benefits that can be represented in a simplified form of "Eight S":

- Size of the market and strong market growth (China has become a strategic battleground for jet engines, Procter & Gamble sells more in Poland than in Italy, and so forth);

- Strong margins resulting from "the novelty appeal" of Western products and services provided by the first movers and government granted privileges (such as market protection or tax holidays);

- Stability (monetary, legal, political) in many post-Communist countries is considerably higher in the Third World;

- Skills available at a lower price (scientific, engineering, and artisanship). For example, GE has discovered that the Hungarian bulb manufacturer Tungsram it acquired has more expertise in tungsten filaments than GE itself. GM's new Opel plant in Eisenach (former GDR) employs 2,000 best qualified workers, who earn only 65 percent of their counterparts in the West and the absentee rate is 2 percent vs. 10 percent in other GM plants in Germany.

- Support (infrastructure, distribution networks, consultancy, legal advice, banking);
- Suppliers capable of lowering manufacturing costs. IKEA's example is classical in this respect but China is an even more spectacular as a source of low-cost supplies;
- Safety cushion protection from excessive risk by placing many smaller stakes of a few tens of millions of dollars each. For example, GM has assembly plants building Opels both in Hungary and in Poland;
- Springboard enabling penetration of other markets. For example, GE intended to use the Hungarian acquisition Tungsram to conquer Western European markets.

Strategies used by Western companies entering post-Communist countries, as identified by Kozminski (1993, 201–215), are intended to take advantage of these potential benefits. These are listed in Table 15.1.

Quite often however, these strategies fail. Why?

Lesson I. Potential benefits resulting from entering post-Communist countries do not exist in a ready to use form. They have to be actively created and developed.

Each of these potential benefits requires "awakening" because in the Communist system it was not used or even realized. How?

1. Market potential has to be reinforced by information and active promotion and by offering of attractive financing as well as buying local products. For example GE is buying several million dollars worth of aircraft parts from China and helping Chinese airlines finance leasing of new jets. Since the beginning of 1992 until the end of 1992, GE has won $500 million in engine orders from Chinese airlines (*Business Week* 1993).

2. High margins result from innovative positioning of the products on the new markets. For example IKEA generally perceived as a low market segment furniture supplier has positioned itself on the higher end of the Polish and Hungarian markets. Government granted privileges have to be negotiated and are usually won in exchange for investment and job creation.

TABLE 15.1.

Viable "Generic" Strategies of Western Companies Entering
Post-Communist Countries

Exploit existing markets through exports

Capitalize on economies of scope and experience (unique products in
   the post-Communist environment)

Take advantage of the uniqueness of location

Maintain your presence and prepare a headstart position for the
   penetration of larger markets

Reduce your costs through use of local resources
   Personnel
   Brainpower
   Facilities
   Market access
   Brand names
   Local suppliers

Develop
   Markets
   Suppliers
   Buyers and distribution channels

Look for local partners to secure
   First and second tier suppliers
   Market access
   Lucrative government contracts
   Reduction of transaction costs through government granted
      privileges (protection, tax, holidays)
   Highly qualified personnel
   Access to natural resources
   Useful facilities
   Access to credit
   Access to emerging capital markets

Become restructuring agent of local and foreign governments and
   supranational organizations (restructuring of "dinosaurs" and
   regions, cleaning of the environment)

---

3. Support of the network's activities has to be created and built
    from scratch. That is why auditors and consultants such as
    KPMG or Arthur Andersen, marketers and advertisers such as
    Satchi & Satchi or Gray, banks such as Citibank or Deutsche
    Bank, law firms such as White & Case, follow their clients in

establishing themselves in the post-Communist countries. Coca-Cola is helping to develop a mass distribution system in Poland.

4. Low-cost local suppliers have to be helped to improve dramatically business infrastructure, manufacturing standards, reliability of delivery, and so forth. Operations of such firms as McDonald's, IKEA, ABB, Thompson Brandt, and others in Central and Eastern Europe show clearly that such assistance pays off handsomely but requires a considerable commitment of time, resources, people, and patience.

5. Highly skilled people are able to perform up to the Western standards only after retraining and in a newly designed and newly staffed work environment. Old habits, old culture, old structures, and most of the old managers have to be removed (Kozminski 1993, 167–191).

> **Lesson II. Actions bringing to the surface business benefits potentially existing in the post-Communist countries can not be implemented without some form of cooperation with local business partners.**

FORMS OF COOPERATION WITH LOCAL PARTNERS

Several forms of cooperation with the local partners can be listed:

- *Outsourcing*—A contractual arrangement between two companies where one company supplies the other with certain components and services;
- *CMT (cut-make-trim) contracts*—These provide for manufacturing garments according to the technological specifications, design and out of material and components supplied by the ordering party;
- *Licensing*—The exchange or sale of design specifications for technologies or products that the recipient companies manufacture and market independently;
- *Joint marketing*—An agreement providing for joint marketing activities that do not require equity participation or the creation of a new corporate entity;

- *Joint product agreement*—A partnership based on joint product or technology development activities that do not require equity participation or the creation of a new corporate entity;
- *Equity-technology exchange*—A contract providing for acquisition of shares in exchange for technologies, products, marketing, manufacturing or distribution capabilities;
- *Joint venture*—An equity-based agreement among two or more firms to form a third corporate entity to carry out specific activities.

> **Lesson III. Jointly owned companies are the least practical and most expensive to run, the most difficult to manage, and the most likely to fail of all the forms of cooperation with local partners. As "solutions of last resort" they should logically follow simpler forms of cooperation to enable the acquisition of sufficient information about prospective partner(s).**

Several indepth case studies performed in European post-Communist countries clearly confirm this opinion about East-West joint ventures (JVs) (Kozminski 1993, 35–47, 103–120). Sources of problems in managing East-West JVs (and by consequence potential reasons of failure) are summarized in the Table 15.2.

TABLE 15.2.
Source Problems in Managing East-West JVs

Western Partner	*Eastern Partner*
Lack of knowledge and understanding of the environment, market and specific company	Lack of understanding of Western business practices
Profit expectations too high	Pay expectations too high
Superiority complex	Inferiority complex
Stereotyping	Stereotyping
Lack of communication	Lack of communication
Lack of intercultural Management	Lack of basic management skills
"Plantation Syndrome"	Militant, politicized trade unions
Poor negotiations skills	Poor negotiation skills

Looking at the problems arising in East-West joint ventures one comes easily to the conclusion that resolution of these problems requires learning one from another, as well as from other sources, to adjust mutually and create a highly performing new entity. Development of learning capabilities must happen on both sides. It has to be noted, however, that the post-Communist part of a joint venture has to undergo a deeper transformation (adjustment to the previously unknown market environment) and that the Western partner has to provide leadership in this process.

It is less obvious, however, but no less important, that the same applies to all other forms of cooperation with the post-Communist business partners, including simple outsourcing. Looking for a common denominator of the restructuring changes post-Communist enterprises have to undergo, empirical researchers unanimously discover the change of the organizational culture as a key factor (Abell 1992, Kozminski 1993). Successful cooperation with Western partners is only possible if "cultural incompetence" inherited from Communism is eliminated. Organizational culture change enables managers to map problems within the context of competitive business environment, find solutions, negotiate, compromise, and cooperate with foreign partners, bringing post-Communist enterprises into the global networks.

> **Lesson IV. Development of valuable, permanent business partners in the post-Communist countries calls for enhancement of learning capabilities on both sides enabling radical change of the organizational culture.**

CHANGING ORGANIZATIONAL CULTURES

The impact of the organizational culture change on performance of the post-Communist enterprises is shown on the Table 15.3. Analysis of factors facilitating and impeding this a dramatic cultural change clearly indicates that such a desired outcome is most likely to happen under specific conditions such as the radical restructuring of the post-Communist partner driven by tough requirements resulting from a dominating strategy of a global network. Some of these factors are listed in Table 15.4.

What cultural characteristics of a Western partner are capable of inducing such change? Research conducted by Cartwright and Cooper seems to indicate that Western companies characterized by

TABLE 15.3.
The Impact of the Organizational Culture Change

Elements of Organizational Culture	Desired Change		Impact on Performance
	From	*To*	
Behavioral patterns	Ritual, pretending, Hierarchy driven Emotional demagogery	Pragmatic, doing, cooperation driven, rational argument	Ability to formulate objectives and cooperate to achieve them
Norms	Egalitarian—Low pay, security	Rewards based on contribution, efficiency	Legitimation of rewards based on contributions
Values	Protection of the weakest, gigantomania, "their property"	Organization survival, promotion smartest, adequate fit, "our property"	Ability to formulate objectives and measure performance
"Philosophy"	Inward oriented, resource maximizing	Outward oriented, client centered, market driven, net result maximizing	Market and client driven organization
Rules of the game	Be like everybody, Information avoiding, Political behavior	Find your niche, Information seeking, Problem solving	Specialization and cooperation to achieve individual and collective goals
"Climate and Feeling"	Mistrust, Closed, Defensive	Positive cooperation, Open, Assertive	Openness and assertiveness

TABLE 15.4.
Factors Facilitating and Impeding Cultural Change

Facilitating	*Impeding*
Management education, training, and development	Resistance of administrative personnel and middle management
Political stability	Political instability, recession, trade union militancy
Clearly formulated, winning strategy	Drifting, fighting for survival
Visible modernization drive	Outdated stagnant technology
Production management improvement—quality orientation	Petrified production management system
Good, rapid feedback from younger work force	Lack of market feedback from older work force
Better educated work force	Uneducated work force
Open information channels	Blocked information channels

a task or achievement culture seem more likely to induce successfully desired cultural change in the post-Communist enterprises usually characterized by the power culture. If a dominating Western organization is characterized by bureaucratic role culture, positive change is less likely to happen (Cartwright and Cooper 1993). This is a hypothesis that has to be tested. The importance of cultural compatibility of Western and post-Communist partners, however, remains unchallenged. Such cultural compatibility can be achieved only gradually through learning (Cartwright and Cooper 1993).

Two possible strategies of cultural change in the post-Communist enterprises can be identified: entrepreneurial, based on individual ownership and building up of a small or medium size firm, and institutional, based on "cultural absorption" of a post-Communist enterprise by a global network characterized by well established management practices. Both strategies are illustrated by in-depth studies of the restructuring of post-Communist enterprises (Kozminski 1993) in Table 15.5.

Different approaches to restructuring the post-Communist en-

TABLE 15.5.
Two Strategies of Cultural Change

Key Elements	Entrepreneurial	Institutional
Driving force	Entrepreneur-manager	System and management team
Preconditions	Private ownership	Foreign acquisition and management control or emergence of "turnaround" management team or both
Style	Informal	Elaborate but functional procedures
Size	Small to medium	Large
Common objectives, instruments	Inducement of the market orientation, strong marketing department; Cost accounting, new accounting system; Improved production management, factory layout, etc.; Elimination of redundant administrative personnel and noncore workers; Linking compensation with performance; Building teams	

terprises by the dominating Western partner are illustrated in Table 15.6 by the cases of GE in Hungary and ABB in Poland.

> **Lesson V. "Cultural absorption" of a post-Communist enterprise by a global network is possible if**
>
> - a winning strategy and gain-sharing make the new situation attractive to the employees;
> - cultural clash is avoided;
> - effective communication system is established;
> - people are proud of their "new identity."

The question arises: What should the Western partner(s) do to produce such a set of conditions?

TABLE 15.6.
Restructuring Post-Communist Enterprises

GE Hungary	ABB Poland
Differences:	
JV managed by large number of foreigners	JV managed by local coached and monitored by foreigners
Priority given to layoff of workers	Priority given to layoff of managers and administrative personnel
"Special" approach to restructuring of tungsram	Application of standard company practices
Gradual change of organizational structure	Radical change of organizational structure
"Import" of experts	Big investment in management development and education and worker training
Modernization financed by parent company	Modernization financed by JV itself
Commonalties:	
Improvement of production management	
New accounting procedures	
Flattening of management structure	
Negotiated layoffs	
Strengthening of marketing	
Modernization drive	

WHAT TO DO?

Formulation and implementation of a winning business strategy is possible only if managers of the network properly do their homework and get to know the new post-Communist partner. Many bad and good surprises can be expected. When GE executives inspected Tungsram's warehouses in France and Germany, $3 million worth of 6 watt car headlights were discovered. Such headlights had not been used since the 1970s. When unsaleable inventories (including cartons of bulbs filled with rocks), uncollectible accounts, and unpaid bills were finally calculated by GE accountants, more than two thirds of Tungsram's official 1988 earnings of $20 million faded away (Tully 1990). At the same time, however, GE was surprise and impressed with research at Tungsram. GE Lighting has established four of the division's nine technology centers in Hungary. Csapody from Tungsram was appointed to head technology for the whole of Ge Lighting Europe (Denton 1993). Only proper assessment to the partner's potential and capabilities enables incorporating it properly into the network's strategy and avoiding bitterness resulting from unfulfilled expectations.

> **Lesson VI. Do your homework. Get to know your partner well. Assess properly and objectively its weak and strong points. Do not concentrate exclusively on bright or dark sides. By all means avoid "labeling" and stereotyping.**

The next potential strategic trap, putting into jeopardy partnerships involving post-Communist enterprises is over-dependence on exports and imports. The unstable commercial and monetary policies of newly emerging post-Communist economies and remaining elements of protectionism make strategies relying entirely (or predominantly) on export of the finished goods and import of components too risky. A solid domestic or regional market base and network of local suppliers are needed. That is why Benetton has encountered serious problems when establishing manufacturing operations in Central and Eastern Europe. IKEA is pushing sales in the region and working closely with the large group of local suppliers. GE has serious problems selling in Western Europe lighting sources manufactured in Hungary. Distribution networks are one of the weakest points of the Communist and post-Communist economies; sound business strategy often requires considerable investment in development of marketing channels.

> **Lesson VII. Do not rely exclusively or predominately on exports from and imports to the post-Communist countries. Develop local market base and distribution channels. Develop local suppliers.**

Mixing expatriates and local managers "under the same roof" is a sure source of conflict because of inevitable pay and benefits differences. A dangerous "plantation syndrome" and serious communication problems often follow. If foreign partners get involved in local politics and take sides in ongoing political struggles things turn from bad to worse. For example, in Russia privileges granted to the foreign enterprises by Gorbachev turned out to be serious handicaps under Yeltsin. Part of the problems GE is facing in Hungary seems to be due to the fact that the whole deal was negotiated with the last communist government.

Expatriate managers are costly and often do not perform adequately under unusual, unstable, and unknown conditions. Adequate selection, training, development, and career planning of local managers becomes a key success factor for the East-West partnerships. Large populations of well-educated young engineers are a natural recruitment base. The "cultural incompetence" factor should not be overlooked. In the initial stages of the partnerships, local managers have to be closely monitored and even sometimes remote controlled by the Western partners. Considerable investment is needed in management education, support, counseling, and consulting. Gradually local managers should be given as much autonomy and responsibility as possible. "Mandarin meritocracy" and "creeping credentialism," to use Peter Drucker's expressions (Harris 1993, 118), should be very carefully avoided, especially when they put poor expatriate managers above more competent locals. Clear performance criteria and objective performance evaluations plus broad responsibilities should help to develop "proactive managers" and eliminate "corporate mandarins" generally perceived as parasitic ceremonial figures. Relying on local managers and investing heavily in them is generally perceived as one of the key factors that contributed to the success of restructuring of ABB Zamech in Poland.

The principle of investing in highly qualified local personnel does not apply exclusively to the managers. It should be also applied to the scientists, technicians, and qualified workers. At ABB Zamech between 1990 and 1992, 1,000 out of 3,400 employees were sent abroad for training in the ABB's centers of excellence in Germany, Switzerland, Sweden, Finland, and the United States. Now Zamech itself has become a center of excellence and a leading manufacturer of gas turbines in the ABB network (Zagrodzka 1993).

Avoiding culture clash calls for quick restructuring without hesitation. Gradual restructuring increases the pain and chance of violent conflict, and enhances the formation of defensive coalitions by individuals and groups endangered by the new "rules of the game." Restructuring has two dimensions: structural and human. Structural reform involves flattening the structure and eliminating of redundant management layers. For example, at Tungsram prior to the acquisition by GE there were eleven such layers; at Zamech before ABB took over, fifteen. Many service departments such as maintenance, catering, legal services, or even accounting have to be spun off.

Administrative, clerical, and middle management personnel have to be drastically reduced. For example, at Tungsram the ratio of white to blue collar workers was 1:2.5 (1:7 in the West). At Zamech management ranks were reduced from 1,200 to 64. To enable turnaround old Communist political appointees have to be eliminated and replaced by local "hungry wolves," young dynamic engineers with some managerial experience. At the same time, however, the "witch hunt" atmosphere has to be avoided.

When the Western partner has management control such radical moves are easier; when not, they have to be induced and negotiated in a more subtle way.

> Lesson VIII. to avoid "culture clash" do not get involved in local politics. Invest in local personnel, especially in local managers, help them to overcome inherited from Communism "cultural incompetence." Avoid using expatriate managers. Eliminate "corporate mandarins" and "plantation syndrome." Offer equal career opportunities for the locals. Restructure quickly without hesitation.

Communication has a key role in integrating post-Communist enterprises into the global networks. The communication problem is fourfold: technology aspect, language aspect, cognitive structure aspect, and communication channel (organizational) aspect. All four have to be attacked at once.

The "technology aspect" is important in the post-Communism countries with an inadequate telecommunication system. In Poland Zamech had to be linked by satellite with ABB's Zurich headquarters. This made possible extensive use of telephones, faxes, teleconferencing, and electronic mail. It also made possible integration of the Zamech's reporting into the overall company reporting system Abaccus.

To cope with the "linguistic aspect" of communication all the key personnel of the post-Communist enterprises have to be trained in English and especially business English. Intensive language training has to become a permanent feature of the restructuring post-Communist enterprises.

The "cognitive structure aspect" has to do with understanding basic modern management notions and tools. All Communist managers are very strongly production oriented with no understanding of marketing and finance, no accounting skills, and a rather primitive hierarchical and formalized approach to communication and managing people. Such basic management "buzz words" as *cash flow, standard cost, income statement,* and *market niche* are completely unknown even to those managers who have some general knowledge of English. At the same time, however, they have good educational backgrounds and ambition to catch up with the foreigners. Adequate educational and management development programs simply have to be supplied.

The "communication channel (organizational) aspect" is the most complex one. It embraces creation of communication platforms such as task forces, joint committees, workout groups, cross-functional teams, and management committees, enabling managers to work together and communicate across national, functional, and institutional borders. Global companies organized in a network form are extremely communication intensive and offer a wide variety of such forms. Managers and core personnel from the post-Communist enterprises have to be involved in them to the fullest possible extend to overcome eventual isolation and marginalization.

> **Lesson IX. All four aspects of a communication system—technological, linguistic, cognitive, and organizational—have to be attacked and dramatically improved at once.**

Pride is an extremely important emotional and motivational aspect of the restructuring process. It enables mobilization and creativity. Promoting pride in the personnel of the post-Communist enterprises implies high expectations and assumes that the local brain power is fully used. The way to accomplish that is to impose on the post-Communist enterprises the same efficiency requirements as on other entities of the network, including the most advanced ones. The secret is to allow no baby sitting but demand quick results at once. Such an approach brings vision into the game. Vision requires setting meticulous benchmarks for all the critical processes against the best worldwide and generates "creative tension" (Burdett 1993). Creative tension produces innovative solutions.

The example of Zamech taken over by ABB illustrates that approach. Financial reporting and accounting system conforming with ABB standards (calculated in local currency and U.S. dollars) was introduced in six months. Cycle times for production of steam turbines were cut in half and became comparable with ABB average. In two years Zamech has become the gas turbines manufacturing center for the ABB worldwide network and has obtained ISO 9,000 certificate. Costs were cut in half and continue to fall. Zamech president Polish-national Mr. Olechnowicz wants to multiply sales volume by factor of five until year 2000. Says Barbara Kux supervising Zamech from ABB headquarters in Zurich: "You can change these companies. You can make them more competitive and profitable. I can't believe the quality of the reports and presentations these people do today, how at ease they are discussing their strategy and targets. I have worked with many corporate restructuring but never I have seen so much change so quickly. The energy is incredible. These people really want to learn, they are very ambitious. Basically ABB Zamech is their business now" (Taylor 1991, 104).

Lesson X. Post-Communist enterprises should comply quickly with the same efficiency requirements the best Western companies are subjected to.

CONCLUSION

Two convergent races are on. On one side, enterprises in the post-Communist countries, suddenly subjected to the challenges of the market economy, have to restructure dramatically if they are to survive. The ones capable of entering global networks sooner than others will be the winners. On the other side, global dinosaurs subjected to increased competition in the crowded markets of the Triad are also hurriedly refocusing, streamlining, flattening their structures, and building networks to keep their place on the worlds 500 list. The ones that will be capable of penetrating and developing faster the post-Communist markets will considerably enhance their competitive advantage. It can be achieved in the most natural way by integrating post-Communist enterprises into the global networks and helping to restructure them.

This adds a new dimension to the high-speed management concept reflecting emerging management practices within the Triad (Cushman and King 1995). This new dimension is the ability to integrate new post-Communist entities into the network, helping to restructure them and develop their natural market and supplier base. The winners have to do it faster and better than others.

The ten lessons from restructuring of the post-Communist enterprises presented here have though more general meaning: they show how Triadic enterprises should deal with the partners from outside of the Triad, to develop them in their best interests.

References

Abell, D. F. (1992). *Turnaround in Eastern Europe: In Depth Studies.* New York: UNDP Management Development Programme.

Burdett, J. (1993). "Managing in the Age of Discontinuity," *Management Decision,* 31: 10–17.

Business Week. (1993). "GE's Brave New World." *Business Week* (November 8): 64–70.

Carnevale, A. P. (1992). *America and the New Economy.* Washington D.C.: U.S. Department of Labor.

Cartwright, S., and C. L. Cooper. (1993). "The Role of Culture Compatibility in Successful Organizational Marriage." *Academy of Management Executive* 7. No. 2: 57–70.

Cushman, D. P., and S. S. King. (1995). *Communication and High-Speed Management.* Albany: SUNY Press.

Denton, N. (1993). "GE Recapitalizes Hungarian Lightning Group." *Financial Times* (March 17).

Harris, G. T. (1993). "The Post-Capitalist Executive: An Interview with Peter Drucker." *Harvard Business Review* (May–June): 115–122.

Kiernan, M. J. (1993). "The New Strategic Architecture: Learning to Compete in the Twenty-first Century." *Academy of Management Executive* 7, No. 1: 7–21.

Kozminski, A. K. (1993). *Catching Up? Organizational and Management Change in the Ex-Socialist Block.* Albany: SUNY Press.

Norman, R., and R. Ramirez. (1993). "From Value Chain to Value Constellation: Designing Interactive Strategy." *Harvard Business Review* (July–August): 65–77.

Taylor, W. (1991). "The Logic of Global Business: An Interview with ABB's Percy Barnevik." *Harvard Business Review* (March/April), 91–105.

Teplensky, J. D., J. R. Kimberly, A. L. Hillman, and J. S. Schwartz. (1993). "Scope, Timing and Strategic Adjustments in Emerging Markets: Manufacturer Strategies and the Case of MRI." *Strategic Management Journal* 14: 505–527.

Thurow, L. (1992). *Head to Head*. New York: William Morrow and Company.

Tully, S. (1990). "GE in Hungary: Let There Be Light." *Fortune* (October 22): 137–142.

Zagrodzka, D. (1993). "Tym Ludziom Nalezy sie Laurka" [Thanks Are Due to These People]. *Gazeta Wyborcza* (January 9–10): 12–13.

CONTRIBUTORS

Ron Cullen is CEO of Performance Management Solutions, a consulting firm based in Melbourne Australia. The consultancy specializes in evaluating and improving the performance of public sector organizations and other organizations with complex service missions. Dr Cullen served as the Director of Finance for Australian Telecommunications, head of the public service agency in Victoria, and head of the Higher Education coordination agency in Victoria. He holds a Ph.D. in Organization Theory from the University of Melbourne and has been involved as a consultant or manager in many public sector change projects. He has published a number of articles on public administration and has led a number of government sponsored reviews of programs and agencies.

Donald P. Cushman is professor of communication at the State University of New York at Albany and holds a Ph.D. in communication from the University of Wisconsin. He has served as a consultant for governments and private corporations in Australia, Bolivia, Canada, Germany, Great Britain, Japan, Korea, Mexico, and Yugoslavia. Cushman has written over sixty articles in journals and ten books including *Message-Attitude-Behavior Relationships* with R. McPhee (Academic Press, 1980); *Communication in Interpersonal Relationships* with D. Cahn (SUNY Press, 1985); and *High-Speed Management: Organizational Communication in the 1990s,* with S. S. King (1994).

Michael Goodman is director of the M.A. in corporate communication program at Fairleigh Dickinson University. He has a Ph.D. from SUNY at Stony Brook and has written two books, including the edited book *Corporate Communication* (SUNY Press 1994). He is associate editor for corporate and organizational communication for the *IEEE Transactions in Professional Communication.* He is an active consultant for such firms as AT&T, Parker Davis, and Grauman Corporation.

John C. Johnson holds a master of arts degree in health care administration from The George Washington University in Washington, D.C. He has spent the past thirty years in hospital and health systems management in various parts of the United States. An active participant in health systems development nationally, he has also contributed to the development of position papers and policies for the American Hospital Association and other national health care groups. In 1987, John Johnson was selected as one of the top twenty-five health system and group purchasing executives in the United States. He is a fellow in the American College of Health

Care Executives and currently president and chief executive officer of Mercy Medical Center in Rockville Center, New York.

Robyn Johnston, M.A. Dip. Ed. has been a lecturer in communication studies at the University of Technology, Sydney, for the past ten years. She lectures in undergraduate programs in the areas of interpersonal, small group, and organizational communication and coordinates the graduate program in communication management. Her research interests lie in areas related to curriculum development in communication studies and training and development. She has presented papers at a number of national and international conferences concerning training and development issues and communication research. She has written articles for professional journals and recently completed a chapter on communication competence for an educational administration text. Johnston undertakes regular consultancy activities in both the private and public sector. These have included short course organizational intervention design in areas related to communication, staff development, and management.

Yanan Ju is professor of communication at Central Connecticut State University. With his Ph.D. in political science from the University of Belgrade, he has taught at China's Fudan University, University of Connecticut, and University of North Carolina at Chapel Hill, and has lectured at various universities or other organizations in Asia, Europe, North America, Australia, and Africa. He has written ten books (English or Chinese) and numerous articles. He also consults in such areas as cross-cultural management, Chinese CBF, public relations, multiculturalism, and organizational communication.

Sarah Sanderson King is professor of communication at Central Connecticut State University. She was chair of the Division of Communication Arts at Marist College and chair of the Department of Communication at Central Connecticut State University. She has been the recipient of $350,000 in grants from such agencies as NEH, NIMH, University of Hawaii, East-West Center, and the state of Connecticut. She was chair of the Department of Communication at the University of Hawaii and has served as fellow or research associate at the University of Chicago, Ohio State University, Harvard University, and the East-West Center in Honolulu. She was a Fulbright Scholar to Yugoslavia. Her publications include *Political Communication: Engineering Visions of Order in the Socialist World,* (coedited with D. P. Cushman); *Human Communication as a Field of Study; Effective Communication Skills: An Interactional Approach;* and *Effective Communication: Theory Into Action.*

Gordon Knowles currently works for a nongovernment organization, The Salvation Army. He coordinates and manages fifty overseas aid projects jointly funded by the Australian government and The Salvation Army in twenty-one developing countries and maintains a keen interest in community in developing countries. Previously he was a research officer and senior electorate officer for a federal member of the Australian Parliament. He worked for eighteen years in the public sector in welfare-oriented areas (police, social security, and housing). He holds a Bachelor of Arts degree (majoring in public administration) from The University of Queensland, as well as a graduate diploma in administration. He was a part-time politics tutor for two years at the University of Canberra. He resides in Canberra, Australia.

Andrzej K. Kozminski is professor of management and director of the International Post-Graduate Management Center at the University of Warsaw. He is also on a regular basis a visiting professor at the University of California—Los Angeles Anderson Graduate School of Management. He has written over 250 scholarly articles in six languages and written several books. His last book *Catching-Up: Organizational and Management Change in the Ex-Socialist Bloc* was published in 1993 by SUNY Press. Kozminski is an active consultant and serves as president of a private training company, the International Business School in Warsaw, Poland. He has been invited frequently as a visiting professor by leading universities in many countries.

Ernest F. Martin, Jr., is head/senior lecturer of the Department of Communication Studies at Hong Kong Baptist College. He received his Ph.D. from the University of Missouri—Columbia in 1971. He previously held positions at Syracuse University, University of Kansas, and Iowa State University. Industry positions included vice-president/general manager of KDNL-TV (Preview), director of research with Cox Broadcasting, senior research project director with Frank Magid Associates, and director of research and marketing for KPLR-TV. Publications include *Professional Interviewing*.

Rodney G. Miller is manager of development at Queensland University of Technology, which includes responsibility for fund raising and alumni relations. He advises nonprofit organizations and foundations internationally on leadership and fund raising strategy and is a core faculty member of the Indiana University Fund Raising School, teaching programs in Australia, Canada, and New Zealand. He has written widely and made numerous presentations on leadership, communication management, and institutional advancement. A certified fund raising executive, awarded by the National Society of Fund Raising Executives (USA), he is a national council member of the Fundraising Institute Australia, chairing its accreditation board. He previously directed the Communication Center at QUT, lectured in the School of Communication, and was the founding editor of the *Australian Journal of Communication* from 1976–1989.

Krzysztof Obloj is associate professor of management, School of Management, University of Warsaw, and director of the MBA program at the International Business School, Warsaw. He has been conducting research in the fields of strategic and international management, and has lectured at universities in the United States, France, Israel, Norway, and Denmark. He serves as consultant to Polish companies and foreign corporations investing in Poland. he is an author or coauthor of over sixty articles published in scholarly journals and four books, including *Management: A Practical Approach, Strategic Management: An Outline of Theory of Organizational Equilibrium* (in Polish), and *Managing in Different Cultures* (in English). His coauthored book on management systems in global environment will be published by Kent Publishers.

John Penhallurick is associate professor of communication and head of the Division of Communication, Media, and Tourism at the University of Canberra. He teaches in mass and organizational communication and has extensive experience consulting for private and public organizations. His current research interests include the use of geodemographics for audience analysis, cognitive mapping, gender and communication, and the analysis of media industries from a resource dependency perspective.

Giuseppe Raimondi is communication manager at IPR—Immuno Pharmacology Research, an Italian firm specializing in high-tech diagnostic kits. He received his M.A. from the State University of New York at Albany in 1993. He received his undergraduate degree in contemporary history from the University of Catanie, Italy, in 1989. He worked previously as a copywriter for a number of Italian advertising agencies.

INDEX

assessment of workplace competency,
262–265, 269–271
ABB Zamech, 320–326
AT&T, 38, 46

benchmarking, 55–57. *See* best
practices
Boehringer Ingelheim Corporation,
114

change skills, 43–47
Challenger, NASA, 101–104
Chrysler, 45–46
coalignment, 1
communication processes, 19
organizational coordination, 23–24
communication and information
technology, 23–24
organizational control, 24–25
audit, 24, 148, 191
organizational integration, 20
climate, 22, 106–109
leadership, 20–21, 35–64
coalignment broker, 21, 42–
43, 74–75
managing discontinuous
change, 21, 58–60
network, 21, 39–42, 51–58
transformational, 20, 36–39,
48–51
teamwork, 22–23, 26–27
community service, 65–81
culture, 287

discontinuous change, 2, 22, 43, 251

gender, 211–212, 222, 290
women, 132, 134–136, 137, 144,
195
GE (General Electric), 47–60, 311–
315, 320–323
gaimianzi, 246
guanxi, 230–235, 240, 248, 288,
297, 298
quanxiwang, 233–235

health care reform, 161–189
high-speed management, 9, 34, 35–
64, 65–81, 143, 242
philosophic perspective, 10–13
theoretic perspective, 13
continuous improvement, 10, 17–
19, 27–29
teamwork
self-managed teamwork, 17–
18, 53–54, 126, 255
New England Town
Meeting, 53–54
cross-functional teamwork, 2,
18, 54
best practices teamwork, 2, 18,
54–55, 256
negotiated linking, 18–19, 55,
315–316, 320, 322
environmental scanning, 10, 13–
15, 55–58, 70–74
value chain theory, 10, 15–17, 40–
42, 56
humanistic rationalism, 228–230

incremental change, 2, 22
industrial relations reform, 251–254
interviewing, 275

333

Jack Welch, 47–60

Kaizin movement, 83

lean production management, 41–42

McDonnell Douglas, DC 10 & C17, 104–106
Maslow hierarchy of needs, 281–282
Mintzberg analysis, 117–124

NGO (nongovernment organization), 127–146

pharmaceuticals, 113–126
pragmatic-humanistic rationalism, 232, 297

private sector management changes, 149–150
public sector management, 147–149
changes, 150–151

Ren/Li, 297, 299
role communication, 245–248
role conflict, 193–197, 206, 209–212
role stress, 191–193

Salvation Army, Australia, 127–134, 136, 138
sipolianpi, 248
stereotypes, 87–89, 93, 316
speed of response, 11–12

TQM, 257–270
Toyota, 41–42, 45–46
Tylenol, Johnson & Johnson, 106–195